MIDDLING FOLK

MIDDLING FOLK

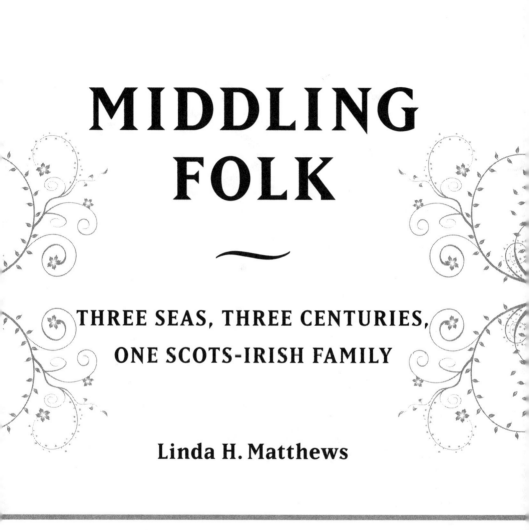

THREE SEAS, THREE CENTURIES, ONE SCOTS-IRISH FAMILY

Linda H. Matthews

CHICAGO REVIEW PRESS

Library of Congress Cataloging-in-Publication Data

Matthews, Linda H.
     Middling folk : three seas, three centuries, one Scots-Irish family / Linda H. Matthews.
— 1st ed.
          p. cm.
     Includes bibliographical references and index.
     ISBN 978-1-55652-969-6 (hardcover)
     1. Hamel family. 2. Scots-Irish—Genealogy. 3. Virginia—Genealogy. 4. United
States—Genealogy. I. Title.
     CS71.H199 2009
     929'.20973—dc22

                                                                      2009025694

See www.middlingfolk.com for genealogical resources including family trees, more
documents and photos, suggestions for additional reading, and more.

Interior design: Monica Baziuk
Map design: Chris Erichsen
Photos courtesy of the author unless otherwise noted

Published by Chicago Review Press, Incorporated
814 North Franklin Street
Chicago, Illinois 60610
ISBN 978-1-55652-969-6
Printed in the United States of America

5   4   3   2   1

For my father

CONTENTS

PART V

THE HAMMILL FAMILY IN THE FAR NORTHWEST
1880–1928

❖

Author's Note

*I*N PUTTING together this account, I have made the most of the amazing resources available to researchers of American and British family history and have documented my findings as meticulously as my sources permitted. But like every historian who attempts to create a coherent narrative from the random leavings of the past, I was confronted with holes in the record that no amount of research would ever fill. I could not bear to leave them gaping. So I filled the holes with fictions of my own devising, following the hints that history offered up.

That does not mean I have blended fiction with fact. The stories are emphatically marked so no one will be deceived as to their nature. Purists can skip them. Everyone else can enjoy these glimpses through the gate that separates the present from the past and our forebears' inner lives from our own.

Now, a word about the spelling of the Hammill name. In Scotland and in America, documents spell it differently from one paragraph to the next. Hamil, Hamill, Hammil, Hammel, Hommyl,

Homel—there is no consistency whatever between 1200 and 1880. In Northern Ireland, however, the name is spelled Hamill with just a handful of exceptions. John Hammill the immigrant brought that spelling with him to Maryland colony—where it quickly fell by the wayside, to re-emerge as Hammill, with a double m, in the late nineteenth century. In the face of this confusion, I have chosen to spell the name Hammill in all cases, and have not altered any of the variations in spelling when I am quoting documents. As for given names, Catherine is occasionally spelled with a K; Neale is sometimes spelled Neal or Neil, and once, phonetically, Nail. I have chosen Catherine and Neale for my narrative, and have left spellings in documents untouched.

The British Isles

PROLOGUE

---

*T*HIS IS the story of a Scots-Irish family that over the course of
centuries made its way from southwest Scotland to Northern
Ireland, then to the Chesapeake Bay region of North America, and
at last to Washington State in the far Northwest.

Because it is the story of an ordinary family, the bulk of their long
history—all those generations passed in North Britain from the
time of the Druids until the very early seventeenth century—can
only be glimpsed as from the corner of an eye, so little documentary
evidence remains for it. Four more generations in Northern Ireland
are likewise impossible to document with anything like precision.
It is only when John Hammill leaves his British home for Maryland Colony, in 1725, that the story coalesces and five generations of
American Hammills come into distinct view. Yet to omit that early
history would be to cheat the story of its beginnings and to hide the
ties that link a distant past to a more recent one, indeed link it to the
present. It seems to me that a hazy background is preferable to none
at all, and so I provide what I can in Part I of this account. When

from time to time a place or individual or event looms brightly through, I make the most of it while wishing there were more.

The story opens in feudal Scotland, then moves to early modern Ireland at the time of the Scots Plantation in 1608 and England's Glorious Revolution in 1688–89. In Parts II and III, the ordered life of the southern colonies gives way to the turmoil of the American Revolution and its difficult aftermath in Maryland and Virginia. In Part IV, the Civil War threatens, overwhelms, and transforms the Hammill family, sending a son to the far West in search of a better livelihood than the ruined South could offer. His story is the subject of Part V.

Throughout the narrative, personal encounters with major historical events show what they entailed for ordinary folk. Wars, economic booms and busts, political upheavals, and social transformations like the abolition of slavery sent family members scrambling to recoup their livelihoods and come abreast of a new present. Private drama, too, plays its part in the story: tragic deaths, business successes and failures, love and loss marked the Hammills as they do every family. And then there is the quintessential American experience of moving westward—pulling up stakes for greener pastures, feeling the risk and also the excitement of moving on.

In short, this account offers what the American story has to offer—a story that in many families remains untold. Tens of thousands of immigrants made the journey from Europe to and then across America. Some managed to carry their pasts with them, in the form of objects, letters, diaries, and most of all in family stories that both shape and encumber those who inherit them. But many others left their pasts behind. Sometimes this was the unintended consequence of moves away from friends and relatives, of huge disruptions like wars and epidemics, or of long intervals between generations, when parents died before their children could hear and remember their stories. And sometimes the older generation feels that there is nothing to say about their life experiences, or no way to say it, or no one who wants to hear it. Unfortunately they are often right about the last of these.

I myself resisted learning my family's story, though my father, Kenneth Hammill, and his sister Roxie Hammill Wilcox spent their retirement in pursuit of its details. Forty years ago, before computers and the Internet, they searched tirelessly by telephone and letter for all they could find about five generations of Hammills in colonial Maryland and Virginia, and three more generations in western Washington State.

It was no secret that they were doing this. My father mentioned details of his research now and then, about the trips he and my mother were taking and the excitement of finding a birth certificate or marriage record that had eluded him for months. But he was reserved by nature, and also far away. He lived in Portland, Oregon, where I was born and raised, and I lived in Chicago. My visits home were never long enough to discuss his work thoroughly, and when we telephoned, we talked about our daily doings and the antics of the grandchildren, not his genealogical discoveries.

So I was stunned when, suddenly, the fruits of his labors began arriving at my door. In the early 1980s I received six fat loose-leaf binders, each a different color, and each stuffed with genealogical charts, photocopies of photographs, typescripts of wills, deeds, licenses, and certificates, with a bit of typewritten narrative, single-spaced, and penciled notes in the margins of discoveries he had made after the pages were photocopied. He had researched not only his family, but the families of all four of his and my mother's grandparents. The mass of material was overwhelming. And then he sent his four-hundred-page autobiography, also typewritten and single-spaced. That was a commitment in itself.

I looked at the autobiography, and we talked a bit about his childhood in western Washington State and his romance with my mother, before my brother and I were born. But I did not study his notebooks. They sat on a closet shelf for the last decade of my father's life and another decade after that. Just a few years ago, I took them out of the closet and lay them on a table where there was some chance I might pick one up.

The light blue binder appealed to me, partly because it was the shortest, and partly because it traced the Hammill history. I knew the family had homesteaded in Lewis County, Washington, in the nineteenth century, and I knew my brother, John William, had been named for his grandfather and great-grandfather Hammill. That was also my maiden name, and it had always puzzled me. Oddly spelled and lumpy, I had no idea where it came from or what it might mean. Maybe the blue binder could offer some answers. I sat down with it. Five years later, this book is the result.

It is a lot of work to write a book, no matter how fascinating the material one has to work with, and the deeper one burrows into the long-ago past, the more one feels oneself growing dotty and obsessed. But I wanted to illuminate the story of these people in the middle, to give an ordinary family the credit that is due.

Historians and biographers build their professions around retrieving the past, filling historical gaps and showing wide conse-quences that are hard to see from the vantage point of a single life. Traditionally, they have favored stories of the influential—people who altered national history or transformed the practice of science, industry, or the arts. More recently, they have concentrated on the lives of the impoverished and disenfranchised: slaves, peasants, excluded minorities, women—those whose stories have been denied or suppressed. I understand why, of course.

But who tells the stories of the people in the middle? They get lost. The experiences and values they reveal seem ordinary, not worthy of comment, even bourgeois or embarrassing. The people who live them are preoccupied with the present and the future. Too often, their descendants have no interest in looking back. Yet it seems to me that these are the most important histories of all. They belong to the people who quietly, century after century, conducted the business and built the livelihoods that made their societies prosper. Their attitudes are difficult to alter or predict, yet they shape culture more profoundly than wars, pestilence, or changes in regime, frustrating as this is to politicians and other leaders.

Middle-class people can embrace new opportunities with a startling fervor. Thomas Jefferson believed that it would take five hundred years for Americans to populate the continent from coast to coast. It happened in less than a century, because tens of thousands in the middle class saw advantage in moving on. Evangelical religion, the industrial revolution, abolition, today's revolution in technology—all of these movements swept the nation and the world because people in the middle made them their own.

And sometimes the middle classes hold firmly to the customs and traditions of their pasts, perpetuating them into the future even as outside circumstances turn their societies upside down. Provisions of the English common law that were established in the distant middle ages continued as a matter of course in colonial America and even after, because both governments and individuals found them familiar and appropriate. Feudal leases became colonial and then commercial leases. In Virginia, fees and rents were calculated in pounds sterling for a quarter-century after the Revolution, because parties to deeds and leases trusted British currency more than they trusted the dollar. Families in the middle strive to protect their own. It is a habit that no ideology is likely to break.

This account shows how the Hammill family passed along its preferences for particular landscapes just as it handed down occupations, religious beliefs, attitudes toward education and politics, and favorite names. It shows individuals leaning into the future against the weight of their pasts. Nations do the same. Why deny it or regret it? The past is alive in the present. It shapes the future every day. If more people embraced this premise, then retrieved and told their family stories to see what they reveal—well, this would be a better world, and a more interesting one, too.

MIDDLING
FOLK

~

PART I

THE HAMMILL FAMILY
IN SCOTLAND AND IRELAND

Western Scotland and Northern Ireland

I

ORIGINS

*T*HE PARISH of Beith in North Ayrshire, Scotland, lies ten or
so miles east of the Firth of Clyde, where the River Clyde
empties into the North Channel of the Irish Sea. From the bluffs
above the Firth, at the town of Largs, one can look west across the
sea to the isles of Great and Little Cumbrae, Bute, and Arran, and
then to the chains of islands and Highland peninsulas that extend
nearly to the northern Irish coast. The view is both spectacular and
enticing. For countless ages, traders, warriors, evangelists, and settlers ventured back and forth across that sea. Often they left progeny
in their wake, and sometimes other traces of their visits.

Cuff Hill, at 675 feet above sea level, is the highest point in the
parish of Beith and in all North Ayrshire. From it one can glimpse
Loch Lomond to the north and the sparkling Firth of Clyde to the
west. At the hill's summit are the remains of a Neolithic chambered
tomb and a great stone that rocked in place for tens of centuries,
until meddlesome humans made it settle by digging under it to find
its fulcrum. The tomb's builders chose their site for that remarkable

stone and for the views around it, of forested landscapes with the Firth in the distance.

Ages later, the ancient tomb and the rocking stone brought Druid priests, called coiffs, to Cuff Hill. There they enacted their rituals, for long enough that the hill took their name. Eventually, Christian evangelists supplanted them. In the ninth century A.D., St. Inan came from the Scots island of Iona to bring the word of God to the pagan Scots. He too favored Cuff Hill for his ministry. He preached at an outcropping of rock near the tomb and the rocking stone, with the wooded countryside stretching out below. The faithful who flocked to hear him called the place St. Inan's Pulpit.[1] Long after his death, the first church built in the parish of Beith was named St. Inan's for the Irish monk.

Among those who gathered to watch the Druid rites and then to hear St. Inan preach were some whose surname eventually became Hammill. They lived in the vicinity of Cuff Hill for numberless generations before and after they took the family name. After 1600, a group of them left Scotland for Northern Ireland and then America. Though these Hammills traveled thousands of miles over many generations more, they seem always to have carried the view from Cuff Hill with them. Its wooded hillsides with water in the distance gave them their vision of home.

Two happy accidents make it possible to locate the family so certainly at such a distant time. First, the Hammills of North Ayrshire were long associated with an estate called Roughwood in the parish of Beith not far from Cuff Hill. The nineteenth-century genealogists and historians who devoted themselves to tracing Ayrshire's long history included them, if only by mention, in their published works. What they have to say about the family takes on a rather hodgepodge quality, for by the early nineteenth century the Hammills were for the most part just a memory in Scotland. One has the feeling that these historians were scrambling to find and render up whatever they could. That they did so is the second happy accident.

If they had not made the scramble, almost nothing at all would be known of the Hammills of Roughwood.

Just below Cuff Hill is Hill o' Beith, where the town of Beith has grown up in the last three or four centuries. Beith—it rhymes with Keith—means birch tree in Gaelic. At one time the hill, like the countryside surrounding it, was thickly wooded. Local placenames like Threepwood (wood of quarrels), Roughwood, Woodside, and Hessilhead (Hazelhead) tell the story. Those woodlands vanished long ago; now the hill o' Beith is crowned by the steep roadways and tall, narrow, picturesque buildings of the town.

High Kirk, square and steepled, built about 1808, commands the town's highest point and is named for its location, not its manner of service. A block or so downhill stands Auld Kirk, tiny and black with age, surrounded by a jumbled yard of toppling gravestones. Its bell, still in place, carries an inscription: "This bell was given by Hew Montgomerie, sone of Hessilhead, anno 1614, and refounded

Town of Beith, North Ayrshire, Scotland.

by the Heritors of Beith, anno 1734." Trinity Church, the newest and largest of Beith's old churches, was built in the middle of the nineteenth century near the western edge of town. All three churches are Presbyterian; all are built of stone. Most other buildings in town are stone as well. Beyond them, the countryside rolls away in a hilly, irregular patchwork of greens and browns, studded with low farm buildings and occasional fences.

Like its woodlands, most of the manor houses of Beith parish have disappeared. The ruins of Hessilhead castle came down just after 1960, leaving a low stone archway half hidden by undergrowth. The house at Roughwood was demolished to make way for a limestone quarry in 1954. Nothing remains at Bradestane but open fields with cattle and stone quarries to the north.[2] Yet through the eighteenth and nineteenth centuries, families of the neighborhood lived in these houses and enjoyed their long histories. Often they were descendants of the families who originally built them.

Located a mile or two southeast of Beith Hill, the Roughwood estate in the mid-nineteenth century consisted of 160 acres in the parish of Beith and 85 acres in the adjoining parish of Dalry, 245 acres in all.[3] The old house would certainly have been built of stone. Two or three stories high, with a slate roof and stone floors, it probably had four smallish rooms on each of the upper stories, and two bigger rooms, the hall and the kitchen, on the ground level. The few windows would have been shuttered against rain and wind, so the house was dark, damp, and chilly except right at the fireside or in the kitchen with its great open hearth. That is where the family gathered, and the cook and other servants, too. Not luxurious, maybe not even comfortable, with heavy oaken doors, great chests for storage, and not much furniture aside from beds, benches, and a table or two, it would have had little in common with the elegant country homes so often pictured in photographs and films. Roughwood was a frugal Scots gentleman's household—nothing less, and nothing more.

The historian George Robertson says that the Hammill family was "very ancient" in the parish of Beith, going back to the year 1371 and possibly a century before. Its coat of arms supports these early dates. One of its devices is a crescent lying on its back, signifying that at least one family member fought in a crusade. Another is a two-pronged, long-handled rake called a shakefork. The shakefork is the symbol of the Cunningham family, North Ayrshire's dominant clan from the mid-twelfth to the mid-fifteenth century. The story goes that a peasant lad of the Cunningham clan once used a shakefork to hide the Scots Prince Malcolm in a pile of hay. In that way the prince escaped his enemies, and he raised that lad to the thanedom of Cunningham as his reward. The shakefork in the Hammill coat of arms shows that they were allied with the Cunninghams when the coat was created.[4]

Accompanying the crescent and the shakefork are a five-pointed star, or mullet, signifying that the owners of the crest were knights, and also a fleur-de-lis. In a Scots coat of arms, the fleur-de-lis signifies an ancient alliance—the "auld alliaunce"—between Louis VII of France and William the Lion of Scotland against the English, their common enemy. That alliance dates back to the thirteenth century, more evidence of the Hammill family's long history in Scotland.[5]

However, no one knows exactly when Roughwood was granted to the family, or who the first Hammill to live there might have been. Ancient charters suggest that the first Hammill to live in Scotland was William de Hameville or de Heneuile or de Hamule. All three of these names are attested at the turn of the thirteenth century, in the reign of William the Lion.[6] William de Hameville witnessed a charter granting fishing rights on the river Solway, in Dumfriesshire at Scotland's southwest border, sometime around 1190.[7] William de Heneuile witnessed two other Dumfriesshire charters between 1194 and 1214. In 1206, Walter de Hamule was granted lands in Lothian.[8] Are these different men or the same one?

The *Oxford Dictionary of Surnames* says that de Heneuile is a variant of de Hameville.[9] De Hamule is probably another variant. All three names would have been pronounced "de Hameville" and are best transcribed that way. As for the inconsistency between Walter and William, given names were abbreviated in the shorthand script of ancient charters. "Wm" could easily be misread "Wr." The historian George Robertson concludes: "Whether this family be derived from this early Anglo-Norman settler, there is no evidence to shew; only, it seems to be not improbable."[10] *The Oxford Dictionary of Surnames* and most family historians and genealogists take a firmer stand, indicating that William de Hameville was the progenitor of the Hammills of North Ayrshire.

The next question, of course, is how "de Hameville" became "Hammill" as the generations passed. Pronunciation is one indication. In Ireland and Scotland, Hammill is pronounced Hommyl. A taxicab driver in Dublin laughed when I introduced myself as a Hammill, pronouncing the "a" as in "apple," the American way. "You mean Hommyl," he corrected me. "Up north where that family settled, they all say Hommyl." More evidence can be found in scattered mentions of de Hommyl, Homyl, and Homel in Scots documents throughout the Middle Ages.[11] These mentions suggest that de Hameville might have become Hammill over time in what was, after all, a very small and lightly populated country.

If the first Hammill in Scotland was a knight by the name of William de Hameville and if the Hammills of Roughwood descended from him, then the surname is not Scots but Norman in origin. Norman! I was very surprised by this—actually, I resisted it. Those Normans were butchers. Moreover, there is no bore like the one who boasts of Norman forebears, especially when the descent cannot be precisely documented. But in fact the association helps to predict the family's social milieu and its religious and political preferences across many generations. In no time at all, intermarriage with local families would have made the Hammills Norman in name but Scots in habit. Eventually de Hameville lost its identity and became just another of the enigmatic surnames one simply takes for granted. De Hameville became Hammill. Who would have thought?

William de Hameville was a few generations away from the Norman named de Hameville who was discharged into England at the time of the Conquest in 1066 or who crossed the Channel to seek his fortune in the British Isles shortly afterward. Scotland welcomed quite a number of these knights and their descendants in the eleventh and twelfth centuries, giving them grants of land, the right to a family crest or coat of arms, and other privileges in exchange for armed service along disputed borders and between feuding clans. With the passage of time, some of these knightly families became rich and influential. Many more evolved or perhaps devolved into the minor gentry of rural districts. The Hammills were certainly among the latter. Still, as minor gentry they took their places in an emerging middle class, a tiny sliver of medieval society that acted as a kind of buffer between the great baronial families that controlled whole regions and the freemen and indentured peasants who far outnumbered everyone else. The Hammills held onto that middle-class status with amazing tenacity. They hold it to the present day.

Not much can be known about individual Hammills through the medieval period except what their status as knights can show. From an early date, the knightly class served their overlords not only as fighters but also as administrators, witnessing documents, sitting on juries, or providing service as ushers or stewards in great households. Increasingly they served as tax collectors, bailiffs, and sheriffs, for as locals they were less likely to antagonize the populace than the "foreign" officers who were appointed by the king.[12]

The scattered mentions given earlier show Hammills in just these roles. William de Hameville witnessed charters around the turn of the thirteenth century. In 1260, John Homel witnessed at an inquest at Irvine, a town not far from the parish of Beith. Andreas Homyl served as bailiff at Roxburgh in the fourteenth century. Another

John Hommyl was master of the Latin grammar school at Aberdeen in 1418. Yet another was bailiff to Sir John Montgomery in 1433. All the while, de Hommyls were keeping up their charters for Roughwood. Such scraps of documentation fix the family securely in its position as minor gentry with administrative responsibilities in their communities.

They also make two other important connections. First is the frequency of the given name John among the Hammills. Together with Hugh and William, John persists as a favorite for six hundred years and more, up to the present day. Hugh and John tend to alternate as names for oldest sons. William is a choice for a younger son, as records from the seventeenth century onward make clear. William de Hameville of thirteenth-century Scotland—was he a younger son, just like the nineteenth-century William Hammill of Washington Territory in the American northwest? I like to think he was.

The other connection to notice is John Hommyl's position as bailiff to Sir John Montgomery in 1433. This mention is the first I know of between the Hammill and Montgomery families, but it is not the last. The two families were closely linked for centuries, in Scotland and then in Ireland later on. Had they been connected even earlier? Montgomery, like Hammill, is a Norman name.[13] The Montgomeries achieved a much higher rank in the British social hierarchy than the Hammills ever did; they may have held that status in Normandy as well. Did the Montgomery/Hammill connection go back so far? It is impossible to know. Still, the duchy of Normandy was sparsely populated, and its social groups clung together both by preference and by necessity. Maybe the two families knew nothing of each other before they lived in Scotland—and maybe they did.

The Montgomeries held several estates in North Ayrshire. The one most often linked with the Hammills was Bradestane (Broadstone), a property of about four hundred acres not far from Roughwood.[14] Like every other landed family in Britain at the time, neither the Hammills nor the Montgomeries owned these properties outright.

Rather, they were feudal tenants: they leased or "held" their lands from an overlord or the king, in turn subletting it to their own tenants, peasant farmers who paid their rent in grain or animals at first, and then, as time passed, in coin.

These peasant farmers were generally indentured to their masters in the early Middle Ages. They "belonged to the land," had virtually no civil rights, could not move without permission, and were protected only by certain vaguely defined customs under the common law. They made up the majority of British subjects for many centuries. Of somewhat higher status was the class of freemen, or yeoman farmers. They did have certain civil rights, and they leased their land for a term of years that varied from place to place and century to century, though it was often twenty-one or thirty-one years. When the term elapsed, the lessee could not assume that his lease would be renewed, even if he could pay the higher rent that was generally demanded when a new lease began. Thus even a freeman's leasehold was not secure.

But gentlemen's leases were "heritable." They could be passed down the generations as long as the family paid its rents and provided the services that its overlord required. Moreover, these leases were written not for a term of years but on three lifetimes. The lease on three lives remained in force as long as one named person was still living, and rents could not be raised for that term. People named grandbabies in them, or magnates of the realm, assuming that the very young or the very rich would live longer than anyone else, and indeed these leases sometimes remained valid for sixty years or longer. They were the precursor of the ninety-nine-year commercial lease that is familiar today.

Properties leased on three lives held the status of freeholds under the law. They represented estates of "dignity," and the gentlemen who held them were known as "heritors," "kindly tenants," or "tenants-in-chief" of the lord to whom they paid their rents. The "heritors" of Beith who refounded the bell at Auld Kirk in 1734 were the gentry of their neighborhood, and they were not too modest to say so.

In England, gentlemanly tenants enjoyed the privilege of voting in parliamentary elections. In Scotland, their privilege and duty was to actually sit in Parliament whenever the king called it into session. In practice, minor gentry like the Hammills rarely exercised the privilege. The trip to Edinburgh, only sixty or so miles away, was fraught with danger, and only the wealthiest and most powerful could afford the armed entourage that such a trip required.[15] Even so, lesser gentry like the Hammills must have made the most of holding the privilege.

By the turn of the fifteenth century, the number of eligible voters in England had grown so large that the English parliament decided to thin their ranks by imposing an income requirement. After 1430, Englishmen could vote only if their freeholds cleared at least forty shillings annually after rents, fees, and taxes. Scotland did not impose the same requirement on those eligible to sit in Parliament, but the "forty shilling leasehold" came to separate gentlemen from yeoman farmers in every corner of Britain.[16]

So it was that on 20 July 1452, Robert de Hommyl appeared before Alexander, Lord Montgomerie, at Ardrossan castle to reaffirm his charters to "the forty shilling land of Roughwood and Bradestane Ward." Fifty years later, on 28 November 1505, another Robert de Hommyl affirmed the charters to the forty shilling land of Roughwood, this time with Hugh, Lord Montgomerie of Bradestane.[17] The Bradestane estate was valued at fifty shillings, but most properties around Beith were valued at the lower amount. It was a Scots parish, after all, and, with few exceptions, its gentry families lived in the bottom tier of their class. Yet, modest as their incomes were, they managed to maintain their rents, negotiate their leases on three lives, pass their estates on to their heirs, and protect their right to sit in Parliament over the course of centuries. Compared with the freemen and peasants who farmed their land, the Hammills with the other gentry families of the neighborhood were privileged indeed.

How did it come to pass that, in the mid-fifteenth century, the de Hommyls paid their rents to Montgomeries and not to Cunninghams? About 1450, a great feud ended the Cunninghams' control of North Ayrshire, and the victorious Montgomeries took their place. Thereafter, the Hammills held their land from the Montgomeries. The relationship between the families continued as the medieval period came to an end and the modern era began. In 1606, as England set about colonizing the world, Hammills followed Montgomeries to Ireland and served them there as agents and retainers. In Scotland, the two families eventually combined—Anna Hammill of Roughwood married Robert Montgomery of Craighouse in about 1725. Though this is the first Hammill-Montgomery marriage for which there is a record, it probably was not the first to take place between the families.

As their descendants increased in number and settled into other parishes, counties, and towns, the Hammills of Roughwood became just one branch of a sizable extended family in lowland Scotland. Most of them were not gentlefolk at all, but found trades or professions by which to support their families. Some left Scotland altogether. Robertson mentions "several respectable merchants in Dublin" by the name of Hammill, and a "Dr. Hammil, Physician to the Emperor of Russia" about 1820! Many others must have stayed in Ayrshire as farmers, artisans, or shopkeepers. Though they undoubtedly made up the majority of family members, these Hammills were not associated with a specific place and thus are very hard to trace.

The Roughwood Hammills formed a thicket of connections with several other North Ayrshire families whose names will resonate in chapters to come. In 1643, Hugh Hammill of Roughwood married Catherine Ralston of nearby Woodside—probably not the first marriage between Ralstons and Hammills. The Semples or Sempills of North Ayrshire became Glasgow merchants with interests in the Maryland tobacco trade. In the seventeenth century, Semples and

Hammills marched together in a state funeral in Ireland. A century later, they did business together in the American colonies.

The Shaws of Greenock married their daughter Elizabeth to Hugh Montgomery of Bradestane about 1587. She and her brother John Shaw accompanied Montgomery to Ireland in 1606, along with some Hammills. In the next century, in Maryland, three Shaw siblings, one named John and one named Elizabeth, married three Hammill siblings. It seems possible that the families intermarried in Britain as well. These favored relationships passed down the generations and then made the transition along with the family from the old world to the new.

The Hammills of Roughwood held their estate through the seventeenth century and into the eighteenth. George Robertson gives the following account of their last years at Roughwood:

> Hugh Hammil of Roughwood, in 1643, married Catherine, daughter of James Ralston of That Ilk, by whom he had a son, Matthew, who married a daughter of Rev. Hugh Peeblis of Mainshill, Minister of Lochwinnoch, by whom he had a son Hugh and a daughter Anna. Hugh sold this estate, about 1736, to Robert Shedden, and afterwards died unmarried. Anna married Robert Montgomery of Craighouse, whose great-grandson, Robert Montgomery, Banker in Irvine, now represents the family of Hammil of Roughwood.[18]

So the siblings Hugh and Anna Hammill were the last to live at Roughwood. Anna married, and her brother Hugh sold out, then died without leaving an heir. Anna and her husband Robert Montgomery had a daughter, Elizabeth, who married Dr. John Witherspoon in 1743. But the Witherspoons, like so many others in the eighteenth century, did not stay in Scotland. Elizabeth became a reluctant immigrant to Princeton, New Jersey, in 1768 when her distinguished husband was offered the presidency of Princeton College.[19] The Witherspoons named their oldest daughter Anna for her Scots grandmother, Anna Hammill. Anna and Robert Montgomery might have had other children who remained in Scotland, but the Hammill name had vanished there, and so had the estate.

Yet the name did not vanish completely. In 1843, a new church was built on the west side of Beith. Now it is called Trinity Church, but for six decades it was called Hamilfield. The land for the church was given by the owners of Hamilfield estate, located right behind it. Today, Trinity Church sits at the east end of the property, and the house called Hamilfield sits at the west end. Together, the buildings occupy about two city blocks. Surrounded by a high cement wall and a garden of trees, Hamilfield is a fine old mansion with wrought-iron gates. Hamilfield Lodge and Hamilfield Cottage, originally outbuildings for the mansion, stand nearby. They are rented to friendly folk who know nothing about the history of the big house beside them. A German couple owns Hamilfield itself. I have not yet solved the mystery of who built this fine home, but my guess would be Robert Montgomery, the banker, descendant of the Hammills of Roughwood.

In 1799, Roughwood passed to the Patricks, relatives of the Sheddens. When Sir William Patrick took over the estate, he found the lands in "a very poor state," the soils clayey, moss-covered, and wet, the farmsteads in ruinous condition. He set about improvements immediately.[20] But the Hammills were not responsible for the property's neglect. They had long since disappeared from Scotland and were established and thriving in Northern Ireland, and by 1799 in the United States as well.

2

A POSSIBILITY OPENS

IN THE spring of 1606, Hugh Montgomery, sixth laird of Bradestane in the parish of Beith, North Ayrshire, shipped servants,
tenants, kinsmen, and as many friends as he could persuade to join
him across the island-filled channel between Scotland and Northern
Ireland to begin a new life in County Down. He was soon followed
by a neighboring laird, James Hamilton of Renfrewshire, and a fair
sampling of all the gentry families of lowland Scotland with their
retainers and tenants. The two lairds did not compel their followers
to join them; Scots lairds were more like country squires than great
lords with almost regal power over their subjects. So what prompted
these people, lairds and followers alike, to move to a notably warlike
region to which they held no historic claim? The answer is simple.
The economic picture in Scotland was bleak, and Northern Ireland
had empty land available for a song.

Scotland is a small country, about the size of Maine, and the least
blessed region of the British Isles if farming is the measure. Three-
fifths of the country is bog, stone, islands, and highlands that are

dramatic to look at but impossible to plant. Even in the southern lowlands, the soil is often sour, stony, thin, or too wet or too dry for crops. Until the eighteenth century, farming methods were unbelievably primitive, far behind those of England or Europe. Peasants insisted on planting ancient but familiar strains of barley and oats whose yields were tiny, barely worth the effort of growing them. People subsisted on oats and on the milk, butter, cheese, fat, and blood (think of blood puddings) that their sheep and cattle provided. The rich lived better, eating meat and drinking wine in good times, but like everyone else they were vulnerable when crops failed and their herds and flocks perished. Short lifetimes and intervals of famine and epidemic disease were the norm.

In spite of kingly efforts to establish central authority, in western Scotland it remained elusive for centuries. In 1600, Glasgow, now so vital a city, had a population of only fifteen hundred. Everyone stole as many animals as they could from their neighbors, and rural security depended on the strength of the local laird and his band of warriors or thugs. The Scots gave us the word *feud*, which has nothing to do with feudalism. It is a northern dialect word meaning "active hatred or enmity," related to the word *foe*. James G. Leyburn, in *The Scotch-Irish, a Social History*, remarks with a certain relish that, before 1800, Scots customs "resembled more those of the time of Beowulf or of the tribes of central Europe during the Dark Ages than those of the present."[1] Thomas Carlyle, also a Scot, called the lairds as a group "a selfish, ferocious, unprincipled set of hyenas." An English traveler in eighteenth-century Scotland found

the landscape a bleak and bare solitude, destitute of trees, abounding in heather and morass and barren hills . . . where the inhabitants spoke an uncouth dialect, were dressed in rags, lived in hovels, and fed on grain [oats], with which he fed his horse; and when night fell, and he reached a town of dirty thatched huts, and gained refuge in a miserable abode that passed for an inn, only to get a bed he could not sleep in, and fare he could not eat, his disgust was inexpressible.[2]

Under these conditions, the question that comes to mind is not so much why people left the country, but why in the world anyone with a choice would stay. But the Scots had few options for migration in large numbers until the turn of the seventeenth century, when England's colonial ambitions opened two frontiers almost simultaneously. One was in North America, and the other was in Ireland.

England had conquered Ireland in the twelfth century, but a great many Irish clansmen didn't seem to know it, especially those in the northern counties of Antrim and Down. In 1600, after decades of fruitless effort and tens of thousands of pounds expended on Irish military operations that never achieved their goal, Queen Elizabeth I sent Lord Mountjoy to the north of Ireland with an army and instructions to suppress rebellion at any cost. Mountjoy complied. He drove out Con O'Neill, chieftain of Down and Antrim, and set about a scorched-earth program of eradication and control that earned him infamy among the Irish, but left upward of half a million acres depopulated and laid waste. Within a few months, O'Neill was helpless in prison, and his former lands were ripe for resettlement.

The first to notice this opportunity beckoning was Hugh Montgomery of Bradestane. He quickly enlisted the support of James Hamilton to take advantage of the situation. I don't want to call them hyenas, but the two Scots lairds certainly had a deep pragmatic streak. They offered the imprisoned Con O'Neill a deal he couldn't refuse. They would buy him out of prison in exchange for two-thirds of his lands. The desperate Con agreed to this, and King James I of England, who in 1602 had succeeded Elizabeth to the throne, after some hemming and hawing signed the necessary papers. Eventually, O'Neill sold most of the rest of his lands to Montgomery and Hamilton.

So in May 1606, just a year before Virginia Colony was established in America, the lairds began transporting and settling their followers in Antrim and Down, the Irish counties nearest western Scotland. Some native Irish remained to contend with, wild men whom the Scots called "wood kerns" (a kern is a lightly armed warrior) because they lay low in the thickets by day and harassed the new settlers by night. Wolves preyed on the settlers' sheep and cattle, even though a bounty was offered on wolves' heads until 1710. But northern Irish soils were deep, rich, and well watered. Its woodlands were thick with oak, beech, birch, willow, and wild game. The Scots settlements prospered. By 1610, Montgomery could raise a thousand fighting men in his parishes, and by 1614, he and Hamilton together could raise two thousand, suggesting a total population in those settlements of about eight thousand.[3]

King James I, a canny Scot by birth, recognized the success of this private endeavor, and in 1610 he expanded it into an enormous state-sponsored program of settlement known as the Plantation of Ulster. English people and lowland Scots were to be proprietors and tenants in Ulster, the traditional name for Ireland's seven northern-most counties. Neither native Irish nor Highland Scots were eligible, they were too wild and too Catholic. Sir Arthur Chichester, the largest proprietor of the English plantation, commented in a letter to King James, "I had rather labour with my hands in the Plantation of Ulster, than dance or play in that of Virginia." Sir John Davies, another prominent Englishman, warned that earlier attempts at settling Ireland had failed, "which will happen to this plantation within a few years if the number of civil persons to be planted do not exceed the number of the natives, who will quickly overgrow them, as weeds overgrow the good corn."[4] King James took the warning to heart. By 1620, when the Pilgrims landed at Plymouth Rock, fifty thousand English and Scots settlers were making their livings in Ulster.[5] By 1640, one hundred thousand Scots, twenty thousand English, and as many more of native Irish populated the north of Ireland.[6]

The Scots migration to Northern Ireland is just one more episode of pioneering in the history of humankind. The crises confronting pioneers throughout that history are remarkably similar. In Northern Ireland and in the American colonies, native inhabitants and wolves were problems that yielded only to extreme solutions. Blood, sweat, and tears when applied to fertile soils produced prosperity and progeny who lived to multiply again, so that empty areas were populated with astonishing rapidity. Place names that twisted the tongue at first quickly became familiar. And people who made the transition from one homeland to another passed along an assumption in the family that if it can be done once, it can be done again, although there is a cost.

The family at Roughwood left no testament, no written word of the dislocation that their move to Ireland brought, both to those who departed and to those who stayed behind. Perhaps the stories they did not write would resemble the two that follow here.

Three Wicked Things

Margaret Hammill, in my thirteenth year

Well, it was so quiet, and so hot—Nurse said it was hot as Lucifer's breath, not fit for good Scottish church-going folk, and what next would come in the world? She sat down on the bench against the dairy wall where the stones are damp and cool, and spread her handkerchief over her face, and went to sleep. Cook was asleep inside the dairy amid the milk basins and pans. I saw her when I went to fetch some buttermilk for Nurse and me. Mother was in her chamber, as every afternoon, and her maid, too. Stillness and heat settled over us like a lid on a pot, and I might have been the last body alive.

I took up my embroidery, where pink roses and green leaves begin to twine across a snow-white field. But my work did not move me. I went to the bucket for water to splash on my face and neck, and then I thought of the river, so cool, so bonny, tumbling along over mossy stones. I took a wee pail in hand and slipped out the door without waking anyone. And that was the first wicked thing.

A flock of crows rose with cries from the riverside when they heard my step. I saw they had been feeding on blackberries, ripe and ready before Cook expected, no doubt because of the heat. I like blackberries warm from the canes, but Cook wants to save them for pies and jam. I filled my belly before my pail, never mind how Cook would scold that I picked without her say-so. And that was the second wicked thing.

And then I saw my stained hands and feet and the purple smears on my apron, pinned over my shift with no frock at all, because of the heat. I stood to my knees in a pool where the water curls and fish hide, and scrubbed skin and apron as well as I could. And then my shift was wet, and I knelt on the pebbles and doused my head and hair, bathing in the river like a boy. And that was the third wicked thing.

But who saw my wickedness? Only the crows, who wheeled back to their feeding when I was done. When Nurse came into my chamber, shamed by her long nap, I sat in a fresh shift, combing out my hair. The pail of blackberries stood in the kitchen for Cook to find. I might tell who picked them, and I might not. For in these strange days when we are a world of women and no breeze stirs, who among us can tell the rules? My father and brothers and uncles and even the plowboys are across the water in Ireland, looking for a new life that they will bring us into whether we will or no.

I like this old life, I have known it for twelve years and it suits me very well. Nurse says I am growing into a fine long-legged lassie right here among the lochs and braes. I do not need a new home. But tenants do not come to me begging for more time to pay their rent, and I remember the sad lifting this spring past, when so many of our sheep and cattle never did rise to eat when the men laid them in green grass by the river. My father says this Scottish land is poor and hard and unforgiving and cannot bear the weight of the people seeking to live upon it. He says we must move on if we can, or risk losing all. And my Lord Montgomerie is pressing him, I know, pressing him to raise men and boats and carry all to the new Irish soil.

When this heat breaks and the wind rises, my father will come home. Nurse or Mother will tell him of my wickedness, if they discover it, and he will remind me of my duty to obey them both. Yet whom will he obey? What would be the greater wickedness for him—to stay here, or to go? And who will be watching him to judge? Does the Lord of Heaven care what he chooses, or only Lord Montgomerie? And think how the crows of Ireland will rise and cry when we come with our pails to pick berries by the river.

Roughwood, summer 1606

Margaret's Nurse Speaks of Beith New Kirk

NEW KIRK! Is that a name? St. Inan's, we called it in my mother's day, for the Irish saint who brought us Christ our Lord back when we worshipped stones and such, God forgive our folly. When I was a wee thing that shared my mother's stool, for in those days we brought our stools from home, the little Virgin still stood in her niche by the font. Country folk dressed her in scraps of silk if they could get it, woolen if they could not, with knitted booties for her naked feet to keep her from the cold. How I loved that little Virgin, and her finery, too. Would she look at me from under her blue hood that was slipping forward over her eyes? She, not old parson, kept my notice through the freezing draft across the earthen floor and the creak of those doors in the winter wind.

I own we were crowded in that small space, with the gentry on the benches and our stools in the aisles. Sometimes folk had to stand in the doors with the rain and wind gusting in. What with the church doors open and the muck in the roads so deep, a good many of a winter Sunday just kept away, said some prayers at hearthside and let it go at that. New

Kirk keeps us Christian by its doors that fit so trim, it could be fairly said. But I do regret that Virgin, now hid away in some loft or attic or in the muddy bottom of the loch for all I know, and the wee lasses nowadays don't have her to study, and my Miss Margaret never once saw her, and that's a shame.

So now we call it New Kirk, and it is new-built on a larger plan, but in same old shape of a cross, and in the old place, if you follow me, with the same wide views all around, high on the side of Beith hill. That's to say hill o' birches in the old tongue. In St. Inan's day, and after, too, oak and birch grew so thick on the hill that wild pigs rooted along the slopes and gentlemen hunted them with hoot, halloo. But the trees have gone to charcoal long since, and some to ship's spars, and a bit that was left to lafts, or galleries, for the quality inside the church, and benches for the rest of us below.

I own those lafts are a very fine thing, for gentle born though they may be, and most of them Montgomeries to boot, how they did squabble and threep in that old church over who sat where! Now each Montgomerie has his own laft, each with its own outside stair, and broad oak boards to sit on, fitted into notches in the walls. Montgomerie of Hessilhead takes the west laft, Montgomerie of Bradestane the east, Montgomerie of Giffen the south, each laird with his followers, of course, and in the north wing is Toun Laft, for the Mayor and such, and those who own town land. We all fit tidy, I own it, and we sing out our hymns with a will, and new parson speaks the sermon in good plain Scots, no more Latin hem and haw. All we lack is a bell to ring us in, though the young laird of Hessilhead told parson one was coming at his order, from the foundry at Edinburgh far to the east. Well, we shall see.

That is to say, some of us shall see. For what is this clamor over Irish lands open to settlement by Scottish folk? My master's laird of Bradestane is determined to seize all that he can fit in his grip, so says Tom Boyd of the Saracen's Head, who in his line of work hears all. We have had lean harvests, sure, and sickness, and our share of misery, but in Scotland that is nothing new. And with New Kirk just now put to rights, how can they think of leaving it behind?

Yet master is tempted, plainly, and if he goes, my darling lassie must go, too—my Margaret, now near thirteen, near of an age to pledge in marriage. Taller than I am by a sight, she is, and than her mother, too, and with a mind of her own. Can I bear to be parted from her, whom I have nursed from infancy? But I can make no such move as they speak of. I am too old, too set in my ways, my people buried here for ages back. Nor does master have need of me in a new place. No, I would but trouble him. I will stay, and my lassie will go, and a hard life she may have of it, wattle and daub instead of stone walls to shelter her, wolves skulking among the sheep, and wild men, too, for all I know, and everything around her new and strange.

No, the young will go, and the old will stay. I'll tend old master and give him his sop, and one day we two will lie in the churchyard, each in our own proper place, and both of us as forgot to the folk as the little Virgin, bless her. New Kirk will be Auld Kirk soon enough, and drafty, and small, and the parish worthies will build anew, I know it. And what of my Margaret, so far from her first home? Well, the old fret and the young get, so they say, and there I leave it, for young miss calls me, and Cook has her pots upon the boil, and today is today, with work enough to get through, though well we know that in the end, time covers all.

Roughwood, summer 1606

Some Hammills accompanied Hugh Montgomery to Northern Ireland or followed him there in the first decade after 1606. Who were they? The record is frustratingly incomplete. Robert and Matthew Hammill, "two Scots," were made denizens of Ireland in 1614.[7] In 1615, a Matthew Hammill was living in North Antrim, barony of Dunluce, as a tenant of the Earl of Antrim.[8] Were Robert and Matthew brothers, and did they move together to North Antrim? Possibly; a Robert Matthews was attested there in the Antrim

Auld Kirk, Beith.

Hearth Money Rolls of 1631. Did Robert and Matthew belong to the Hammill family of Roughwood? That is impossible to say, other than to observe that the Roughwood Hammills did sometimes choose the given name Matthew for their sons. Eventually, a sizable community of Hammills grew up in North Antrim in and near the barony of Dunluce, presumably around the lands tenanted by Matthew Hammill.

Another pair of Hammills with the given names John and Hugh are attested in Ireland in the early seventeenth century, not in Antrim but in the county of Down. John and Hugh participated in Sir Hugh Montgomery's funeral, which took place with great pomp in September 1636. "Hugh Hammill of Roughwood" accompanied a great many other Scots and Irish gentlemen in the funeral procession, while John, identified as Sir Hugh's "gentleman usher," marched with the laird's personal attendants as a member of the Montgomery household. One of many Roughwood Hammills who attended Montgomerys as bailiffs and in other roles, John must have been living in County Down as long—or nearly as long—as Sir Hugh himself.

John and Hugh Hammill can be traced to the first decades of the Scots migration because Sir Hugh's grandson William Montgomery took the trouble to mention them in his wonderful "Memoires" of the Montgomery family, which he wrote sometime in the 1690s.[9] A more enjoyable introduction to these Hammills can scarcely be imagined—except the one that John and Hugh might themselves have written.

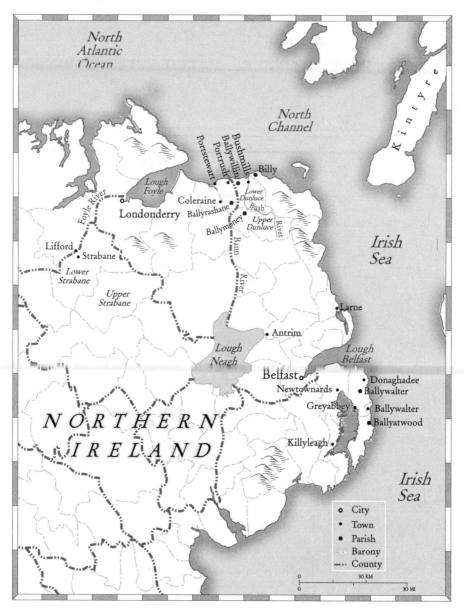

Northern Ireland

3

Scots-Irish Pioneers, 1606–1641

———————— ❦ ————————

ILLIAM MONTGOMERY was born in 1633, so he did not witness the beginnings of the Scots plantation firsthand. In his "Memoires," he explains that the old men who had followed Sir Hugh from Scotland entertained him with their stories when he was a boy. I believe him, and I believe history bears out his claim that the early days of the plantation were productive and for the most part unmarred by violence. William gives a lyrical account of the Scots immigrants' first months in County Down, where they took shelter in three parishes of the eastern Ards Peninsula that Lord Mountjoy had scoured clean of Irish settlement some years earlier. William does not dwell on the destruction that preceded this Scots pioneering; new inhabitants of an old region never do. Rather, he portrays the energy and excitement that Montgomery and his followers poured into their enterprise. He shows immediately that he is quite aware of the parallel between Ireland and America as colonial destinations early in the seventeenth century:

> In the spring time, Aⁿnulo 1606, those parishes were now more wasted than America (when the Spaniards landed there), but were not all encumbered with great woods to be felled and grubbed, to the discouragement or hindrance of the inhabitants, for in all those three parishes aforesaid, 30 cabins could not be found, nor any stone walls, but ruined roofless churches, and a few vaults at Gray Abbey, and a stump of a castle in Newton, in each of which some Gentlemen sheltered themselves at their first coming over.
>
> But Sir Hugh in the said spring brought divers artificers with him, as smiths, masons, carpenters. . . . They soon made cottages and booths for themselves, because sods and saplins of ashes, alders, and birch trees (above 30 years old) with rushes for thatch, and bushes for wattle, were at hand. And also they made a shelter of the said stump of the castle for Sir Hugh, whose residence was mostly there. . . . and some of the Priory walls were roofed and fitted for his Lady and their children and servants, which were many, to live in. . . . Now every body minded their trades, and the plough, and the spade, building, and setting fruit-trees, etc., in orchards and gardens, and by ditching their grounds. The old women spun, and the young girls plyed their nimble fingers at knitting,—and every body was innocently busy. Now the Golden peaceable age renewed, no strife, contention, querulous lawyers, or Scottish or Irish feuds, between clanns and families and sirnames, disturbing the tranquillity of those times; and the towns and temples were erected, with other great works done. . . .[1]

William explains that Sir Hugh's "Lady," Elizabeth Shaw Montgomery, with her six children and many servants, came to Ireland soon after her husband and sheltered in an old priory until a suitable home could be built for the family. She was as enthusiastic a supporter of the Scots plantation as Sir Hugh, seeing to it that water-powered grist mills were built in all three parishes and encouraging the home manufacture of linen and woolen cloth, bringing down prices of both flour and textiles for the immigrants because they no longer had to be imported. In short order, the Irish settlements were exporting grain and cloth to Scotland.[2]

No list has survived, if one ever existed, naming the servants and other members of her extended household, but John Hammill, a child as young as six or seven, might have been among them, attending the Montgomery offspring or acting as a page for the laird and his lady, as had been the custom among gentry families in Britain and Europe for ages past. It is almost too easy to imagine him as a pretty little boy with gentle manners, running errands, tending the family pets, practicing horsemanship with the Montgomery youngsters, carrying her ladyship's sewing box or spinning wheel from room to room, fetching Sir Hugh's handkerchief or walking stick when he went out, and thriving on the excitement of his adventure in this new homeland.

When John was old enough, he became Sir Hugh's gentleman usher, an intimate member of the Montgomery household. At his master's death, John took his place in the ceremonies that honored the viscount's passing. The viscount was embalmed on his death in May 1636, and his body was held until September so that dignitaries from all over Britain and northern Europe could attend the ceremony. It was planned in meticulous detail, and every detail had its significance. William's description of the event opens the door to a different world. [3]

Two "conductors, with black truncheons" led the way from the tower where Sir Hugh's body had been held to the church where the funeral took place. After the conductors marched seventy-six alms-men, "the year current of his Lordship's age," walking two and two in their black gowns and carrying black staves. After them came the servants of all the "Gentlemen and Esquires" attending the funeral, marching two and two, and then, after two trumpeters "sounding the death-march," a standard bearer, the "horse of mourning" with his groom and a footman, more servants, and various "Divines," at last marched the gentlemen and esquires themselves. There were thirty-seven of these. Hugh Hammill of Roughwood was number twenty-six, marching with Robert Adair of Ballymenagh, number twenty-seven. Each of these gentlemen marched in the position appropriate to his station. Hugh Hammill was not the first of the group, but he was not the last, either.

There was much more. Seventeenth in the procession was Neil Montgomery of Langshaw, carrying a cushion that held the viscount's coronet with a "circolet" about it. Nineteenth was "the defunct's Gentleman Usher, named Jno. Hamil, [who] walked bareheaded next before the King at Arms." In that formal age, John's bare head expressed the profoundest bereavement, humility, and respect. His lord's death represented a private as well as a public loss to him. Neil Montgomery, who marched a step or two ahead of John, was probably also a gentleman servant to the viscount, and I surmise that he and John Hammill knew each other well. Perhaps they had grown up together, perhaps were taken into the viscount's service together. Did they name children or grandchildren for each other? I would say, maybe.[4]

After the King at Arms, who carried the dead man's weapons, came the hearse, drawn by six horses draped in black, followed by the chief mourners—members of the deceased's immediate family —their servants, and any number of ordinary men and women in black, marching to the parish church with "the great Bell. . .tolling all the while." Important guests were accommodated inside the church, and the others stood outside during the service.

Dr. Henry Leslie, Bishop of Down and Connor, preached Sir Hugh's funeral sermon, indicating that these Montgomerys worshipped as Anglicans.[5] Like many of the first wave of Scots settlers in Ireland, they conformed to the beliefs and practices of the Established Church. Their Anglican faith set them apart from two more radical Protestant groups of the time. Oliver Cromwell and the Calvinist Puritans dominated southern England by the 1630s. Presbyterians, or "Covenanters," were flourishing in Scotland. Soon after Hugh Montgomery's death, his son and heir "split with his Scottish connections in opposing the covenanting movement while they supported it."[6] Such doctrinal splits, always rancorous and sometimes violent, divided countless families in decades to come.

Not many years after this elaborate funeral, the tranquility of the settlement era was shattered. What happened in Ulster in 1641 is what might have happened in the American colonies if the native peoples of North America had not perished in droves of diseases like smallpox but lived to rebel on a gigantic scale, abetted perhaps by such foreign powers as France or Spain. Driven wild by religious persecution and the loss of their ancestral lands, the Catholic Irish rose in a desperate, bloodthirsty rebellion throughout the country that lasted nearly eleven years and resulted in tens of thousands of deaths, some from battle and many more from deprivation and disease.

An end to the carnage came in 1651 in the person of Oliver Cromwell, the Puritan scourge or Lord Protector of England, whichever you prefer, who had staged a revolution against the ungodly practices of the Established Church in England and had supported the execution of the king, Charles I. He came to Ireland with his troops and "in one dreadful campaign crushed the opposition of Catholic and Presbyterian alike.... His 'pacification' of Ireland was so thorough that it left scars on the country that have never been forgotten or forgiven."[7]

Cromwell died in 1658, and the Protectorate ended a year later when monarchy was restored under Charles II. But the Irish rebellion and Cromwell's suppression of it wiped out more than six hundred thousand people. This annihilation effected a profound social transformation. After Cromwell, Northern Ireland was predominantly Scots. Moreover, that Scots population was now for the most part Presbyterian.[8]

There is no snarl like that of religion in Ireland in the seventeenth and eighteenth centuries, and I am not going to try to comb it out. I will say that a family's religion predicted its politics and its class, and that antagonisms between different Protestant denominations were as savage as those between Protestants and Catholics. Cromwell's Puritans were Calvinists, and so were the Scots Presbyterians, yet they fought like cats and dogs. The Presbyterians for their part hated Irish Episcopalians, though both fought on the Royalist side in favor of monarchy and the restoration of the Stuart kings. During Cromwell's Irish campaign, Scots Presbyterians called Irish Anglicans "the malignants."[9] Such divisiveness was a primary reason for Cromwell's defeat of both groups.

The Montgomerys were Royalists, and they did their part to resist Cromwell in the short, brutal year of his occupation. Sir James Montgomery, William Montgomery's father, lost his life in the aftermath of the fighting, in the winter of 1651. William gives considerable detail in his memoir regarding the Irish Rebellion and Cromwell's occupation—he lived through both. His parents fled with him, an eight-year-old, in 1641 from County Down, where "ye whole country (round about us) was in flames," to Strabane, "a town full of Brittish inhabitants,"[10] and on to Derry. He left Ireland altogether during the Protectorate, to pursue his studies in the safety of Glasgow.

William remembered that his father gave certain of his followers commissions in the Royalist army between 1648 and 1650. Sir James Montgomery appointed "Math. Hamil, whose son, Hugh, built B. Attwood house, with David Ramsey his servants, to be Lieuts. under his command, Jo. Hamill, the First and Second Viscounts' Gentleman, he made Quarter-Master."[11] To rewrite this more clearly, Sir James made his servants Matthew Hammill and David Ramsey lieutenants in the army, and he made John Hammill, gentleman to both the first and second viscount, his quartermaster. In addition, he says that Matthew had a son, Hugh, who later built Ballyatwood House in the parish of Ballywalter, County Down.

John Hammill is the bare-headed gentleman in the first viscount's funeral procession. He continued as "gentleman" to the second viscount, another Hugh Montgomery, until that Montgomery died in 1645. If John Hammill moved to Ireland in 1606, then by 1650 he must have been fifty at least. Yet he was ready to serve in the army, and the army was ready to have him. I suppose this is not too surprising. A capable man could be an effective quartermaster at fifty, since it is not a combat position but one of logistics and supply.

A lieutenant, however, must be ready to fight. Lt. Matthew Hammill must be at least one and maybe two generations younger than John. Could he be a son of that Matthew Hammill who leased land on the north Atlantic coast in 1615? Was he a near relation of John, the gentleman usher?

Intriguingly, a Matthew Hammill, Laird of Rockwood, is named in a list of 260 persons of influence who as Presbyterians were to be removed from Ulster to Munster in 1653.[12] I cannot find a Rockwood in Ulster, but it would be very easy for a clerk to mis-hear or mis-write Roughwood as Rockwood as he took down a list of names. I think this is a Presbyterian Matthew of the Roughwood family who came over from Scotland to help fight Cromwell and stayed too long, perhaps in an attempt to convert his relatives. What happened to him or how exactly he fits into the family tree, I do not know, but he certainly indicates a link between the Hammills of Roughwood and County Down and those of North Antrim.

Now, what of Hugh, Lt. Matthew's son, and his house at Ballyatwood? William Montgomery gives more detail:

I kept a clerk named Hugh Hamill, whose father Lt. Mathew was an old servant to my father, ... & haveing an unsollicited kindness for ye said clerk: .... I wrote for him, & imployed him, and meaning to improove him, I allowed largely on him, every term, to attend my Attorney on record, also called Hugh Hamill, that he might learn to practise for others, & he acted very duty fully, and was well rewarded: he gained credit above all those who had been subsherifs before him, insomuch that he was imployed several years successfully; and gott to be under Senschall to the earle of Clanbrazill; he then maryed & built B. Attwood house where his son & heir now lives.[13]

Now there are two Hugh Hammills to sort out. One is William Montgomery's attorney of record, probably a middle-aged man, and the other is the clerk William sends for because he has "an unsolic- ited kindness" for this youngster. I don't know how the two Hughs are related; already, in the mid-seventeenth century, a thicket of Hammills has established itself in Ireland. Young Hugh lived some distance away from William Montgomery, for he was summoned by letter. Did he come from North Antrim? If I could prove that, I would have some ground for arguing that the Matthew Hammill attested there in 1615 was this young man's grandfather.

In any case, the younger Hugh Hammill acted dutifully and prospered. William Montgomery explains that he was employed as a law clerk and then for some years as a subsheriff of County Down, and he performed so impressively that Henry Hamilton, the second earl of Clanbrassil, lured him away from the Montgomery establish- ment to become underseneschal, or understeward, to his elaborate household at Killyleagh. Sir Henry died in 1675 at the early age of twenty-eight—some say he was poisoned by his wife, the spoiled and self-absorbed young beauty Alice Moore. Hugh's duties as understeward began some years before Sir Henry's death, probably in the early 1670s, and ended when Lady Alice died in a fit of fever and frustration, on Christmas Day, 1677.

During her very brief widowhood and second marriage, to Lord Bargeny of Ayrshire, Scotland, Lady Alice relied on Hugh Hammill as one of her "great agents and confidants" in securing her interests in her first husband's estate.[14] After she died, and perhaps with some relief, Hugh sided with Sir Hans Hamilton, one of Sir Henry's five heirs, and spent the last years of his own life trying to end the interminable lawsuits over the estate. Hugh Hammill of Ballyatwood died between 16 September 1678, when he signed yet another business letter to Lord Bargeny about the lawsuits, and 1681, when he was noted as deceased in a list of Hamilton tenants in County Down. In this list, he was styled as Hugh Hamill, Esq., and he held leases for two townlands in the parish of Ballywalter—Ballyatwood and Ballyrussely—as well as a block of real estate in Ballywalter Town. However he may have been related to the Hammills of Roughwood and the Hammills of North Antrim, Hugh Hammill of Ballyatwood had done very well for himself.[15]

William Montgomery ends his remembrances of the Hammills who served his family with the suggestion that it was Montgomery patronage and "improvement" that enabled Hugh the clerk to build and then live happily ever after in his house at Ballyatwood with his wife and "son & heir." But it seems to have been Hamilton patronage that Hugh acknowledged in the end. A few generations after his death, in the mid-eighteenth century, two County Down wills name Hans and Hans Mark Hamill as heirs to Ballyatwood. Hans was a favorite given name among the Hamiltons.[16]

Improbable as it may seem, another Hugh Hammill of gentry status, roughly contemporary with Hugh of Ballyatwood, lived in northwest Ulster less than one hundred miles from County Down. He can be found in 1679 and 1680, signing leases on properties in County Donegal around the town of Lifford, just across the river Finn from the larger town of Strabane in County Tyrone.[17] Hugh Hammill of Lifford may seem like one Hugh Hammill too many for those reading this account. Yet of all the Hughs touched on in this chapter, he is most important to the story.

Judging by his death date in about 1709, Hugh of Lifford was some years younger than Hugh of Ballyatwood. He may have been a native of Strabane, the town that William Montgomery said was "full of Brittish inhabitants" in 1641. One of these was a John Hammill who, in a deposition dated 1674, gave his age as sixty-five.[18] Could this John Hammill be the gentleman usher of the 1630s and 1640s, now grown old and living with family members in County Tyrone? Was he the father of Hugh of Lifford and Hugh's younger brother William? Did Hugh and William Hammill share a grandfather or great-grandfather with Hugh of Ballyatwood? At the moment, none of these questions can be answered.

Hugh of Lifford married Elizabeth Creighton on Friday, 9 May 1670. Her older brother, Col. Abraham Creighton, was an army officer who twice served as High Sheriff of County Fermanagh.[19] I imagine that Elizabeth met Hugh through her brother. When Hugh took the lease on the Lifford estate, Creighton was one of his guarantors. But Hugh and Elizabeth did not live at Lifford, though Hugh owned mills and plantations there. They preferred the city life in Strabane, where Hugh energetically acquired town properties throughout the 1680s.

Hugh Hammill of Lifford served as High Sheriff of County Donegal in 1682 and 1685. He was a member of parliament for the borough of Lifford in 1692. These appointments show that he, like many Hammills in Ireland, conformed to the beliefs of the Established Church. Like his in-laws, the Creightons, and many others who had immigrated to Ireland in the early seventeenth century, Hugh of Lifford worshipped as an Anglican.

Hugh of Ballyatwood and Hugh of Lifford prospered in the mid- to late seventeenth century in part because no dramatic outside events intervened to slow them down. The years between 1660 and 1685 were calm in the British Isles. King Charles II held the throne, no revolutions rocked the ship of state, and everybody worked to mend livelihoods that had been battered in the upheavals of the 1640s and 1650s. In Northern Ireland, prosperity was often linked to the manufacture and export of linen cloth. Planters raised flax on their lands and milled it in their factories, then exported linen to booming markets in the American colonies and elsewhere. Businessmen of Scots heritage grew rich, especially Anglicans. Presbyterians were also able to thrive, though government discriminated against them in many ways, creating a reservoir of resentment and bad feeling even as their numbers increased every day. Catholics struggled to get by and had almost no civil rights at all, but that was nothing new.

By the late seventeenth century, Northern Ireland was brimming with Hammills. Though the relationships among them cannot be established, it is clear that many were businessmen, including those who, like Hugh of Ballyatwood, began their careers as functionaries in aristocratic households. Besides the lawyers, accountants, real estate speculators, and merchants whose activities rose to public notice, many other less conspicuous Hammills were undoubtedly making their livings as farmers, shopkeepers, and weavers or other kinds of artisans—the middling folk of their time and place. In the early nineteenth century, they can be found operating as carriagemakers, blacksmiths, and grocers throughout Ireland's northern counties.[20] Almost certainly, they conducted those same businesses and trades in the seventeenth and eighteenth centuries as well.

The late-seventeenth-century political calm that enabled British citizens to prosper ended in 1685 with a terrible jolt. Charles II died in that year, leaving the crown to his Catholic brother, James II. James's ascension to the throne brought as much joy and relief to the Catholic Irish as it did shock and horror to the Protestants, who feared repression if not extermination at his hands. The Ulster Scots, conformist and nonconformist both, welcomed the news in 1689 that the Protestant Prince William of Orange, backed by powerful interests in England and Europe, had landed in western England to attempt the throne for himself. His arrival in Cornwall began the conflict known in textbooks as the Glorious Revolution. In the course of it, Catholic rule of England was defeated forever and the English Parliament became more powerful than any king. By chance, Ireland was the battleground, and Hugh Hammill of Lifford and his brother William were in the thick of the struggle.

4

Hugh and William Hammill
and the Siege of Derry

M OST AMERICANS have heard of the Battle of the Boyne, when, on 12 July 1690, William of Orange's armies defeated those of James II, sending him fleeing to France. But that battle was, in terms of outcome, a mere formality. The war had been won a year earlier, at the Siege of Derry, when the citizens of that town, among the northernmost in Ireland and the major town in County Derry, held out against the besieging Catholic army for one hundred five days, until reinforcements from Prince William arrived to destroy James's hopes completely.

The Siege of Derry is the nexus of powerful myth today just as it was three hundred years ago. It was one of the few times—perhaps the only time—that events in Ireland reached international significance and indeed changed the course of European history. Reverend John Graham, whose *History of the Siege of Derry* was completed on 1 January 1829, began his account like this:

"As Ireland was doomed to be the arena upon which the fate of the liberty of the West of Europe was to be decided, so was it from this island that James II received the first intelligence of the Prince of Orange's designs against him."[1] Graham, who was passionately Protestant in his allegiances, referred to James as "the Royal bigot," and reported that the king "was heard to say, that a 'Protestant stunk in his nostrils,'" and his Chief Justice threatened that "before the expiration of one short month," the Protestant rebels of England would "be seen hanging in all parts of it like bunches of onions."[2] These comments, or rumors of them, were not encouraging to Protestants anywhere in the realm.

James's strategy was to engage William from both Ireland and England. He sent one army southwest from London to meet William's troops coming up from Cornwall, and a second army north from Dublin to Northern Ireland, where it would sail across to Scotland, join regiments of Catholic Highlanders, and march south to trap William's forces from the rear. As James's Irish army, reinforced with French soldiers and advisors, advanced northward,

> the Irish in all places were assembled in great bodies, killing the cattle of the Protestants ... so that many who had lived in great plenty and hospitality now wanted the common necessaries of life, and had nothing left to prevent them from starving. ... The horses of the gentlemen and farmers were seized for the king's service, and brought into the garrison towns, where the Popish soldiers lived at free quarters in the houses of Protestants, by which these unfortunate people were reduced to such a state, that many of them were not left a morsel to eat or a bed to rest upon.[3]

These events, or rumors of them and much worse, reached Ireland's north far in advance of the soldiers and drove many hundreds of Protestants off their land into Derry, where they felt somewhat safer behind the town walls. This was normally a city of perhaps ten thousand, but its population more than doubled just before the siege, swollen by soldiers and refugees. In the winter of 1688, the town began to muster men and build fortifications for its defense under Lieutenant-Colonel Robert Lundy, the military governor and a Scots Episcopalian. Yet on 7 December 1688, when the Irish army first became visible across the River Foyle, panic and indecision reigned among the town leaders, including Lundy. Thirteen apprentice boys, famous now in song and story, took it upon themselves to close and bar the town gates in the very face of the enemy.

Lundy's indecisiveness continued, and the Derrymen began to suspect his loyalty to their cause. When the fighting began in earnest, in April 1689, their suspicions were confirmed. Lundy abandoned the town, slipping away by night to safer shores. The town council hastened to arrange a new military command. As everywhere in Ireland

Londonderry Cathedral viewed from the city walls, Londonderry, Northern Ireland.

at that time, tensions between Protestant denominations had been running high in Derry. But the crisis precipitated by Lundy's flight drew the townsfolk together; Anglicans and Presbyterians set their antagonisms aside and found a way to share the cathedral between them. Though the senior officers were Anglican, most townspeople, soldiers, and junior officers were Presbyterian.[4] Hugh Hammill, one of eight colonels appointed to defend the city, was Anglican like the rest of the top command.

Col. Hugh Hammill distinguished himself in several battles, the first on 14 April, near Lifford on the River Finn, when he and Captain Crofton "fought all through the night and inflicted heavy casualties on the enemy."[5] He engaged the enemy once more on 25 April, at the battle of Pennyburn Mill, where after brisk fighting the Protestants were forced to retreat, and again in early May, at the second battle of Windmill Hill. Here Hugh was wounded. A versifier of the siege tells us:

> While Col. Hammel did the foe pursue,
> Through his left cheek a pistol bullet flew.

Reverend Graham, who quoted these lines in his history, said it was "a small bullet" that apparently did no permanent harm, though it must have left a scar. Hugh no doubt regarded it as a badge of honor.[6]

The hostilities soon reached the town of Derry itself. Here is a contemporary description of the Catholic army's first attack on its walls, given by none other than William Hammill, Col. Hugh Hammill's younger brother:

> The horrid Ingines of War ... play'd upon the City, [and] with the utmost Vengeance, set it on Fire in several Places at once, and the thin Paper Buildings soon shiver'd into Pieces, and dropt in upon the Heads of the poor frighted Inhabitants (few of which had ever

heard the noise of a Cannon before). . . . So that nothing was to be seen over the whole Place, but Fire, Smoak, Ruins, and Horrid Death, Pain and Anguish in a Thousand different Aspects, nor to be heard but Dying Groans, the sharp accented screeches of Dread and Pain; the falling of Houses, and the Cannons roaring for more Prey and Slaughter. . . . *Death* began to appear among them now in another Shape, viz. *Famine*: . . . and first they began with eating their *Horses*, till all the *Troops* were reduced to Foot; and when these failed, they fed upon *Tallow* and *Starch*: And when all fail'd, they had recourse to the Salt Hides from the *Merchants* Warehouses, for the Carren [carrion] they had before eat up.[7]

Rev. Graham added: "The pale and emaciated victims of hunger were every day seen collecting wild vegetables and weeds, and all kinds of sea wreck, which they devoured greedily, to the total ruin of their health."[8] Money became almost without value. By the time the English relieved the siege on 7 August 1689, Derry was teetering at the point of collapse.

But the town's troubles were not over. When James's army began its retreat, it pillaged its way south to the seaports where ships waited to carry the men to safety:

They that had Estates, had their Mansions Plunder'd and Destroy'd, their Corn and Cattle taken away; and the Fields being Uncultivated and Unsown, their Hopes of a Harvest were likewise entirely cut off. . . . [Within the city,] Every Cellar was a Grave, where many Dead Carcasses lay piled one upon another, in Stench and Rottenness, without Shroud or Coffin to cover them; where they saw without a Figure, that *Corruption is our Father, and the Worms our Mothers and Sisters:* Mothers saw their Children, Husbands their Wives, and Wives their Husbands, in the manifold and foul Embraces of loads of Vermin, that gorg'd and wanton'd upon them without Controul.[9]

But the worst of it was that England never compensated the Derry defenders for their victory. Hugh Hammill's service continued through the siege and afterward. He was appointed one of six commissioners to represent Derry in a parley demanded by the besieging army, and he with many others signed the victory address that was sent to Prince William when the siege was lifted.[10] And what was his reward? The relieving English officer, Major-General Pierce Kirke, immediately demoted him, putting him "under the command of Captain White, to the severe injury of one of the most distinguished defenders of the city." Graham commented:

> Hamill went to London to remonstrate against this unjust act, and to solicit compensation for his losses, and a remuneration for his acknowledged services. The tradition, in Lifford, records his disappointment; his only reward, according to it, being a civil reception and the present of a gold laced hat.[11]

Patrick Macrory, a recent historian of the Scots experience in Ireland, sums it up:

> The true soldiers of Derry, the citizen army that had borne the heat and burden of the siege, were now to be treated by the English government with a shabby meanness that almost passes belief. Charles Fox, the Paymaster of the Forces, had reported that the eight Derry regiments, from the dates of their commissions to the end of the siege, were owed nearly £75,000. . . . a House of Commons Committee, investigating the matter in 1705, found that . . . the total debt due the garrison was now £134,958 3s. 3d., of which so far less than £10,000 had been paid. And this was simply the total of ordinary pay owing to men who had served as soldiers of King William and did not take into account money spent on horses, arms and accoutrements, most of which had been found by the officers and men from their own

pockets.... The ex-soldiers of Derry appointed Colonel Hamill of Lifford, 'noble Hugh Hamill,' as agent to pursue their claims, a thankless office which in 1698 he handed over to his brother, William, who was living in England at the time. For thirty years William Hamill battled on to no avail and finally, having spent thousands of his own money on the hopeless task, found himself imprisoned for debt.[12]

William Hammill died in Newgate Gaol in 1721, soon after he published his vehement pamphlet entitled *A View of the Danger and Folly of being Publick-Spirited and Sincerely Loving One's Country.* The bulk of the pamphlet copies his accounts of what was spent on Derry's defense and presents the letters and petitions that he, Hugh, and others submitted to Parliament, kings, queens, and noblemen through the thirty years that William served as agent for the debt. He calculates that the arrears of pay for the Derry defenders is by 1721 at least £195,000,

> for want of which, or any part of it, these thirty-three years,
> to purchase the common necessaries of life, those of them who
> were so unfortunate as to survive the flame, the pestilence
> and the sword of the enemy have been left by their fellow-
> subjects (for whom they suffered these hardships) to drop into
> their graves one after another through hunger, cold and other
> extremities of misery; and many of them could not have found
> graves to lie down in, their poverty being such that few had
> enough to fee the parish officers.
> ... We have lost all our estates, our blood and our friends
> in the service of our country and have nothing for it these
> thirty years but royal promises, commissions without pay,
> recommendations from the throne to Parliaments and reports
> and addresses back to the throne again, finely displaying the
> merits of our services and our sufferings and the justness of our

claim. . . . Good God! What have we done or left undone to be
treated after such an unheard-of manner?

But it was no use. The war was over, Ireland was no longer a
threat, and Parliament preferred to use the state's funds to discharge
other obligations. William died maintaining that he had spent four
thousand pounds of his own money pursuing his suit and relieving "several of his own principals, being in a starving and miserable
condition, and still lies under weighty debts, all of which has now
reduced your Petitioner to want in his old age."[13]

The last few pages of the pamphlet present "Mr. William
Hamill's Private Case." He does not provide what the genealogist
most desires: his parents' names, his and Hugh's places and dates of
birth, and the names of their siblings, wives, and children. But what
he does provide is both useful and eloquent:

William Hamill, is Brother and Heir of Col. Hugh Hamill,
Deceased; who was one of the Colonels of Londonderry; of an
Estate of about 1000£. per Ann[um], and was by much, the most
Active Man in that Memorable Siege, and kept a Diary
of the same: He was look'd upon as the Spring of their Actions,
and the First in their Councils. When King James sent to
desire some of their Number to be sent out to treat with him
(the Colonel being the Principal Man) he was Tempted with a
promise of Twenty Thousand Pounds, to be lodged in any of the
Banks abroad; if he would disert his Party, and not Return to the
Garrison: Which he Bravely Rejected; tho' his Estate was then
very much Incumbered.

After that Great Affair was over, he was appointed Agent for
those Regiments; and when he came to England, he was hand-
somely Received at Court, particularly by Queen Mary: He
followed these Peoples Claims, with all the Application and
Address imaginable; but the former Incumbrance upon his

Estate, with about 3000£. Damage, done to his *Mills* and *Plantations*, by the Enemy; together with the Expence of Soliciting these Claims, and the Money he did at several Times Advance, to the Indigent Officers, who had no dependance but upon their Agent; having Script Him of his whole Estate; The Thoughts of that, together with the Disapointments he met with at Court, first effected his Head, and soon after broke his Heart.

Mr. William Hamill, having thus lost his Brother; likewise the Prospect of an Estate of 1000 Pounds a Year, to which he should have succeeded: However to the Agency he succeeded, at the earnest desire of all concern'd.

He likewise followed their Claims, with all the Dexterity of a Man of Business; to which he has been accustomed from his Youth, but with his Brothers ill Success and hard Fate; For besides His Charges in Soliciting for above 20 Years; he has been obliged, as Agent, to Support many of the Officers while Living, and to be at the Charge of Burying several of them when they Died in Want; till he has spent and laid out above 4000£. which was his All; not doubting in the least but that a Debt of so much Merit, as that, for which he was soliciting, would not only have been Justly and Honourably Paid; but that some Singular Marks of the Nations Gratitude, would have been shown to every Body concern'd in it.

William has given a neat summary of Hugh Hammill's life and death, suggesting in his reference to "Mills and Plantations" that his brother might have been engaged in the linen industry, and explaining that James's retreating armies destroyed that source of livelihood, further compromising his encumbered estate. However, the Creighton family—Hugh's in-laws—took a different view:

In 1670, Col. Abraham Crighton's sister had married one Hugh Hamill of Strabane, Co. Tyrone. Eight years later, Hamill purchased Lifford (for £3,450) from Richard Hansard of Ballind-rait, Co. Tyrone ... with money largely borrowed from Crighton, and following the purchase, Hamill fell into increasingly serious financial difficulties. . . . By 1707, General David Creighton had obtained all or most of the Lifford estate as a result of foreclo-sure or other action to recover the money owed by Hamill.[14]

This dismissive paragraph ignores the events that followed the Siege of Derry and suggests that Col. Abraham Creighton should have known better than to trust Hugh with his money and his sister. But William believed that Hugh died half-mad and heartbroken, crushed by his financial losses and the deeply insulting failure of his suit at court. Did his wife, Elizabeth, survive him to live as an impoverished gentlewoman dependent on her older siblings? Since Hugh left no living child, the answer might be no—she might have died years before her husband, in a childbirth gone wrong, or as the victim of a fever that took her life before she became a mother.

And what of William? He described himself as a skillful "Man of Business, to which he has been accustomed from his Youth."[15] He may have been a linen exporter; he moved to London to facilitate his business dealings, and, though it broke him in the end, he was wealthy enough to furnish thousands of pounds of his own money to the support of the Londonderry troops. His pamphlet demonstrates all the paraphernalia of an eighteenth-century gentleman's educa-tion: quotations in Latin and Greek, classical allusions, Biblical pas-sages, and a good deal of rhetorical skill. He considered himself a gentleman, and styles himself as such on his title page. But though he clearly belonged to Northern Ireland's economic and business elite, he was not a member of the governing class, and he and his brother bore the taint of trade. Perhaps that told against them in the rarefied atmosphere of the royal court.

William's pamphlet is the only document I know of that was cre-ated by a Hammill to communicate with the public, to express not only the facts of a great wrong but something of a private life, a personal history. I close these excerpts from William's pamphlet with a brief passage expressing his political views:

> Whatever others may think of the Martyrdom of King Charles
> the First, I confess I could never read the Tryal and Sufferings
> of that Prince without droping a Tear, nor yet without some
> sensible pleasure, in the mean time, to find in him to his last
> Breath, so rare an Instance of Fortitude and Courage in his brave
> defence of the Fundamentals of our happy Constitution.[16]

William Hammill supported the "presence and regular Administration of a Lawful King," defended the British Constitution, and was moved to tears of pain by Charles's execution and no doubt tears of joy when the monarchy was restored. He was a Royalist, and an Anglican. Of course.

5

John Hammill the Immigrant

―――――――――― ❧ ――――――――――

*T*HE SIEGE of Derry and the Battle of the Boyne were fought
in the last twelve years of the seventeenth century, when the
Scots settlements in Ulster were about eighty years old. From a population of a couple of thousand in 1606, four or so generations of
natural increase and continued migration from Scotland had produced a population of some three hundred thousand Scots in Ulster
by 1690. Among this burgeoning population were a good many
Hammills. Those who lived in the Strabane area and in County
Down have been relatively easy to trace, some because they themselves rose to prominence in their communities, and others because
their influential patrons chose to mention them in family accounts.
A third large cluster of Hammills in Ulster was centered in North
Antrim, in the Barony of Dunluce on the Atlantic coast. This was
the home of the Matthew Hammill who in 1615 was a British tenant
of the Earl of Antrim. John Shaw was a tenant of the same earl in
the 1620s—maybe a relative of Elizabeth Shaw Montgomery, the
wife of Sir Hugh Montgomery of Bradestane. These North Antrim

Hammills have left fewer accounts of themselves and their doings than the others, but they certainly prospered. Within a few decades, the Hammill family had proliferated amazingly in North Antrim.

In 1631, when muster rolls were drawn up to see how many fighting men could be raised in the Scots counties, eight Hammills were counted among the Earl of Antrim's British tenants in the Barony of Dunluce. Of these, four were named John, including one junior, one was Hugh, and one was William. How many individual families are represented? I would say between three and six, all of them closely related. Matthew Hammill was not counted, suggesting that by 1631 he was deceased.

About forty years later, in the Hearth Money Rolls of 1669, eleven separate Hammill households were counted in North Antrim. Three were headed by Johns, three by Hughs, two by widows, and there were also households for Robert, Thomas, and Brian Hammill. Eight of these households were located in the Barony of Dunluce. Six were in Upper Dunluce around the town of Ballymoney, and two were in Lower Dunluce on the Atlantic. These families were undoubtedly closely related as well.

The poll taxes for North Antrim returned between 1666 and 1669 show a John, a Patrick, and a Neale Hammill living in the townland of Killycarn, parish of Skerry, Barony of Lower Antrim, some miles south of Upper Dunluce. Are they brothers or cousins or a father with two sons, and do they represent one household, or two, or three? It's impossible to say. Clearly, the family is expanding into new territory, and here for the first time among the Hammills is the given name Neale. I like the idea that this name Neale was originally a tribute to Neil Montgomery, who marched with John Hammill in Hugh Montgomery's funeral procession in 1636. But Neale is a popular Scots given name—there may be no connection at all.

The name persists for several generations among the Antrim Hammills. In 1704, a Neil Hamill was Ruling Elder of the Presbyterian church in Kilraughts parish, Upper Dunluce. By 1715, this Neil had become commissioner of the church. In 1728, a Neale Hamill was living in Tornaroy, in the parish of Derryaghy near Belfast. In 1743, Neale Hamill was a member of the Presbyterian Synod in an area of Antrim known as The Route.[1] Was he the same Neale Hamill as the one in Tornaroy in 1728, or a different one? And how were all these Neales of Northern Ireland related to the infant Neale Hammill who was born in Maryland Colony in about 1743? For the given name Neale pinpoints the branch of the North Antrim Hammills that produced my seven-times-great-grandfather, John Hammill, who left Ireland to begin a new life in Maryland in the first quarter of the eighteenth century.

John Hammill surfaces for the first time in colonial land records for Charles County, Maryland, on 26 January 1726. He had a son whose name, spelled phonetically as N-a-i-l, is mentioned just once in a will, and he also had a grandson Neale, his daughter's child. That name Neale links the Maryland Hammills to the cluster of Neale Hammills in North Antrim, their place of origin. The spelling N-a-i-l seems to confirm that John Hammill came from Ireland. What pronunciation could be more Irish than Nail for Neale? Like mail for meal, it's a giveaway.

At Chicago's Newberry Library, I found a topographical survey of North Antrim made in 1838. The survey indicated that Hammills were buried in the eighteenth-century graveyard in Ballywillin Parish, North Antrim. It went on to say that about forty people emigrated from Ballywillin to America each year, usually in September. Three small ships a week called at the town of Portrush bound for Liverpool, and three or four called each week that were bound for Glasgow. The statistics would have been similar a century earlier. So many Irish Protestants left Ulster between 1725 and 1729 that the English Parliament appointed a commission to investigate their departures, fearing that every Protestant in Ulster might leave home for North America.

Also at the Newberry Library, I found a small book by the Reverend T. H. Mullin called *Families of Ballyrashane: A District in Northern Ireland*. Ballyrashane is the parish adjacent to Ballywillin on the west. Hammills were mentioned in that book, but they dated to the early nineteenth century. Then, on page 207: "John Hamill of Ballymacvena appears as a surveyor in the parish in 1725.... John Hamill's name actually goes back to 1716, but part of the townland name is eaten away, and only Ballyma——— appears. It can be safely assumed that this is intended for Ballymacvena, as in 1725." I could not believe my luck.

In Charles County depositions, John Hammill gave his age often. It is easy to calculate that he was born in 1692 or 1693. In 1716 he would have been twenty-three or -four, an adult in his home parish. In 1725, he disappeared from Ballymacvena to appear a few months later in the records of Maryland. Very possibly he took one of those Portrush packets that departed in late September, depositing him in his new country in November or December 1725.

How can I be so certain that this John Hammill was my seven-times-great-grandfather? It is because John of Ballymacvena and John of Charles County, Maryland, were both surveyors. The Charles County inventory of John Hammill's estate includes instruments for land measurement and a book on land surveying. Many of the depositions he gave in Charles County had to do with boundary disputes, for he was often called on to help resolve them. I have a photocopy of a plat of survey that he drew and signed in 1745. The names, the dates, the occupations converge too neatly to be coincidence. And there is one more link that I will turn to later in this chapter—the link of religious faith.

But though I am certain John Hammill of Ballymacvena became John Hammill of Charles County, Maryland, I cannot begin to explain how he was related to John the gentleman usher of County Down, or to Hugh and William Hammill of the Siege of Derry, or to Hugh of Ballyatwood and Hugh of Lifford in the counties of Down and Tyrone. I simply do not know. Impatient readers will wonder why I took them on that multichapter tour of the Ulster Hammills if John the immigrant was no relation, or related at such a distance that it could hardly signify.

But I say that to know John's relatives, even distant ones, helps to understand him and the framework that produced him. More tireless research in Ulster archives might reveal the missing connections. And I think these Hammills might have been quite closely related. John was born during the lifetimes of both Hugh and William. He was of an age to be a grandson to William, or a grandnephew. Judging by the names John gave his American sons, his own father's name was Hugh. If I could show that the William Hammill who wrote the pamphlet had lived or done business in North Antrim before he moved to London, if I could show that William had a son named Hugh—you see how tantalizing the possibilities might be.

But even if John was only distantly related to Hugh and William Hammill, he would certainly have known that they were kin. He would have felt their fury with the English, and, when Hugh died a ruined man and William perished in debtor's prison, he would have felt their disgrace. Not surprising if four years later, in 1725, he decided to take his talents elsewhere, to a place where they would be appreciated, not punished. So often the English government missed the obvious consequences of the path it chose to take, especially in Ireland.

Was John the immigrant a member of the minor gentry, like the Hammills of Roughwood, Ballyatwood, and Strabane? Nothing suggests that he was. I think the Hammills of North Antrim, like their descendants in Maryland and Virginia, farmed and also operated family businesses or practiced a profession or trade. John was a surveyor; in the early nineteenth century, other Hammills in North Antrim worked as blacksmiths and coachmakers; some were grocers or merchants or dairymen. Today Hammills, including plenty of Johns, Hughs, and Williams, are listed in North Antrim communities as lawyers, doctors, businessmen, farmers, educators, and more.

North Antrim was and is a prosperous region of Northern Ireland, a good place to make a home. Ballywillin, John Hammill's home parish, extends from the Atlantic coast inland in a narrow rectangle. Its name means "mill town" in Irish. Its largest community is the town of Bushmills, named for the water-powered mills that since time immemorial have operated where the River Bush flows into the Atlantic, grinding grain and processing wool and flax. Since 1608, at the dawn of the Scots plantation in Ulster, Bush waters and local barley have been malted, then distilled into the famous whiskey that carries the Bushmills name.

Ballywillin soils are fertile. An 1837 topographical survey of the parish remarks on their "excellent state of cultivation." Today, flourishing green fields and pastures crowd nearly to the ocean's shore. The parish lies just three miles northeast of Coleraine, in County Derry, and shares that city's prosperous heritage. Wealthy individuals traditionally built their "elegant lodges and pleasing villas" along Ballywillin's coast. The Victorian resort town of Portrush, grown a bit seedy, still boasts its elegant seafront hotels. Inland are "pleasantly situated" villages, each with its "handsome and spacious" gentlemen's residences, many of them lived in today.[2]

Another survey comments, "There have always been schools in this parish," and continues, "The inhabitants are chiefly of Scottish descent and possess much of the Scottish habits, customs and dialects; they are very comfortable in their circumstances and manner of living.... They are intelligent and well informed, and seem to have a desire for knowledge and information."[3] That is a good description of John Hammill the immigrant and many of his American descendants.

The ruin of an old stone church can be found today in Ballywillin parish. The 1837 topographical survey describes it as "an ancient, spacious, and handsome edifice, in the early English style, ... said to be the only one in the diocese or county, built prior to the Reformation, in which divine service is now performed; it has neither tower nor spire, but being situated on an eminence it is visible at the distance of several leagues at sea."[4] Now the church is roofless and nearly floorless, with grass growing up between flat tombstones that once lay inside. But its walls still stand on that "eminence," and the views from the ruin are spectacular, looking out over rolling farmland to the Atlantic Ocean, a wide ribbon of blue in the northeast.[5]

For historians of the Hammills, the treasure of the church lies in its vestry book for the years 1710–55, and in the line of six Hammill headstones outside the ruined church walls. The oldest legible stone commemorates John Hammill of Ballymacilvenon, who died in 1820, age sixty. So he was born in 1760. John Hammill the immigrant left the parish only forty years before this other John was born. Both Johns came from the townland of Ballymacilvenon or Ballymacvena—these are variants of one townland name.[6] Here is the root or heart of the North Antrim family that produced the immigrant John.

Now, what was the denomination of the Ballywillin parish church? Was it Catholic? No, the parish had not been Catholic since the Reformation. Was it Presbyterian, as Americans would tend to expect? No again. The church was Anglican. It was Established Church, in the seventeenth and early eighteenth centuries, the church of the prosperous and the successful. John Hammill was Anglican, like many of his Ulster relatives. When he went to America, the family social and religious affilations went with him. Formed in Scotland and continued in Ireland, they took root in America as well. John was a Hammill, a member of a family that holds to tradition. His Anglican faith is the final link identifying the Irish John Hammill with the American one.

At the beginning of this chapter, I mentioned several Neale Hammills who were not Anglican, but Presbyterian. Other Hammills were Presbyterian, too. In 1706, two John Hammills were

Ruins of Ballywillin Parish Church, Ballywillin Parish, Northern Ireland.

Ruling Elders of the Presbyterian synod, one at Templepatrick and one at the presbytery of The Route. A James Hammill was Ruling Elder at Cootehill that year.[7] So religious divisions occurred among the Hammills as well as among Montgomerys and other Ulster families. Did heated arguments fly and men stomp out of their cousins' houses over questions of traditional church hierarchy—bishops versus elders? Did daughters break their parents' hearts by marrying into the wrong faith? I imagine they did.

I had assumed that John Hammill the immigrant, like the vast majority of Scots-Irish, was Presbyterian in Ireland, whatever he may have become in America. This line of thinking caused me innumerable problems as I tried to place John Hammill in his Maryland context, and in following it, I ignored a whisper of family lore that said the Hammills were "always" Episcopalian—how could I dismiss one of these few precious clues to the past? Most Ulster Scots came to America as Presbyterians, but John Hammill did not. He kept to his traditional beliefs at a time of religious divisiveness. The strongly Anglican colony of Maryland appealed to him in part because he shared its faith.

John was one little pebble in a landslide of men and women who left Ulster for America in the early eighteenth century. For the country they left behind, their departure was cataclysmic. By most estimates, just under a quarter-million Ulster Scots entered the colonies before the Revolution. Northern Ireland lost a third of its inhabitants in the space of fifty years. Whole villages were decimated. Parishes could not afford to maintain their churches and schools. The young men vanished, leaving old folks and women at home to live out threadbare lives. Those who profited were the colonies, and the merchants and sea captains who transported the immigrants to their new homes.

Before 1731, English trade regulations excluded Ireland from the lucrative tobacco economy, but a lively secondary trade existed in the export of household goods, horses, linen cloth, and indentured servants to the colonies. The return cargo for Irish ships consisted of grain and flaxseed, especially the latter. The colonies produced the seed with the help of indentured labor from Ireland, and the Irish raised the crop, manufactured the cloth, and shipped low-priced linens back to the colonies, in a trade that increased steadily after 1705. Small port towns in the far north of Ireland carried on a surprisingly large share of this activity. In the autumn months, ships left the harbors of Derry, Larne, and tiny Portrush on a tightly synchronized schedule, carrying linens and people to the colonies and sailing home loaded with seed for the spring planting.

These ships took on a handful of paying passengers in addition to their cargoes of indentured servants, if they could. Two or three full fares offset a bit of the captain's risk and were well worth the extra provisions required for those traveling abovedecks. At the time John Hammill booked his passage, the fare from Ireland to the colonies was about six and a half English pounds. That was a lot of money—about six hundred dollars in today's currency. Only about a fifth of immigrants to the American colonies were able to pay their own way. I am quite sure that John Hammill was one of them.[8]

I see him booking passage on one of the many packets leaving Portrush Harbor in late September 1725. His family comes to the wharves to bid him farewell. Catherine, the sister I imagine for him, weeps to see him go. He says to her, "Kitty, don't cry." His father, Hugh, and his brothers Neale and William shake his hand. He boards the little ship and leans over the rail into the cold wind that blows steadily out of the northwest, across the sandy dunes surrounding Portrush Harbor. Sailors are shouting, the sails shudder and fill. The ship heels and scuds eastward. Portrush vanishes in a bank of cloud; Scotland's western coast looms up. But John is not going back to Scotland. He is continuing the family's journey westward, crossing the ocean that his forebears have lived beside for centuries.

Hard as it is to leave home, it is harder still to be left behind. If he had a sister Kitty, she might have written a letter to John in Maryland that read something like this:

❖

To Mr. John Hammill in the care of Mr. John Chandler
Port Tobacco, Maryland Colony
August 7th, 1726

My Dear Brother,

I pray this letter will reach you before the year is out, so that you can honor our father in your thoughts during the year of his passing. For our dear papa departed this life yesterday, Tuesday the sixth of August, at about four o'clock in the afternoon, in great peace, it seemed. Our Uncle Neale and Reverend Kirk attended at his last moments. He is to be buried tomorrow and Uncle and Aunt have opened their house to the guests who will flock no doubt to the church and to the supper afterward. I will help Aunt in the kitchen but have little provision to contribute to the supper aside from our good apples and a wheel of cheese left in the pantry from last summer's dairying.

For my dear, things have grown so meager here it frightens me. The young men are gone away by the dozens to America, mostly to Penn's colony, it seems. I almost dread the packet coming for it brings their letters in bundles, enticing their brothers and sisters to come to them in their new place. But if in those bundles is a word from you, then I am still grateful to have them.

I can find no able men to do our farm chores or help with the harvest, such as it is at this time. Papa and I managed to get in some potatoes and cabbages and a couple of acres of oats and barley, no wheat this year at all. Your heart would choke you if you could see the state of our fields and fences and our house, which stands in need of nearly every repair that can be imagined. And I sold Betsey with her new calf to Mr. Gleason in town. I needed that bit of money for papa's care and of course his burying.

I tell you this not to shame or trouble you but as preamble to what I now must say. My dear, I have accepted Reverend Kirk's offer of marriage, as papa begged me to do while he could still speak. "Marry Mr. Kirk," he said, and I whispered to him that I would.

Now it is no secret that Mr. Kirk has sometimes annoyed me with his attentions. What was it you once said? "He drones like a bagpipe, always on one note, and that note mi! mi! mi!" But he is kind enough and can shelter me, also well enough. I cannot think of living with my Aunt, good soul that she is. Mr. Kirk at least plays his pipes only briefly each day. He is silent a good deal of the time, and absent a good deal as well. But my Aunt—she chatters from morning to night, incessantly, as she always did. No, I think I am doing what is best for my comfort and happiness. I will stay here in the house through Christmastime and will be married in the New Year. I believe our Uncle Neale will take over the lease of the land, he or our cousin Hugh.

Well, my dear brother, may this find you well and happy. Our father passed his blessing to me, to pass to you, which I now do. Also sealed here are six gold coins that papa kept for you, and his ring. I have kept his pocket watch for my son, should I be fortunate enough to have one. For I am not so old—not yet thirty, though Aunt takes on as if I were a hundred. Well, I am not, and when I am done mourning, I will re-trim my bonnet with pink ribbons, like a girl. Why ever not? Pray think of me, as I do of you.

Your sister Kitty

Ballywillin Parish
Kingdom of Ireland

The North Atlantic Coast, County Antrim, Northern Ireland.

PART II

CHARLES COUNTY, MARYLAND

1725–1778

Charles County, Maryland

6

John Hammill,
Tidewater Planter

---⟨❧⟩---

IN THE Chesapeake region of North America and in the northern British Isles, water and land jockey for dominance. Knobby Scottish headlands crowd into the Firth of Clyde and the North Channel of the Irish Sea. In Northern Ireland, the Rivers Bush and Bann spill into the Atlantic along the Antrim coast. Lough Foyle and Strangford Lough to the west and south pull seawater deep inland, turning fresh water brackish with the tides. Across the Atlantic, the Chesapeake Bay mingles seawater with fresh, creating a huge estuary that divides Maryland's eastern from its western shore. The immense Potomac cuts Maryland away from Virginia. Runs like the Patuxent and the Wicomico flood into it from the Maryland side, and wide-mouthed creeks like the Neabsco, Quantico, and Occoquan pour in from Virginia. These areas are defined by water and to a large extent draw their livelihoods from it. Fishing boats, water-powered mills and factories, and great ships engaged in transatlantic commerce have been familiar sights in these places for centuries.

A young man whose early life was passed in Northern Ireland might find the geography of the Chesapeake familiar, even reassuring. He might relax at the sight of sloops and schooners and dugouts in every waterway, and at the sounds of seaport life—ships being loaded and unloaded, sailors shouting, men and women and children milling about on the wharves. He might look twice at the slaves being herded on and offshore, and at the huge hogsheads of tobacco being rolled down plank roads to the waterside, though even those sights would be familiar if he had boarded ship at Glasgow or Liverpool. And he might rejoice at the signs of prosperity he saw everywhere around him, and at his good fortune in arriving safely at his destination, so carefully chosen. For he has put ashore in Charles County, Maryland, in the Chesapeake Tidewater, the place "best laid out for trade of any in the world."[1]

By 1725, Charles County, on Maryland's Western Shore, had been producing tobacco for the Atlantic trade and fortunes for planters and merchants for more than fifty years. It was no longer mired in the seventeenth century, when deaths exceeded births, population growth came exclusively from immigration, and lifetimes were so short that family and community networks remained rudimentary.[2] By 1725, its population was about three thousand, fairly balanced between the sexes, increasing naturally. Communities had grown enough to support small commercial centers. Port Tobacco, the county seat, contained the courthouse, a few dozen homes, several public houses, or "ordinaries," artisans' shops, a church, and a nascent public, or "free," school.[3]

At that time, about 80 percent of Charles County residents were free and white. The rest were indentured servants, convict laborers, or slaves. In the seventeenth century, indentured servants worked as field hands and laborers, but by 1725 those roles were more often filled by slaves, and indentured servants worked in the trades and as teachers.[4] During the term of their indenture, they could be bought and sold, as in this newspaper advertisement from the later eighteenth century: "To be Sold—a schoolmaster, an indentured servant that has got two years to serve. N.B.—He is sold for no fault any more than we are done with him. He can learn book-keeping, and is an excellent good Scholar."[5] When their indentures expired, these servants joined the free community, and many prospered. Slaves, of course, did neither.

About half of Charles County planters owned slaves by 1750. In 1725, the percentage would have been smaller but still significant. This human bondage is hard for modern readers to stomach, but it is a fact of southern colonial life. Next to land, slaves were a colonist's most valuable asset. Often, slaves and other commodities were purchased with tobacco rather than hard currency, because tobacco was plentiful and money was not. The value of tobacco rose and fell with the Atlantic markets, so its purchasing power fluctuated constantly. Even so, it was the most common medium of exchange throughout the South until after the American Revolution.

The vast majority of free whites in Charles County raised tobacco for export, and other farm products for their own subsistence. Because tobacco was so labor-intensive and so hard on the soil, smaller planters put in fifteen or so acres at a time and let the land rest after four years. The acreage under tobacco cultivation thus shifted constantly. Fifty or sixty acres divided between tobacco and other crops were considered essential for the support of a family. Men who owned fewer than two hundred acres were considered small planters, and they were the majority; those who owned two hundred to five hundred acres were "middling" to "upper-middling" planters, and they represented about a quarter of the whole. The remaining quarter of Charles County landowners, those who owned five hundred to several thousand acres, formed the county's gentry class.

These gentry families were wealthy by colonial standards. They could send their sons back to Europe to be educated and could build comfortable, well-furnished homes. But the Maryland gentry were rarely as wealthy or as impressively pedigreed as their counterparts in Britain. They were mostly immigrants who had made good. In their prosperity, they did what came naturally, passing their money and their connections from one generation to the next. From among the gentry came justices of the peace, sheriffs, constables, and magistrates who kept order, took censuses, collected taxes, and made meticulous records of community life in the colonies, just as they had done in Britain for centuries.

Most people in Charles County worshipped in its four Anglican churches. Though Maryland had been founded by Catholics, by 1725 it was predominantly Church of England in practice. In the colonies as in Britain, between 1689 and 1718 Catholics were by law excluded from voting and holding political office. The anti-Catholic bias continued throughout the colonial period, driving away some Catholic families who had prospered there in the first century of settlement. Still, Charles County always had a substantial minority of Catholics. St. Ignatius Church on Chapel Point, near Port Tobacco, was and is a county landmark, and the Jesuit order of St. Thomas that built it was the largest single landholder in Charles County throughout the colonial period.[6] Until Methodism made an appearance in Maryland's Eastern Shore around 1780, denominations other than Anglican or Catholic seem virtually not to have existed there.

Southern Maryland in 1725 was about as secure, prosperous, and beneficent a place to live as the New World had to offer. It was a tightly knit society, but not so tight that newcomers were unwelcome. A young man of the Anglican faith, with some education, a profession, and some money in his pocket, might do very well there, comfortable as he was with the language and the culture, familiar as he was with the transatlantic marketplace, where tobacco and other goods were almost feverishly being bought and sold. And so John Hammill stepped off the boat into this Chesapeake culture, and made his start.

Two Charles County land records reveal John Hammill's first business transactions in the New World. In the first, dated 21 January 1726, he purchased a fifty-acre property called Wilderness, on Zekiah Swamp. This enormous swamp remains a major feature of the landscape in southern Charles County. He paid two hundred pounds of tobacco for what was probably excellent tobacco land, muddy and rich. The transaction gives John's occupation as "planter," but he may have bought the tract as a speculation. Only eighteen months later, on 13 June 1727, he sold Wilderness to a Scotsman named Magrah for sixteen hundred pounds of tobacco. Even allowing for instability in tobacco values, John has turned a profit on this transaction.

More interesting than his profits are two other details provided in the second land record. In June 1727, John's occupation is given as schoolmaster, not planter—and his wife, Sarah, waived her dower rights in the sale.[7] In a matter of months, this young man has married, made some money, and settled in as a schoolmaster, a solid citizen of the community.

Maryland's 1723 "Act for the Encouragement of Learning … in the several Counties" stipulated that in each county, taxes would be collected for the purchase of a tract of one hundred acres and the income from the property would be used for the support of a schoolmaster. In addition, the master would receive an annual salary of twenty pounds sterling.[8] Charles County, like the other counties of colonial Maryland, found two difficulties in implementing this highminded Act. One was finding qualified instructors. Schoolmasters were to be "capable of teaching well the grammar, good writing, and the mathematics," "of pious and exemplary lives and conversations," and "members of the Church of England—if such can conveniently be got."[9] The last clause indicates that often they could not be got, conveniently or otherwise.

The second difficulty lay in collecting the taxes to pay that twenty-pound salary or its equivalent in tobacco. It was a good deal of money—for instance, it was the wage paid to William Proctor, tutor to the family of William Byrd of Virginia, in 1739.[10] Most counties could not or would not pay what aristocratic William Byrd offered, and so the free schools envisioned by the Act were slow in coming. John Hammill provided an answer to one of Charles County's difficulties, for he was both educated and an Anglican. He may also have accepted something less than twenty pounds per annum, thereby resolving the other trouble as well. For a man just off the boat, newly married, with some money to spend but nothing like a fortune, a schoolmaster's salary would be welcome even if it was less than the stipulated sum. It was like finding money in the street—a bonus, a gift.

John might have taught in the school associated with Christ Church, William & Mary Parish, where he and his family worshipped for decades. The rector of Christ Church, Reverend Mr. Hugh Jones, ran a school there between 1726 and 1732.[11]

However, John could just as well have taught at the Charles County Free School, newly built in 1726 on the outskirts of Port Tobacco. The courthouse was in Port Tobacco, and John was obviously very handy to it. His name appears frequently in court records as witness, testifier, and deposer between 1726 and 1735. His in-laws, John and Ann Chandler, also lived in Port Tobacco, and I think John Hammill may have lived with them in his first years in Maryland. Certainly he spent a good deal of time at their home, for in short order he was married to their daughter Sarah.

At either school, John was likely to have taught mathematics. As a surveyor, he would have mastered arithmetic, geometry, trigonometry, and mapping. He might have learned some mathematics at his own parish school in Ireland and more through private study at home. Many studied the surveyor's craft—or "mystery," as some documents call it—on their own.[12] He could probably also instruct in English literature and history. Though his parish school education would have given him some knowledge of Latin grammar and classics, it seems unlikely that Latin was much in demand among the ordinary youngsters of Charles County or their parents. Young gentlemen bound for school in England were tutored in Latin and Greek at home.

I like to imagine that John put ashore at Port Tobacco and lodged his first night or two at one of the public houses near the wharves. Perhaps he stood a round to his fellows there; perhaps the ship's captain, well known to the locals, put in a good word for him before weighing anchor and heading out to other ports. A fellow country-man might even have met him at the quayside—John Shaw, for instance, whose family had immigrated to Charles County in the sev-enteenth century, or Dr. John Curry, a county resident who became one of the Hammill family's close associates in later years. Either might have introduced him to John Chandler, a member of a well-established Charles County family who perhaps had a room to let to the right man. The Chandlers may have helped John decide that the Wilderness property was worth purchasing. They may have taken him with them to Christ Church on Sunday mornings, where he would have met Reverend Jones and his fellow parishioners, soon-to-be neighbors and business partners. They found he was able and also willing to teach, and recommended him to Reverend Jones or to the county magistrates as a possible master for the new Free School.

And in the Chandler home he met Sarah, their oldest child, pretty and smart and almost seventeen. At thirty-three, John was a likely match for her, maybe what her parents had been waiting and hoping for. They do not consider John too old for their daughter. On the contrary, it pleases John Chandler that his future son-in-law is a man he can talk to, ready to take on the responsibilities of family life. Soon John and Sarah are married. But they continue to live with her parents in Port Tobacco for a few years more, until the babies start to come and John has acquired a suitable property for the family to live on. John pays for their room and board, and Sarah helps as she always has done with the housework and her younger siblings. It is an ideal situation for both of them.

This is a pleasant bit of novelizing. How much of it is supported by fact? No birth date survives for Sarah Chandler, but she probably was the oldest child in her family. John Chandler was born by 1674, as he witnessed a deed in the Charles County land records in 1695, presumably having reached the age of twenty-one. He died about 1735. Two of Sarah's brothers were born in 1714 and 1720, when their father would have been between forty and fifty.[13] A sister, perhaps the youngest child, married a man who was born in 1724.[14] A birth date for Sarah of 1710 would seem realistic, since young girls in the colonial period reached their majority "at Age Sixteen Years or Day of marriage, which[ever] may happen first."[15] As for John and Sarah living in Port Tobacco with her parents, it is one way to explain the fact that John did not purchase a property he kept hold of until 1731. I think John and Sarah Hammill stayed in Port Tobacco with the Chandlers until 1736. Such melded households were very common in colonial times, helping the young folk to get a start while providing care and support to the old.

The link with Dr. John Curry is less tenuous than one might imagine. Surnames in the records of colonial Maryland reveal a solid Scots and Irish presence. John Hammill witnessed a deed for the Douglass family, did business with a McGraw and an Abernathy, married his children to Shaws, and sat in church with Judith O'Cane Penn. O'Cane, like Hammill, is one of the most frequently attested names on Ballywillin parish gravestones.[16] Curry, too, is a very common Northern Irish surname.[17] I have long wondered whether these two Scots-Irish men came to America together. Land records show only that Dr. John Curry became a business partner of John Hammill's in 1749, and continued as an associate of the family after John's death in 1765. Either John Curry or John Shaw might have helped to persuade John Hammill that life in the colonies made sense for him.

John Hammill's tenure as a schoolmaster seems to have ended within a few years. When he bought and sold land throughout the

1730s and 1740s, he was always described as a planter. He seems to have enjoyed making land deals with his neighbors. In 1733, he sold twenty acres called Hamill's Discovery to Francis Posey. Captain Barton Smoot bought thirty acres of Baker's Addition from John in 1742. In 1736 and again in 1740, John purchased land in St. Mary's County, which adjoined Charles County to the south. In the first, John purchased 135 acres he called Hammill's Town, and in the second, he joined with several other investors to purchase 138 acres called St. Andrews Rose. These properties did not remain in his estate, so I assume that they were speculations.

Like virtually every British colonist in Maryland, John was also interested in purchasing properties he could hold for his lifetime and then pass on to his heirs. He acquired Ashbrooke's Rest, 150 acres, on 22 February 1731, and Promise, a hundred acres, on 29 March 1736. He bought an adjoining fifty-acre tract called Baker's Addition in July of that year, and he kept twenty acres of it as a permanent supplement to Promise. A thirty-three-acre tract called the Gammon Enlarged is named in his will. John acquired Partner's Purchase, 164.5 acres, on 4 September 1738.[18] Ashbrooke's Rest, Promise with Baker's Addition, and Partner's Purchase with the Gammon Enlarged made John Hammill the proprietor of nearly five hundred acres of Charles County land by 1740. His St. Mary's County property brought the total up to seven hundred acres for the time that he held those tracts. Even without them, John Hammill had achieved the status of a solid upper-middling planter within fifteen years of his arrival in Maryland.

Ashbrooke's Rest was in Durham Parish, on the west side of Charles County. This parish stands on bluffs above the Potomac, so Ashbrooke's Rest may have been relatively high, in summer less vulnerable to the clouds of mosquitoes that plagued low-lying property. It had to have been in easy reach of a creek to facilitate the shipping of tobacco, but the land description does not mention a creek by name, so its exact location in the parish is not clear. Nor is it clear whether John and Sarah Hammill ever lived at Ashbrooke's Rest. I don't think they did, for they seem always to have worshipped at Christ Church in William & Mary Parish, to the southeast, rather than at the Durham Parish church. John Hammill might have leased the land to another planter, or he might have sent a crew of slaves with an overseer to work it during the busy season, checking in himself from time to time. Eventually, his second son, John Jr., took ownership of Ashbrooke's Rest, but at the time of John Jr.'s early death, in 1760, he apparently was not living there, as no household goods are mentioned in his will.

Promise and Baker's Addition were on Pope's Creek overlooking the Potomac, just north of Christ Church in William & Mary Parish. Like Ashbrooke's Rest, they included some higher land where a house and other buildings might catch the breeze and escape mosquitoes in summer. I think the Hammills lived on these tracts, for they were not deeded over to an heir until John Sr.'s death in 1765. The largest property, Partner's Purchase, lay low, along Cuckold's Creek and the Potomac, south of Christ Church. It was valuable as tobacco land but probably not ideal for a household—it must have been muddy and infested with mosquitoes all summer long. John's oldest son, Hugh, was deeded this land at his majority, and he was living on it when John Sr. signed his will in 1764.

A plat of Partner's Purchase appears in the land records, showing an oddly shaped parcel divided among three owners. The plat is not signed, but John Hammill may have drawn it for the clerk to copy, as he did other plats. One section is owned by John Howard, later by Dr. John Curry. John Hammill owns a second section, and a small rectangular section is labeled "Newman's Pretensions." Apparently some controversy simmered over this property. As late as 1757, members of the Newman family were petitioning the colonial assembly to recover land on the Potomac once belonging to George Newman, deceased.[19] John obviously questioned the validity of that claim—"pretensions" is not a flattering term. I like to imagine John's

A View of the Potomac from Cuckold's Creek, Charles County, Maryland.

voice echoing in this word as he made an insider's joke for those who watched him draw the plat.

As a southern colonial planter, John Hammill owned slaves. Deptford, Jacob, Pete, Charity, Jenny, and a boy named Harry are slaves named in his will. The inventory of his estate made a couple of years later lists a Negro man of thirty-nine years, "a Negro wench Jane," and four children, two boys and two girls. The men and older boys would have worked with John and his sons in the fields, and the women and older girls in the house and farmyard with Sarah. Probably they lived in a separate cabin, not in the Hammill home.

John supplemented his slave labor with the labor of convicts. This notice from the *Maryland Gazette*, Thursday, 11 September 1760, mentions one by name: "John Hamill, in Charles County, reports a runaway convict servant man named John Ware, an Englishman, about 23."[20]

The American colonies were jettison points for thousands of impoverished young men held in British prisons. Planters took them on as free labor until they worked out their term of imprisonment or ran away, a very frequent occurrence. Since they looked and spoke just like their masters, they could disappear into the woods or across a river and leave no trace. Very likely, John Ware made it across the Potomac and into a new life with no harm done to him, and John Hammill was out the money he had paid for this young man. But he might have owned the indentures of other convicts who were not so adventurous.

As a free white male in his community, John witnessed numerous wills, deeds, and land transactions over the years. On 21 January 1726, in his very first weeks in Charles County, he witnessed the sale of a property called Skidmore to Francis Posey, and Francis then witnessed John's purchase of Wilderness. John also made appraisals; in one, the John Rigg case, 18 November 1735, he and three others, "good and lawful men of the bailiwick," appraised a black horse at 350 pounds of tobacco. He surveyed privately, as several plats indicate. And in the case of James Abernathy, "late of the County Armagh in the Kingdom of Ireland, ... weaver," John can only be aiding a countryman in need. On 23 October 1739, James sold two lots in Charles Town (another name for Port Tobacco) "in consideration of the sum of five Thousand pounds of Good sound Tobacco," to John Hammill. On 21 December, two months later, John sold them back to James for the same consideration. It isn't clear what crisis James was trying to avert—he obviously needed cash in a hurry—but whatever it was, John seems to have helped him get around it.

John also made frequent depositions regarding disputes over land boundaries. In one of these, I wonder if again I hear John's voice, articulate and intelligent before the court: "John Hamill, aged fifty-two years or thereabouts, being Sworn on the holy Evangelists of almighty God, declares that some years ago, when a Commission was Executed to prove the Boundaries of a Tract of Land Called Todershell's Gift..."

"Some years ago, When a Commission was Executed to prove the Boundaries of a tract of Land." Is that boilerplate, like "being Sworn on the holy Evangelists of almighty God," or is the court recorder taking down John's own words? If the latter, this fragment shows how succinctly he could speak. No wonder his community made use of him in every way it could.

Yet John never became a vestryman, sheriff, magistrate, or other county official, nor did he join the county Department of Survey, headed for many years by Robert Hanson, whose plats and signature are ubiquitous in the Charles County land records. Why not? He did not belong to the gentry class. He was a newcomer, and, though he prospered, he did not own acres in the thousands. In Britain, his education and his training as a surveyor might have put him "above" the Chandlers, Penns, Smoots, and Poseys, who were shoemakers, blacksmiths, boatwrights, and carpenters by trade. In Maryland, they melted together in the same pot. Subtle class distinctions were eroding. The middle was growing larger and less differentiated in terms of status. The American middle class was being born, right there in the Tidewater.

In the old country, few or none of these families would have owned property or leased large tracts. In Charles County, they speculated in land—buying, selling, trading, and also farming it. They named their properties exuberantly: Monday's Disappointment, Robey's Vexation, Hamill's Discovery, Hamills Outwitted, Smoot's Trifle, Smoot's Fishpond, The Widow's Venture, Perry's Last Chance—gleefully expressing their fears, hopes, triumphs, and daily ups and downs. Their fanciful naming parodies the upper-class tradition of naming estates. These planters have made a game of it, as if they can't contain their excitement over this amazing new life in the colonies. They were living the immigrant's dream. Plain people owning property, purchasing consumer goods, passing their possessions on to their children—creating a patrimony for them, if you will—this was America's contribution to the old way of the world. And these eighteenth-century planters, these ordinary plain folk, knew it.

Plat drawn and signed by John Hammill, 29 October 1745.
꙳ Courtesy of Maryland State Archives

7

Sarah Hammill
and Her Household

BEHIND THE men of Charles County, so busy in their public world, were the women. They did not share the status of their husbands, brothers, or fathers. The political sphere was closed to them; they did not vote or serve as magistrates or take on any other public role. Wives owed obedience to their husbands. Fortunate girls were taught their letters at home, but they certainly did not go to school. Single women had the same legal rights as men; they could travel, earn money, buy and sell property, sign contracts, and have recourse to the courts to protect those rights. But a married woman was invisible under the law. Her rights were forfeited to her husband; as an individual, she had no legal status at all.[1]

However, in the eighteenth century this was true for women everywhere in the world, so far as I am aware. I am struck not so much by the legal oppression of colonial women, but by how humanely they were treated in the courts given the law and custom of the time.

John Hammill's marriage was noted in county land records because Sarah, his wife, acknowledged the sale of Wilderness in 1727. Every time a man sold a property, the magistrates took his wife aside and asked her whether she would suffer by the transaction:

December the 20th, 1739

Then came John Hamill before me the Subscriber (one of his Lordship's Justices of the Provincial Court) and acknowledged the within written Indenture to be his act and deed ... and at the same time Sarah the wife of the said John Hamill relinquisht her right of Dower of in and unto the said Lots of Land and premises, being first by me Examined apart from and out of the hearing of her said Husband and declaring that she relinquished her rights aforesaid voluntarily and freely without being Induced thereto by threats or fear of Ill usage from her Husband or any dread of his Displeasure. Examined acknowledged and Certified the day and year aforesaid

By Geo: Dent[2]

Within the legal framework of the British courts, the American colonies took some trouble to protect the well-being of married women.

Married women testified in court and signed documents as witnesses. When, on 12 October 1751, Joseph Douglass and his wife, Elizabeth, "out of Natural Love and Affection" deeded one Negro child apiece to their two youngest children, Sarah Hammill signed her name as witness along with John. She did not sign with an X, "her mark," but with her signature. If Sarah Hammill could not read and write before her marriage, John the schoolmaster would surely have taught her to do so afterward.[3]

Although Sarah and John were married by 1727, no surviving child was born to the Hammills until 1733. Possibly babies were born earlier who did not live, or the couple were frequently separated in those first years, or Sarah was simply too young to sustain a pregnancy until a few years after her marriage. Once she got started, the Hammill children were born about two years apart—seven of them, five boys and two girls. No birth dates are recorded for them. Eighteenth-century families in the Chesapeake were not required to register births and deaths, and people often kept these events within the family, celebrating births and burying the dead on their own lands instead of in the churchyard.[4]

However, land records suggest that Hugh was the oldest. His father deeded Partner's Purchase to him in 1754, presumably when he reached his majority. Thus Hugh was born in 1733. He was almost certainly named for his paternal grandfather, following the Scots and Irish tradition. John Jr. received the deed for Ashbrooke's Rest in 1756, suggesting a birth year of 1735. Stephen was married by 1763, and John Jr.'s will implies that he, like his two older brothers, had reached his majority before 1760. I think Stephen was the third child, born about 1737 and named for his mother's brother, Stephen Chandler. Sarah, Catherine, and Neale were next, born perhaps in that order between 1739 and 1745. William Chandler was the youngest, born by 1746 as he was an executor of his father's estate and therefore had come of age by 1767.[5]

Where and how did John and Sarah Hammill raise their children? Land transactions suggest that the family lived for decades at Promise and Baker's Addition, on the southeast side of Pope's Creek near Baker's Creek and the Potomac. The best guide to how they lived is provided by the inventory of John Hammill's estate, made on 19 June 1767, two years after his death. A transcript of the inventory follows. Values are given in pounds, shillings, and/or pence, which are set off by colons or periods.

Inventory of the Goods and Chattells of John Hamill Dec'd appraised by these the Subscribers being First Qualified According to Law

1 Negro Man 33 years of Age . . . . 35.

1 Negro Wench Jane 32:10

1 Negro Boy Aged 12 Years . . . . 18.

1 Negro Girl Aged 10 Years. . . . . 18.

1 Negro Child Aged 3 Years . . . . 14.

1 Negro Child Aged 1 Year . . . . 10.

3 Cows and Calves 5:5

1 Cow with Calf. 1:10

1 Stear 4 Years old 1:15

3 two year Old Stears . . . . 3.

1 heiffer 3 years Old. 1:15

2 ditto 2 years Old & 1 Barron Cow 3:8

3 Yearlings. 3:2:6

1 Horse . . . . 2.

1 Old Mare 10

1 young ditto . . . . 1.

5 Barrows. 2:3

15 Shoats 3:15

2 Breeding Sows 16

1 Sow and piggs 12

1 Bed and old furniture Bedstead

Cord and Hyde. . . . . 4.

1 do. and old Silk Rugg and

old Bla[n]kett 3:10

1 old ditto and Rugg & Quilt 2.10

1 old ditto 1:3

3 Iron pott Racks 15

1 Iron pestill 6

1 Cupboard 9

2 old Chests 10

1 old Warming pan 1:6

1 Brace Spice Mortar and pestill 6

1 pair of old fire tongs . . . . ._9

1 old griddle 1

1 Coarse hackle 5

1 Fine ditto 2:6

1 old Oval Table 10

a parcel of Earthen Ware 4

a parcel of Old Books 10

12 ct of old Pewter 4

9 of pott Iron 8:2

1 old Anchor and Cable belonging

To a flott [float] 10

1 old broad hoe 1 narrow do. 2

1 old Narrow Ax 2 Iron Wedges 7

3 turkeys 9 Ducks 6

7 Dunghill fowls 1 Barrell of Corn 11:9

a parcell of Wooden Ware 3

2 Slaughter hydes 1 mutton ditto 15

a tight Cask Containing 460 Gallons 19:2

1 pair of Cart Wheels 12:6

1 Sett of Land Instruments . . . . 1.

1 Spade 5

a parcell of Old Lumber 10

1 Book of Surveying 10

1 pair of Chais Wheels . . . . 1.

a man's Saddle 6

1 Candle Mold 1

. . . . 181:5:10

This terse listing provides physical evidence for John's profession as surveyor in the set of land instruments and the book on surveying.

It stints on details: for instance, the titles of the old books, and exactly what items were in the parcels of old earthenware, woodenware, and pewter. Nevertheless, it gives a vivid impression of the Hammill farmstead and the household that Sarah Hammill created and managed for her family through the thirty-eight years of her marriage. At the same time, it places the Hammills squarely within their colonial Chesapeake culture.

Yes, they owned slaves, by far their most valuable possessions. The inventory opens with six Negroes, two adults and four children aged twelve, ten, three, and one—possibly a family. John and Sarah Hammill may at one time have owned as many as eight or ten individuals.

After its slaves, the family's wealth lay in its livestock. In this, the Hammills were absolutely typical for their time and place.[6] They owned sixteen cattle, including four cows with calves—milkers—and three heifers that would become milkers before long. In addition, they owned twenty-three swine. Like the Chesapeake colonists in general, they ate very well, enjoying plenty of milk, butter, cheese, beef, and those great staples of the southern diet, bacon and ham. The three turkeys, nine ducks, and seven "dunghill fowl," or chickens and geese, mentioned later in the inventory provided eggs as well as meat, and feathers for comforters and pillows. The family's three horses would have served as work animals, as transportation for John and his sons, and possibly as racers in their best days, for horseracing was a favorite leisure activity in the Chesapeake. All those Race Streets in southern towns led to the track or even served as the track in colonial times.

The inventory moves incongruously from a sow and its "piggs" to four beds with "old furniture Bedsted Cord & Hyde." Possibly this indicates that the inspectors have stepped from the barn into the family home, but it may also be that they have simply moved to the next most valuable grouping of possessions, the family beds. Again, the Hammills are typical for their time and place: "Through the eighteenth century, all groups continued to spend more on bedding than on any other functional grouping of equipment."[7] The Hammill beds, valued at more than eleven English pounds together, must have been prized family showpieces. Probably the two best ones stood in their main room for guests to sit on and admire.

As beds in colonial inventories go, these are valued near the top of the range. Rich men might pay almost anything for a bed and its "furniture," which might include tapestry or embroidered hangings, fine linen sheets, silk coverlets, and feather-stuffed mattresses, but a great many ordinary families slept in beds valued at under one pound, most of these not sitting on bedsteads at all, but placed directly on the floor. The word *ditto* used after the first furnished bedstead and the bed values, all above one pound and two quite a bit higher, convince me that all the Hammill beds had bedsteads. Cord and hide mattress supports were the best—a tanned cowhide was stretched taut with rawhide cords that could be tightened around pegs attached to the wooden frame. As ever, the trick was to keep the "bed" itself—the mattress—well supported so it did not sag. Mattresses could be stuffed with straw, flock, or feathers. Many inventories specify the mattress stuffing. I wish this one did.

Again judging by their value, I don't think the Hammill beds were curtained, but their "furniture" certainly included sheets, pillows, and covers. Quilts and blankets are named in the inventory, and so are bed "ruggs." Woolen bed rugs were heavy, thick coverings, very warm but not elegant. Dr. Samuel Johnson, in his 1757 dictionary, calls them "mean." A silk bed rug, however, was an impressive luxury, very fashionable and desirable in the first half of the eighteenth century. Web sites describing colonial furniture say that no silk bed rugs have survived into the present—silk is delicate, and probably the rugs were used until they fell apart and became mattress stuffing. It pleases me to imagine that this silk rug, perhaps a cherished gift, was spread over John and Sarah's bed.

After the four beds comes other household furniture, including kitchenware like the three iron pot racks and iron pestle, the fire tongs and old griddle. I wonder if the pot racks were used inside the fireplace to hold cooking pots steady over the fire. Again, the inspectors may be walking around the family's main room, taking account of the pot racks, pestle, cupboard, warming pan, two old chests, and spice mortars as they pass by. The coarse and fine hackles are combs for pulling processed or "broken" flax into fibers that can be spun. Other inventories from the Hammill neighborhood mention bundles of flax, spinning wheels, and linen cloth, suggesting that many families produced linen for their own use. Maybe Sarah and her daughters did, too.

Then comes the old oval table, the parcel of earthenware, the old books, twelve pieces of old pewter, and nine pieces of pot iron. The earthenware and pewter are valued at four shillings each, among the lowest values in the inventory. Probably the pewter consisted of old forks and spoons, maybe six and six. The earthenware might have been old mugs or a few plates. The books could be relics of John's teaching career, or collections of sermons or Bibles, or even Shakespeare's plays. It is impossible to say. But the nine iron pots and spice mortars suggest that the Hammills took trouble over their cooking. One pot might have been an iron teakettle, for what British immigrant could do without his mug of tea in the morning?

The next items are an old anchor and cable for a float, two old hoes, and an axe with two wedges, suggesting that the inspectors have stepped out of the kitchen into a separate storeroom or shed. The turkeys, ducks, and other fowl are mentioned here, with their barrel of feed corn—perhaps they scratched in the dirt outside the kitchen door, between the house and shed.

The remainder of John Hammill's movable estate seems to be a hodgepodge of belongings set in the shed for safekeeping. They include a man's saddle, a pair of chaise wheels, and a pair of cartwheels, but no chaise or cart. It may be that when all the children were at home and their lives were in full swing, the family used both a chaise and a cart. Sarah and her daughters may have enjoyed driving or being driven in the chaise. The cart was meant for farm work, especially transport of tobacco hogsheads down to that float anchored by its cable in the creek or river. A flatboat could then come by to collect the great loaded barrels.

Old lumber, a parcel of woodenware, three animal hides, and a spade are noted, and a tight cask holding 460 gallons, for cider or ale. Perhaps the family had some apple or peach trees and made their own cider from the fruit. The candle mold suggests that they might have tended a beehive or two, eating the honey and using the wax for candles. Or they might have made tallow candles from the leavings of their slaughtered cattle.

The men of the family, both free and slave, would have seen to the tobacco crop and also a field or two of Indian corn. Throughout the colonial period, corn, not wheat, was the staple grain, and bread, mush, cakes, and puddings of milled or otherwise processed corn a mainstay of the Chesapeake diet. Wheat flour was a luxury. The Hammills would have taken their ripe corn to a local mill and brought the flour and meal by cart in bags or barrels to the farm.

The spade and hoes are the only cultivating tools mentioned. Can a farmstead exist without a plough? In the early days of Chesapeake agriculture, the answer is yes. Ploughs were expensive imports, and slaves who had been born in Africa did not know how to use them. They prepared the soil with simple hand tools, substituting labor for equipment. By the mid-eighteenth century, however, fields were typically prepared for planting with the plough.[8] The Hammills must have hired out their ploughing, for one spade and two hoes could not have done the job even if the family was old-fashioned enough to prefer hand cultivation. The slaves used them in the garden, on potatoes, cabbages, peas, carrots, turnips, and any number of other vegetables.

Now, how does the Hammill household stack up beside those of other Chesapeake colonists? Historians Lois Green Carr and Lorena S. Walsh have constructed an "Amenities Index" by which to evaluate Chesapeake living standards before the American Revolu-tion.[9] Indicators of affluence in this culture include sleeping off the surface of the floor, more than one way to cook food, and seasoning food with home ground spices — imported pepper, cinnamon, nut-meg, and clove. Sarah Hammill's home scores quite high by these measures. Her nine pots show variety in cooking, and the "brace" of spice mortars, or two of them with pestles, indicate carefully pre-pared, well-seasoned meals. The Hammills enjoyed their creature comforts, by night in their well-furnished beds, warmed by the bed-warmer in winter, and by day at the table.

And I doubt that they ate from wooden trenchers or the com-munal pot, reaching in with their knives, chunks of cornbread, or wooden spoons. People who owned spice mortars, a cupboard to store them in, and an oval table to dine on could afford to eat from plates using metal tableware, even though the inventory does not name these things explicitly. Tableware and earthenware or china plates are other signs of affluence in the colonial Chesapeake.

So are books and jewelry. John Hammill's inventory includes a number of books. It does not mention jewelry, but John Jr.'s will of 1760 names a pair of silver shoe buckles and twenty-three imported bone buttons, laid aside for the next time his mother and sisters made up shirts. Even William Chandler, the youngest and poorest of the Hammill children, at his death owned a "stone ring"—that is, a ring set with some kind of semiprecious stone.

It appears that Sarah and John Hammill raised their family com-fortably, as one would expect of a couple whose movable wealth comes to 181 pounds, 5 shillings, and 10 pence. The Amenities Index authors define "the rich" as "those with more than £225 in movable wealth" before the American Revolution.[10] Like the number of acres he owned, the value of John Hammill's moveable estate put him in the upper-middling sector of Tidewater colonists. He and his family were not quite rich, but they were very far from poor.

And this brings me to the puzzles in the inventory—to the things it does not include. Where are the old clothes—shirts, jackets, aprons, petticoats, shawls? Where are the extra bedsheets, pillowcases, hand towels, and napkins? Are there no chairs for that oval table, no candles with holders, no dipper or ladle or knives? Every kitchen, no matter how spartan, had to have knives. Where are the Negroes' necessities, the "Negro bedding" and "Negro cloathes" mentioned in so many other Charles County inventories? Can it be that the Hammills owned four milk cows but no milk pans, no butter churn or "trott," no cheesecloth or strainer or butter paddles? So many small items of domestic utility are missing from this inventory that come up time and time again among the possessions of less prosperous men. The "box of iron and heaters," for instance. A family of five sons and two daughters with no way to iron clothes? Not to mention the handful of luxuries that are counted in the property of less affluent men, like the "2 glass bottles" or "Delph punch bowl and six Delph plates" that belonged to James Martin, whose inventory, totaling sixteen pounds and change, directly precedes John Hammill's in the account book.

The answer is not that the Hammills did not own such things. It is that this inventory was made two years after John and Sarah died. Their farm and animals and slaves are being cared for, but no one is living in their house. The slaves must be staying with one of the grown-up Hammill children, Hugh and his wife Elizabeth, perhaps. They have been brought to the farm especially for the inventory, where all has been neatly organized and prepared for the inspectors. But every sign of ordinary daily life has vanished.

Where did all those missing items go—the teapot, the irons, the tablecloth, Sarah's best shawl, the family knives? Sarah Hammill inherited all of them at her husband's death, but she died just four months after him.[11] My own experience suggests that after John was gone, perhaps sensing that her life, too, was drawing to a close, she told her children what family goods she wanted them to take, more often and in more detail than they cared to hear. Hugh, Stephen, and Catherine, all married before 1765, and even young William Chandler were using the family cutlery, chairs, and extra sheets, the napkins, old clothes, and candleholders. The young take the best of what the old have accumulated. It was and is the way of the world.

LAND RECORDS and the Hammill inventory and wills capture a good deal of this family's Charles County life. One more resource reveals John and Sarah Hammill within their community. Remarkably, a scrap of the Christ Church vestry book has survived for the Sunday of 8 June 1752, and, even more remarkably, it contains the pew assignment for John Hammill.[12] Sorting out and identifying the people named in this fragment places the Hammill family squarely among their Maryland neighbors and kin:

Pew 14   *Notley & Sarah Maddox, Edward & Ann Smoot*
Pew 15   *Judith Penn & Notley Dutton*
Pew 16   *John Hammill & Jane Penn*

Who are these people? First, only the heads of families are listed. John Hammill and Jane Penn are not sitting alone in pew 16. John's wife and all seven of the children are sitting there too. On this June day in 1752, they range in age from nineteen to five or six. In pew 14 sits Edward Smoot, John's brother-in-law. He is about twenty-nine, married to Sarah Hammill's youngest sister, Mary. With Edward and his wife are their three oldest children, first cousins to the Hammill youngsters. Ann Smoot is not Edward's wife but an unmarried sister or, more likely, a widow in the family. She may have children sitting with her as well.

Jane Penn and Judith Penn are Sarah Hammill's aunts, sisters-in-law of Sarah's mother, Ann Penn. They are great-aunts to the Hammill children. Jane is the widow of Mark Penn. Judith's full name is

Judith O'Cane Dutton Penn. She is the Judith O'Cane whose family may have come, like John Hammill, from Northern Ireland. Her first husband was Matthew Dutton, and her second was John Penn. Both are deceased.

Notley Dutton is Judith's oldest son from her first marriage. His brothers Gerard and Thomas may be sitting with them, as well as the youngest child, who was born after Matthew Dutton's death. Notley's wife and children might be squeezed into the pew as well. These Duttons are not blood relations of the Hammills, but second or third cousins by Judith's second marriage to John Penn. Pews 14, 15, and 16 are full to overflowing with the Penn-Chandler clan of William & Mary Parish. These kinfolk have become John Hammill's extended family in America.

This picture of the extended Chandler family is not quite complete. Sarah Hammill's brothers, John and Stephen Chandler, may be sitting elsewhere in Christ Church with their families, or they may worship at one of the other county churches. The William Penn Sr. family is not mentioned, either. William was yet another brother to Ann Penn, Sarah Hammill's mother. He may already be deceased, and his wife, Elizabeth, may already be married to her second husband, Col. Richard Harrison. Jezreal Penn would be sitting with his mother and stepfather at their church, elsewhere in the county. A second cousin to the Hammill children, Jezreal in 1752 was a boy of maybe ten.

Though Edward Smoot of Pew 14 has only his immediate family and Ann Smoot sitting with him, his brother John and any number of other Smoots may be filling different pews in Christ Church. Sharing Pew 14 with Edward Smoot are Notley Maddox and his family. Sarah Maddox is not his wife but an unmarried sister or widow. Like the Smoots, the Maddoxes are old-timers in Charles County. In generations to come, their children and various Hammill children will marry. It is tantalizing to imagine that with Notley and his wife sits their small daughter Elizabeth Maddox, five or six years old. Does Hugh Hammill, an adolescent of nineteen, even notice her? More than thirty years hence, and after a very great deal of living, she will become his second wife. Elizabeth Maddox, Edward and John Smoot, Jezreal Penn, and Col. Richard Harrison will all find their way into this book later on.

Christ Church, William & Mary Parish, still stands in southern Charles County, not far from the Hammill property called Partner's Purchase. The little brick church, built in 1692, has been meticulously preserved and maintained. No additions mar its simple lines, though new stained-glass windows were put in near the turn of the twentieth century. Its ancient graveyard stands around it, shaded by a giant tree. Inside the church, the original crossbeams, black with age, support the peaked roof and whitewashed walls. New pews are arranged in three rows: eleven pews in each of the side aisles, and eight pews in the center. The church could seat fifty people, maybe a few more. A simple altar at the front was decorated with flowers on the frigid January day I visited, and sunshine poured in through the colored glass. It was lovely—just as lovely as it must have been on Sunday, 8 June 1752, when the Hammills took their places for the service.

I see them gathered all together on that summer Sunday, the old taking comfort in the familiar ritual of the service, the young restless and itching to get out and enjoy the day. John Hammill sits at one end of Pew 16, beside his daughter Catherine, whom they call Kitty. In 1752, she was about ten. Neale and William are little boys of eight and six, squirming in the pew. The big boys, Hugh, John, and Stephen, sit shoulder to shoulder, a head taller than their mother and sister Sarah, who is about thirteen. Their great-aunt Jane Penn sits on the aisle, behind her sister Judith in Pew 15.

Of them all, only John Hammill can compare this church, this moment, with the great stone church in Ballywillin Parish that overlooked the sea. Does he think back, missing his own family and distant British life, or does the little brick church comfort him in its simplicity? Probably neither, for John Hammill was a practical man. For the people who lived it, that Sunday morning slipped past quicker than it can be described.

In the course of the 1750s, both the Hammill family and colonial Charles County reached their maturity. Between 1725 and 1760 the county's white population tripled, to about eight thousand, and the black population rose to nearly five thousand, from 19 percent to 38 percent of the total, giving thirteen thousand people altogether.[13] Even in 1725 the county had been a thriving commercial center. By 1760, it was entering its golden age. White families prospered, their casks of tobacco finding a ready market all over Europe as well as in Britain. In exchange came slaves, sugar, molasses, rum, and spices, silk and cotton fabrics, fine china and earthenware, looking glasses, books, and guns. The Hammill children grew up in these boom times and by 1760 began to take their places in a consumer culture, probably confident that it would last forever.

By 1760, Hugh, John Jr., and Stephen had all reached their majority. Hugh, living at Partner's Purchase, was probably already married, maybe even a father. John Jr. had taken the deed for Ashbrooke's Rest but was unmarried and apparently still living at home. Cath erine, at eighteen, had a suitor, Joseph Shaw. Maybe Sarah had one, too. Even Neale and William, the youngsters, were in their teens. John Sr. was sixty-seven or sixty-eight, his wife about fifty-two.

I imagine this prospering family on New Year's Day 1760, celebrating the year that has passed and the one that has just begun. Is it soft-headed to hope that the slaves in their cabin have new clothes, the day free of work, extra firewood, and a few fat hens to stew or roast, with double measures of cornmeal, buttermilk, and bacon? Such a gesture might heighten John and Sarah's enjoyment of their own holiday feast.

A great ham steams on their oval table, or a freshly roasted turkey, or both. The tall pudding stuffed with imported raisins and figs sits on its pewter or earthenware platter, ready to be served. Mugs hold cider made from their own fruit, or good English ale. Friends and neighbors fill the room, the young perching on the two chests and on the beds so their elders can sit on the chairs. A delicious meal, a round of toasts, and the winter night draws in. Guests depart; the Hammill family stays a moment all together, and then John and Sarah retire easy and content to their bed with its warm blanket and old silk "rugg," sharing a moment of satisfaction with what they have made of their lives.

8

THINGS FALL APART

―――――――――――――― ❧ ――――――――――――――

IN THE ten years between 1760 and 1770, all but one member of
John and Sarah's family perished. Six died in the first half of the
decade—John, Sarah, and four of their grown or nearly grown children: John Jr., Sarah, Neale, and Stephen. John Jr. signed his will on
21 January 1760, when he was about twenty-four. John Sr. signed his
on 21 May 1764. Neale and Sarah, both named in John Jr.'s will, are
not named in their father's. They have died in the intervening four
years. Sarah Hammill died four months after her husband, in 1765.
Stephen Hammill perished late that same year. He left a widow,
Asinah Wilder Hammill, and two babies, Sarah and John. John's
birthday was 6 October 1763, and Sarah's 23 June 1765.[1]

By December 1770 two more were gone: Catherine Hammill
Shaw and William Chandler Hammill. William died sometime in
the first few months of 1770. He, like his brother John, was about
twenty-four at his death. The inventory of his estate, made on 17
April 1770, reveals a young man with few possessions. He owned
two horses sixteen and nine years old, a valise, some old clothes, and

a ring set with a stone, for a total value of twelve pounds, nineteen shillings. His sister Catherine also died in 1770, possibly in child-birth. Her husband, Joseph Shaw, was left a widower with three children, the youngest a newborn named Catherine for her mother. Catherine was the sixth of the Hammill children to perish before she was thirty. Only Hugh, the oldest, remained alive.

Countless differences exist between life today and life two hun-dred years ago. People no longer "humbly Crave allowance" for a hearing in court, or weigh the "dignity" of an estate before purchas-ing it. Girls are not considered adult at sixteen. Few today travel primarily by water or on horseback, or live and work on farms amid a thicket of kin. No one owns slaves. And almost no one plans a life around the imminent threat of death. Of all the differences between the past and the present, this last must be the most profound.

Charles County record books brim with arrangements for the support of orphans and parents' efforts to secure property to their young children, motivated by the uncertainty of their own survival. John Sr. and Sarah, his wife, were fortunate enough to die what in the eighteenth century would have been considered "natural" deaths, John in his early seventies, and Sarah in her midfifties. But six of their children survived the perilous years of infancy and childhood only to die in their teens and twenties, when they should have been most resilient. What ended their lives?

Accidents are one possibility. Country life was full of bizarre mishaps that killed both young and old. Drownings, runaway carts and wagons, fires, falls from roofs and haylofts, children strangled by dangling ropes or trapped in wells—all these are attested in the *Maryland Gazette* over the years. Young women died in childbirth, and young men had their own special risks: guns exploding, boats overturning, horses bolting, tobacco hogsheads weighing a ton apiece careening down wharves to crush anyone in their path.

But disease had to be the most frequent killer. Tuberculosis killed George Washington's older brother, Lawrence. Malaria, spotted fever, and yellow fever, all insect-borne, came and went cyclically throughout the seventeenth and eighteenth centuries, especially in warmer areas like Maryland and Virginia. In the Hammill family, where John Jr., Neale, Sarah, Stephen, and their parents died in the space of five years, I suspect an epidemic disease, and smallpox is at the top of my list.

Smallpox was one illness in Europe and quite another in America, as the colonists were quite aware. European children were exposed to the disease as they grew up, acquiring immunity almost as a matter of course. But in the colonies, children could easily reach adulthood without ever having been exposed. Thus when smallpox struck, it was generally deadly.[2] In the seven years between 1760 and 1767, flare-ups caused frightening epidemics with high mortality in both Maryland and Virginia.[3] In Baltimore, the disease was so devastating that in February 1765, Dr. Henry Stevenson, "the most successful inoculator in America," opened an inoculating hospital in that city and also visited Prince George County, Maryland, to treat people, but he didn't make it as far south as Charles County.[4] In any case, inoculation was very expensive and also risky. The Hammills might not have ventured it even if it had been available to them.

John Sr. was probably immune to smallpox, as he had been born and raised in Britain, but his children would have been very vulnerable to it. One avenue they might have taken to protect themselves probably never occurred to them. They might have avoided using convict labor in their homes and on their plantations, for these prisoners were often carriers of virulent infection.[5] The Hammills and many others in their community relied on convict labor in spite of this. John Hammill was looking for a runaway convict in September 1760, just months after John Jr.'s death. The following entry appears in Stephen Hammill's business accounts: "Crop Tobacco and Transfer due to Col. Richard Harrison per Judgment against this Account ... on account of the Deceased becomeing Special bail for Richard Ratcliff, runaway."[6] It appears that Richard Ratcliff was working for Col.

Richard Harrison when he ran away, and that Stephen had provided Ratcliff to Harrison in the course of his business. There is no other reason why Stephen would post bail for a convict worker. Clearly, Stephen had been associated with Richard Ratcliff, who could easily have exposed him to smallpox or an equally virulent disease.

The risk of infection from convicts and the ships that carried them into Chesapeake harbors became so great that "in 1766 the Maryland Assembly passed a quarantine act 'to oblige infected ships, and other vessels coming into this Province to perform quarantine.'"[7]

Could such a quarantine have protected John, Neale, Sarah, and Stephen Hammill? It is impossible to know, just as it cannot be known for certain that smallpox took their lives. But the quarantine might have helped.

Stephen's sudden death, so tragically disruptive for his newly begun family, produced several pages of running accounts between 1766 and 1769, when his estate was finally settled. Preserved in the Prerogative Office of the Charles County courts, these accounts provide birth dates for Stephen's children, and they reveal what happened to Asinah, Stephen's widow. In 1767, Stephen's account was administered by "John Shaw and Asinah his wife." John was the oldest brother of Joseph Shaw, Catherine Hammill's husband. Stephen's widow Asinah thus became a double sister-in-law to Catherine, by marriage on both sides of the family.

In addition, these records give a fascinating though incomplete picture of a young man's business life. As was traditional in British families, Stephen's older brothers had been deeded land when they reached their majority. Stephen, the third son, became a businessman. The transcripts of his accounts name many of his customers, including Dr. John Curry, his uncles Edward Smoot and John Smoot Jr., his first cousin John Smoot, his second cousin Jezreal Penn, and Jezreal's stepfather, Col. Richard Harrison, who had lost Richard Ratcliff, the convict laborer.

Predictably enough, Stephen's two biggest creditors were Glasgow tobacco merchants: John Semple and Company, and John & James Jamison and Company, whose factor was John Craig. It seems most likely that Stephen acted as a subfactor or middleman between the tobacco growers in his area and the large companies that purchased the crop for export. Stephen collected the crop as his neighbors produced it, fronting them money or credit. He consolidated the leaf, had it inspected, and delivered it to the Scots factors, who in turn fronted him money or gave him credit on the crop's sale. Stephen also at times provided labor to his customers, and perhaps other things like the great wooden hogsheads in which tobacco was packed, or other necessary supplies.

John Semple belonged to the Semple family that, like the Hammills, originated in southwest Scotland and sent a mourner to Hugh Montgomery's funeral in 1636. John Semple and James Jamison were business partners in the 1750s, operating a big store and trading center in St. Mary's City, a town in St. Mary's County, which adjoined Charles County on the south. Semple was a sharp dealer who got into and out of considerable trouble in both Maryland and Virginia before the end of the century.[8] By 1765, he and Jamison had parted ways. But in 1750, when Stephen was about thirteen and ready to learn a trade, his father John Hammill may have apprenticed him to these two Scotsmen.

Few family records remain of the Hammills' early years in America, but there is one. Stephen Hammill's grandson, John Hammill Poston, owned a Bible that passed down the generations with a handwritten note tucked inside. The note says that John Hammill came from Scotland, and that Stephen Hammill "came up to Charles County from St. Mary's County, with his father."[9] The note offers remembered information not quite accurately, long after it was given, but it is valuable on two counts. First, it shows that John Hammill considered himself a Scotsman even when he moved to the colonies, and that his parents and grandparents felt they were Scots long after the family moved from North Ayrshire to Ireland.

Second, it supports the connection between Stephen Hammill, John Semple, and James Jamison that is so briefly hinted at in the Prerogative Court records. What could be more plausible than that John Hammill proposed his son Stephen as an apprentice to those fellow Scotsmen, possibly family acquaintances? John Hammill took his son down to St. Mary's City to begin his apprenticeship, and when it was done, John went down again to bring him home. Thus Stephen and his father came up to Charles County from St. Mary's County, together.

A few more insights into Stephen's short life and brief marriage can be drawn from a land transaction that was not recorded until three years after his death. On 28 June 1768, the Charles County Office of Land Patents recorded Stephen Hammill's patent of a tract called Sena's Delight. "Sena" is surely an affectionate nickname for his wife, Asinah. The patent concerns Stephen's property Ashbrooke's Rest, which Stephen's father purchased as a tract of 150 acres from Margaret Ward in 1731. Stephen has looked into the land records and old surveys, and has determined that the original patent, issued in 1673 to "a certain Thomas Ashbrooke," guaranteed the "Liberty to Correct and amend any Errors in the Original Survey and add any vacancy thereto contiguous." The next owner, John Ward, exercised that guarantee, adding 120 acres of vacant land adjacent to the original tract. He called the addition Ingerstone, and it was not included in the tract that John Hammill purchased from John Ward's widow in 1731. Stephen has gotten to the bottom of all this. He had both tracts resurveyed on 13 July 1764 and repatented the whole as a 264-acre tract called Sena's Delight, paying five pounds fourteen shillings for the vacant acreage.[10] He was a clever fellow, this Stephen.

I have built an image of this young man that may do his brothers an injustice. I see him as the go-getter in the family, the son who inherited his father's energy and good judgment. Unlike John Jr., Stephen left no silver shoe buckles behind him. Instead, he left a wife he adored, two babies, and a promising future as a business-man and planter. If he had been the survivor instead of his oldest brother, Hugh, would the family's fortunes have evolved differently in the political and economic upheavals that were fast approaching? Of course, no one can say.

William Chandler's life is as intriguing as Stephen's, though in quite a different way. John Hammill Sr. added a codicil to his will in November 1764, not long before his death. Here it is:

> Whereas by my will dated the 21st day of May 1764 I have given
> and bequeathed unto my son William Chandler Hamill one
> hundred acres of land being part of a tract of land called Promise
> and Bakers Addition as by the said will more fully appears,
> now it is my full intent meaning will and desire that if my son
> William Chandler Hamill should disturb or offer to disturb or
> dispossess my son Stephen Hamill in his possession of that tract
> of land called Ashbrooke's Rest whereof he now stands seized,
> that then the aforesaid two tracts of land called Promise and
> Bakers Addition should be the right and title of my son Stephen
> to him and his heirs forever. As witnessed my hand this 11th day
> of November anno 1764.

Is John anticipating a problem, or has William already expressed his anger and dismay that Ashbrooke's Rest has gone to Stephen rather than to him? John Jr. received Ashbrooke's Rest from his father when he came of age in 1756 and willed the property to his younger brothers, Neale and William, at his death in 1760. By 1764, Neale, too, was dead, and William was still a minor. Therefore the property reverted to John Sr., who passed it to Stephen. William is to receive a different property, Promise, with a thirty-acre supple-mentary tract called Baker's Addition. I think this was the Hammill home place, where the children grew up. William Chandler would have been intimately familiar with every inch of Promise.

The codicil presents a tempting situation for the novelist within. John Sr., weak and ill, might have imagined a conflict that did not exist. Or William, eighteen years old and rebellious, might have been furious with his father at overturning John Jr.'s will. John Sr. was determined to impose his authority and control his youngest son. Apparently Ashbrooke's Rest was the more desirable property and therefore appropriate for Stephen, who was older, married, and had a family of his own. Perhaps the land was better situated or more productive. In any case, William wanted it, and he did not want Promise.

How did this situation play out? In real life, Stephen held Ashbrooke's Rest for less than a year. When he died, the property went to Hugh, the oldest son and heir-at-law. Five years later, William also died. The inventory of his estate names Hugh as executor. William's uncles, Stephen Chandler and John Smoot Jr., were next of kin. John Smoot, William's first cousin, was named as a creditor.

The historian notes that William was borrowing money from his cousin, but cannot say why. Nor can she explain where William is living or what he is doing with his time. The novelist, however, can portray him as bent on a young man's pleasures, not attending to the property he inherited, perhaps living hand-to-mouth with his cousin John Smoot, three years his junior, and John's wife, Elizabeth, simmering with grievance and anger against his family. Could William have perished violently, thrown from a horse or drowned in a fall through rotten ice as he raced in a sleigh on the Potomac? Or did fever take him, aggravated by horrible winter weather?

The first months of 1770 brought in "a kind of Greenland winter." So said Jonathan Boucher, an English visitor to Maryland and Virginia that year. George Washington recorded in his diary that "on the 26th of January, snow began to fall in tons.... By the 29th, when the storm ended, the snow was up to the breast of a tall horse everywhere—the deepest I suppose the oldest man living ever remembers to have seen in this country."[11] Whether the winter was to blame or not, William Chandler died before April 1770, when the inventory of his estate was made. His properties, Promise and Baker's Addition, and any money left after his debts were paid, went to his oldest brother, Hugh.

So many deaths in so short a time must be acknowledged somehow. In the two inventions that end this chapter, I put words in the mouths of newly widowed Sarah Hammill and William Chandler, her youngest son.

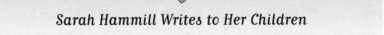

Sarah Hammill Writes to Her Children

FOR MY children, should I bee took suddenly from you as God help me I fear may bee if this heaviness about my chest should not abate, for I am uneasy by night and by day, tho may be it is but grief for your dear father, only our Maker knows.

I have not your father's skill with pen and ink but yet must write this note for your father thought it not needful that I have a will, and these are my wishes as well you know and I trust you to honor them, my dears.

Kitty, to you one suit of bed linen and my clothes, which may do for your Negro women if not for you, but if your child be a girl my blue silk scarf might do for her tho it have one little spot at the hem, and your old bolster and cover that is still in the house, and my best tablecloth with the gold stripe and napkins that we wove and sewed together my dear, and for your husband Joseph your father's best vest with silk front and stuff sides.

Hugh, to you and Elizabeth the steel knives and strop and grindstone and the good pewter spoons tho I fear one spoon bee lost but yet there are seven, which will do you well, and one set of bed linen withal and your father's gold ring which he had of his father long since, and for your little Kitty, the worked linen throw that lies upon my marriage chest, bless her.

Stephen to you and Asinah the six yards of diaper and the hemmed towels in your father's Irish chest and one suit of bed linen and the wooden chairs which tho of an age with the table and but two in number will still serve, and the black iron candle holders that your John so likes to toy with, the darling, and for baby Sarah the knitted hood and gown that lies upon my needles by my chair.

William Chandler to you your father's mourning ring set with a black stone, the which he purchased to honor my father at his passing, and but for that one silk vest, also your father's clothes, and one set of bed linen, for tho you are not yet settled in life still you must sleep clean, and the copper candle holder with four wax candles for to light your way, and I pray you will honor your father in your thoughts and deeds and not kick against the pricks of his desires.

And my dears I pray you will share and share alike all the remaining estate according to your father's will and wishes for they are well known to you.

Your loving mother Sarah Chandler Hammill at Promise, William & Mary Parish, County of Charles and colony of Maryland, 30 June 1765

❖

William Chandler Hammill Speaks His Rage and Loss

DO NOT kick against the pricks of your father's wishes, my mother says in her last words, and not spoke direct to me but in a crumpled note. She would not say it outright for fear of my rant. Yet I do kick, and I do rant. My brother gave me that land and it was mine by his will—the will he had to dictate breath by breath, too weak and too much oozing with the pox to touch a pen, my god I never can forget that sight, and he the handsome one, his skin so white, his blue eyes pierce my dreams. And by his will, his desire, as well, for he cared for me, my brother did, my brother John.

Curse the others, that stiff stick Hugh, that Stephen, look at him, strained and scrambling at the wharfs all the day, "Yes, sir, no, sir, let me see to it, sir," those two puking infants ruining his nights, I have no pity for him. He made that life, no kind of life for a young man. Not for me. Not for my brother John either, he did not care to marry but loved his fine horse and his clothes, loved to cut a figure in the town, ride up to church with dash and a flourish, the girls simpering around him, the silly fools.

I was to have John's land, Ashbrooke's Rest, high above the river with such a breeze as angels' wings might make. But no, my father took it from me, he gave it to Stephen against my brother John's desire, he threatened to disinherit me—yes, so he did, it is there on the paper, heavy as the stone on my brother's grave: "If my son William Chandler should disturb or offer to disturb or dispossess my son Stephen in his possession of that tract of land called Ashbrooke's Rest, then the two tracts of land called Promise and Baker's Addition should be the right and title of my son Stephen to him and his heirs forever."

I have no wish to live at Promise. What promise does it hold for me? My parents' spirits hover here, their things still in the house, the milk cows in the yard lowing for my mother's touch, my dying brothers John and Neale, and my sister Sarah too, always before my eyes. She was a second mother to me, I called her "little mama," so they say. How their skin broke and oozed, how they tossed and moaned, how hot they were, and then how cold. Oh god, how came it to be that I am so alone in the world?

Promise, 17 September 1765

❀

But in the end, it was William's brother Hugh who was left alone. The oldest child in the family, Hugh was about twenty-seven when the cascade of deaths began, and about thirty-seven when it ceased.

The loss of his parents and six siblings cost him a good many of his closest personal connections, and at the same time they made him heir to the bulk of the family wealth—the land, the slaves, the livestock, and the household goods that his parents had accumulated throughout their lives, excepting only what passed to Stephen and Catherine's surviving spouses. By the death of his relatives, Hugh gained freedom of choice and security, the gifts of a comfortable inheritance. Was he fortunate, or unfortunate? Perhaps he was both.

Christ Church, William & Mary Parish, Charles County, Maryland.
Built in 1694, this is the church where the Hammill family worshipped from 1726
to 1774, and where John Hammill might have taught school.
A plaque in the church commemorates the Reverend Neale H. Shaw,
grandson of the immigrant John Hammill.

9

HUGH THE HEIR

―――――――――――― ❦ ――――――――――――

EATH CAN be a generous provider, of family records as well
as of goods. The wills, inventories, and business accounts produced by the deaths of John and Sarah Hammill and their children
reveal details of their lives that are captured nowhere else. Hugh the
heir did not die in Charles County, and the transactions preserved
in court records under his name offer more enigmas than answers.
His wife, Elizabeth, for instance. Who was she? Her given name
comes up frequently in Charles County Land Records, but not her
maiden name, nor the names or birth dates of her children. Only one
document, preserved in the archives of Virginia after the family left
Charles County, indicates that in 1780 Hugh and Elizabeth had a
living daughter named Catherine.[1] As to Elizabeth's identity, circumstances offer a suggestion—a strong suggestion, in my opinion—but
no firm answer. And there are other questions raised in court records
that both beg and resist interpretation where Hugh is concerned.

I believe that Hugh was married to Elizabeth Shaw, one of six
children of John and Elizabeth Jenkins Shaw of Charles County.

Parents of the eighteenth century often chose marriage partners for their children from a single family; the Hammills and the Shaws certainly did so. Elizabeth's younger brother Joseph was married to Hugh's sister Catherine. John Shaw Jr. married Stephen's widow, Asinah Wilder Hammill.[2] Very probably, Hugh and Elizabeth Shaw were married about 1760 in a match arranged by their elders, when Hugh was in his later twenties and Elizabeth, born 20 September 1739 and hence six years younger than her husband, was about twenty-one. Like Hammill, Shaw is an old Scots surname. The families may have shared a cultural kinship that drew them together in colonial Charles County. It is even possible that they were distantly related.

The Shaw and Hammill offspring were linked by ties other than marriage. Philip Shaw, born about 1733 and hence close to Hugh in age, moved to Virginia some years before Hugh and Elizabeth; eventually, the two families leased land near each other in Prince William County. William Shaw, another of Elizabeth's brothers, witnessed a deed of sale for Hugh in 1768, and a Jane Shaw witnessed the will of John Hammill Jr. at his death in 1760. All these details reinforce the likelihood that Hugh's wife was Elizabeth Shaw, but they do not offer proof. This is just one instance where circumstantial evidence is the best that can be mustered regarding Hugh Hammill.

Hugh's father, John, appears in court records as a rising man, firmly ensconced in his community and following a life path that was as traditional as it was transparent. John married, acquired land, secured properties to his sons as they came of age, married off his children, and saw to his will and the disposition of his estate before his death at the respectable age of seventy-two. Hugh, on the other hand, sold his father's possessions rather than adding to them. He rarely testified, witnessed, or gave depositions before the court, and for a good many years he was utterly absent from the records of Charles County. Even so, land transactions recorded in his name reveal something of his whereabouts, companions, and difficulties in the years directly preceding the American Revolution.

Some of these transactions seem rather surprising. For instance, in 1768 Hugh sold Partner's Purchase to a man named Joseph Douglass. In 1771 he sold eighty-four acres of Promise to Benjamin Douglass.[3] Why did Hugh divest himself of these two valuable properties from his father's estate? Promise had been his parents' home, and Partner's Purchase was his own inheritance, deeded to him when he came of age in 1754. Why did he sell it so soon after his father's death—why did he not live on it himself? And who were these Douglasses that Hugh was so ready to do business with?

The second question is not so difficult to answer. Benjamin and Joseph Douglass were Hugh's first cousins by marriage as well as old friends of the Hammill family. Their parents, Joseph and Elizabeth Douglass, had asked John and Sarah Hammill to witness a deed of gift for them on 12 October 1751.[4] Fifteen or so years later, the Douglass's daughter Elizabeth married John Smoot, John and Sarah Hammill's nephew.[5] After his own siblings perished, those Douglass and Smoot cousins were among Hugh's nearest living relatives. It might have pleased Hugh to sell family land to these young kinsmen, especially if he did not need it himself.

Yet the Douglass brothers owned Partner's Purchase and Promise for only three or four years. On 15 November 1773, Hugh repurchased them both. Benjamin and Joseph Douglass planned to relocate to Dorchester County, on Maryland's Eastern Shore, following their sister and her husband, John Smoot, to the other side of Chesapeake Bay. In buying the properties back, Hugh made the move easy for them.

But Hugh was still determined to sell Partner's Purchase, and he had figured out another way to do it. His second cousin Jezreal Penn bought it from him that same November day in 1773, "in Consideration of the Exchange of Lands and also for the consideration of nine shillings Sterling Money."[6] The cousins swapped land, and then Hugh turned around and sold Jezreal's former property for a pretty penny. The buyer was John Hoskins Stone, a rich young merchant of the county. He paid "Four hundred and Eleven pounds and fifteen Shillings" for the land.[7] That was a lot of money. A gentleman and his family could live decently though not luxuriously on one hundred pounds a year, and a tradesman's family could live on fifty.[8] Hugh did very well by the transaction.

But more questions beg for answers. Why was Hugh in such a hurry to sell his property? Was he under pressure to clear outstanding debts? The court recorded a third transaction for Hugh Hammill on 15 November 1773. It was the mortgage of his "negro girl Lety" to his brother-in-law, John Shaw, for a consideration of "forty-three pounds seventeen shillings three pence of common money," or about four hundred dollars.[9] Hugh clearly needed money, and he needed it fast. Perhaps he owed a good deal to the tobacco merchants who had advanced him credit on the sale of his leaf. Or maybe he wanted to finance his move from Maryland to Virginia. Or perhaps it was both.

Hugh's sale of land to John Hoskins Stone is his last transaction in the records of Charles County for nine full years. Between November 1774 and April 1783, while the American Revolution was being fought and won, Hugh was an elusive figure in his home county. Was he helping to defend his country? Though he was forty-three in 1776, Hugh was not too old to fight. In Maryland during the American Revolution, military service was mandatory for free white males between sixteen and fifty; fifteen hundred men mustered up in Charles County.[10] So Hugh was well within the age of mandatory service. However, his name does not appear in the published muster rolls for Charles County.[11] Nor does it appear in the census ordered by Charles County commissioners and carried out piecemeal between 1775 and 1778.[12] More puzzling still, when in 1778 the Maryland Convention required that every free male over eighteen sign an Oath of Fidelity to the State of Maryland or be deported as a loyalist, Hugh Hammill's name does not appear in the listings for Charles County.[13]

Could it be that Hugh was not sympathetic to the Revolution? That suspicion grows when one discovers that Hugh's Uncle Edward and his good-for-nothing younger son, William Groves Smoot, were accused of trafficking with the enemy in the course of the war—the only men in Charles County to be so accused. Charges against Edward were dismissed on 23 December 1777. William Groves was not so lucky: "At the March session of the court in 1778, William Groves Smoot was arraigned and accused of bartering provisions for rum and sugar on board of the enemy's ship. It is the opinion that his action was due more for the thirst of alcohol, as no gold was exchanged, rather than for any sympathy with the British."[14]

It may be that Edward Smoot was brought into the fracas as the father of twenty-three-year-old William, not because he was caught red-handed on a British ship. Or it may be that he could not resist an opportunity to lay in a stock of rum and sugar, in very short supply among the colonists since the embargoes on British goods had been enacted in the early 1770s. Whatever blot this adventure might have made on Edward Smoot's character, it seems not to have lasted. He became a county magistrate after the war, and died a rich and apparently respected man in 1795.

Hugh did not flee from the colonies as a Loyalist at the outbreak of the war, nor was he deported as a troublemaker to Halifax or the Caribbean. In fact, he did sign the Oath of Fidelity, on 28 February 1778, the last day it was possible to do so. He signed it in Dorchester County, on Maryland's Eastern Shore, rather than in Charles County, where his properties were. Moreover, he signed with an X—"his mark." That X is the only time in three centuries of family records that a Hammill signed with a mark. One can only conclude that Hugh had doubts about the Revolution and was not about to set his signature to any oath supporting it. An X would do to save his land.

It could even be that Hugh moved to Virginia in part because its governor at the outbreak of the Revolution was a Loyalist: Governor John Murray Dunsmore, who later was run out of the colony in ignominy.[15] Hugh could certainly avoid service in the army more easily in Virginia, a larger and less tightly organized state than the notably militant Maryland.

But these suggestions do not explain why Hugh was in Dorchester County in the first place. Could the reason be one of religion?

Dorchester County was a hotbed of itinerant Methodism during the Revolution, and the Hammill family "dissented" from the Episcopal faith at some point, to become Methodist. Could it be that the first Methodist in the family was Hugh—or more likely, Elizabeth, his wife, who brought Hugh and any children into the faith along with her? A man who was the lone survivor of a family of nine might seek solace in evangelical religion. Moreover, the Methodists were pacifists. That might explain Hugh's puzzling absence from the muster lists.

It was an intriguing possibility. The itinerant preachers who so tirelessly combed Delaware and Maryland's Eastern Shore in the late eighteenth century poured their hearts, hopes, and experiences into the journals they kept of their travels. The journals show how important women were in establishing the small Methodist societies or "classes" that became the backbone of the movement. This was appealing—maybe a pathway to the women's side of the story, so sorely wanting in this narrative, lay here.[16]

And Methodism was exciting! Anglican clergy resisted the itinerants violently, pulling them from their horses, throwing them in the mud, stomping them, driving them out of town. The Method-

Hugh Hammill's "mark" on the Oath of Fidelity, Dorchester County, Maryland, 28 February 1778. ❧ Courtesy of Maryland State Archives

ists would stand in a town square or on the steps of a church on Sunday, and begin singing hymns at the top of their voices. When a crowd gathered, they preached. Sometimes they ended up in jail, and their supporters staged dramatic rescues. And then there was the question of their political sympathies. John Wesley, the founder of Methodism, was not only a pacifist but an Englishman thoroughly loyal to the crown. All Methodists were suspected, not unreasonably, of being the same.

These itinerants, and the historians who came just after them in the early nineteenth century, kept detailed lists of those who provided them with shelter, food, money, and a friendly ear, partly so that future traveling preachers would know where they could safely stay. What a gold mine! I dug in it tirelessly for several weeks, but in the end could find no evidence that Hugh Hammill or any of his associates were Methodists in the last two decades of the eighteenth century.

Well then, what was Hugh doing in Dorchester County in February 1778? Of course, he was visiting his Smoot and Douglass relations. In 1770 Hugh's uncle Edward Smoot had purchased a tract of thirteen hundred acres called Rehoboth on the Nanticoke River in Dorchester County. Shortly thereafter his son John and daughter-in-law Elizabeth Douglass Smoot moved to Rehoboth, followed by Joseph and Benjamin Douglass and then another brother, Alexander. One historian comments rather smugly:

> John Smoot settled about 1771 upon "Rehoboth" where he
> constructed Liberty Hall, a spacious Geor   gian mansion,
> now one of the showplaces of Dorchester County. At the
> census of 1790, he had 41 Negroes on his plantation, being the
> largest slave owner in the county. . . . John Smoot before his
> death controlled a number of mercantile establishments on the
> Eastern Shore—besides the store at Northwest Fork Bridge,
> he had one at Crotchers' Ferry. In his concern at Vienna he had

Alexander Douglas as his partner, and then there was a lumber firm of Douglas & Smoot, near his seat of "Rehoboth," where also stood a mill.[17]

Edward Smoot provided an opportunity to his son, and John made the most of it. He served as a captain in the Dorchester County Militia during the Revolution, became a county magistrate, represented his district at Maryland's first State Assembly, and died a rich man in 1793, two years before his father. Through John, the Douglass brothers become successful as well.

Hugh, like his Smoot and Douglass relatives, also moved out of Charles County in the course of the American Revolution. He was living in Prince William County, Virginia, by 1778, maybe as early as 1775, soon after he made that land sale to John Hoskins Stone. That was why he did not muster up in Maryland at the outbreak of the war. But the Oath of Fidelity caught him off guard. He had to sign it to protect the Maryland tracts he still owned. Otherwise the state would confiscate them, if his neighbors didn't do so first.

I believe that Edward Smoot smoothed the way for his nephew Hugh just as he did for his son John Smoot and John's brothers-in-law, the Douglasses. An indenture dated 25 May 1764 between William Mitchell of Prince William County, Virginia, and Edward Smoot of Charles County, Maryland, shows Smoot purchasing a tract of 153 acres in Prince William County, on Powell's Creek near the town of Dumfries. The tract lay just across the Potomac, an hour at most by ferry from western Charles County. I think Hugh moved to the Powell's Creek tract at his uncle's invitation, to oversee Smoot's tobacco plantation there. Ties of kin predict that Smoot would do something of this kind for Hugh, and this land record suggests how he might have done it. Other records show that Hugh Hammill lived in or near Dumfries for two decades at least. Once more, circumstantial evidence makes a very strong case. Only the last word, the final proof is missing.

10

GOOD-BYE TO CHARLES COUNTY

---—❦—---

*W*HY DID Hugh Hammill move out of Charles County? I did not want him to sell his father's properties or to abandon old family associates like the Chandlers and Penns. I did not want him to stop worshipping at Christ Church, where his parents took him all his childhood. Colonial Charles County cast a spell that I hated to see broken. Such a busy, bustling, conscientious place, taking care of widows and orphans, settling disputes, organizing land transactions, keeping meticulous accounts. Bold signatures appear in the record books, huge folio volumes containing hundreds of pages written out in beautiful, usually legible, script. Pretty little plats decorated with sketches of oak leaves and "saplins" accompany deeds and bills of sale.

The social world of colonial Charles County seems to have been exuberant, even joyous. On the brink of the American Revolution, in 1774, an Englishman named Nicholas Cresswell visited the county and in his journal wrote of the charming girls dancing at a harvest festival "without stays," of the slaves, who seemed "as if they had forgot or were not sensible of their miserable condition," and of the people in general, who "appear to live very well, and [to be] exceedingly happy."[1]

As for the natural world, court documents evoke it in nearly every word. Consider these lines from John Hammill's deed to Baker's Addition, recorded 4 October 1736:

> ...begining at a bounded Locust a bound Tree of a Parcel of
> Land called Marsh Land runing thence with a Straight Line to
> the head of a Creek called Bakers Creek so high as the tide Ebbs
> and flows, thence binding with the Swamp on the east and south
> side of the Swamp to a bounded white oak....[2]

The twice-daily flood and ebb of the tide, the marshy land laced with creeks, rich soils imperceptibly giving way to swamps thick with locusts and oaks—water was and is ubiquitous. The fact made accurate property descriptions nearly impossible before surveyors could measure from reference points that were not themselves subject to alteration or disappearance. A "bounded" tree was one that someone had declared to stand on a boundary line. What happened when the tree rotted or was cut down? Or when people forgot which tree marked the bound? Maybe it stood about where the high tide reached—or maybe where the tide ebbed, who can say? And what if the swamp contracted in a dry summer, or overspread its usual area in a wet one? No matter, the deed says the property contained "by Estimation Thirty-seven acres more or Less." In tidewater regions, sometimes more, sometimes less was good enough.

Physically, Charles County today is not much changed from what it was in the eighteenth century, if the visitor can look beyond paved roads, telephone wires, and pockets of urban sprawl that pop up suddenly just off the main highway. Much of the land is still wooded, so, though it is surrounded by water, one does not see this except from high ground, cleared ground, or right at the brink of a creek or the Potomac. At shoreline the water and land interpenetrate, so that in winter the sun dazzles as it glances from icy streams onto dry yellow fields that seem almost to stand in their midst. Zekiah Swamp, enormous just as it was three hundred years ago, at first glance is woods, until one sees the ice glinting between the saplings at their roots.

On low land and high land, wide fields spread, sometimes full of cattle that wander across unpaved side roads at their whim. A few McMansions stand, naked on their three-acre lots. Washingtonians have discovered that western Charles County is a commutable distance from the city. I saw several beautiful old farmhouses, half hidden by branching pines or shade trees, bare in winter, of course. Small settlements of house trailers and middle-class homes, many of brick, clustered now and then at a crossroads with a bar or old-time grocery. The eighteenth-century churches, also small and built of brick, stand intact, in perfect repair, surrounded by the tombstones of their parishioners. Familiar names appear on the churchyard headstones: Dutton, Penn, Chandler, Smoot, but none go back as far as the early eighteenth century.

Except for the main highway, where traffic speeds ceaselessly day and night, the roads were nearly empty on a winter day. The wind was ice cold. Two ruts of mud and ice led off the highway at Cuckold's Creek, on the Potomac, where Partner's Purchase lay. At the end of the ruts spread the Potomac, wide as a lake or bay, with a modern bridge just visible in the far distance, linking Maryland and Virginia. Pope's Creek Road skirts the Potomac on higher ground, the big river catching the sun from the edge of stubbly fields.

Maryland's southernmost counties have a timelessness that even the fast-food restaurants along Highway 301 cannot dispel. I drove many miles through that golden countryside, exploring. My companion was the radio, tuned to WKIK Country. The tunes seemed almost too appropriate: "She's gone, gone like a freight train, gone like a Civil War soldier, bang bang, gone like a '59 Cadillac..."

The past, both visible and hidden away in the state's voluminous archives, seemed to be as alive as the present—weighed just as much, somehow.

But huge numbers of Charles County residents did just as Hugh Hammill, Philip Shaw, John Smoot, and the Douglass brothers did, around the time of the war. Why did these families leave the county that had been so good to their fathers and grandfathers? What changed in southern Maryland after 1770? Of course, between 1776 and 1782 the Revolution was fought and won, with gigantic consequences for all the former colonies as well as for Great Britain. But even before the outbreak of the war, life in the Tidewater was growing problematic.

First was the issue of credit and debt. British merchants extended easy credit to tobacco growers in the strong market years of the 1760s and early 1770s, and most growers took full advantage of it. Between 1772 and 1774, however, European markets for tobacco contracted sharply, and merchants began to call in the loans that had provided so many households with consumer luxuries from teapots and sugar to pistols and clocks. No one wanted to buy their tobacco, so small to middling planters were hard-pressed to raise what they owed. Some were reduced to selling household goods or even their land to avoid being hauled off to prison. When Hugh sold land to John Hoskins Stone for 411 pounds sterling, some of that cash almost certainly went to pay off consumer debt. As one historian drily comments, "[t]he credit contractions of 1772–74 triggered substantial conflict between planters and merchants."[3]

Then, too, land prices in the Tidewater had been rising steadily throughout the eighteenth century. "Between the 1750s and the 1770s, a time of no inflation, land prices multiplied four times—from ten to forty shillings an acre—in … Western Shore tobacco-growing areas."[4] Tobacco growers could no longer expect to buy new land cheaply when their old land was exhausted by tobacco cultivation, unless they were prepared to move west to the tobacco frontier, or to central Virginia or the Carolinas. Many families did just that. Others sold the land they owned but stayed in or near their home counties as tenants, "because they figured they would earn more money by leasing good land near markets than by owning land isolated from trade centers."[5]

The Charles County that welcomed John Hammill in 1725 had vanished. In 1775 it was fully populated, maybe overpopulated. Its soils, once so fertile, so superbly suited to tobacco cultivation, were depleted, though land prices did not yet reflect this fact, and its tobacco could no longer compete with that produced on virgin acreage to the west and south. In 1725, John Hammill had looked at his Irish homeland and decided he could do better in the colonies. Fifty years later, his son looked around at his Charles County home and judged that Virginia, across the Potomac, was a better place to be.

Just one of John Hammill's descendants stayed on in Maryland. He was Neale Hammill Shaw, John Hammill's grandson, second child of Catherine Hammill and Joseph Shaw. Neale's sisters, Elizabeth and Kitty, followed their father to Virginia and then to Orange County, North Carolina, around 1795, along with their husbands and children. Neale stayed behind. He married Ann Ford, daughter of a well-to-do Charles County family that lived at Black Friars, a comfortable, even distinguished, home for the late eighteenth century. Brick, with glass bay windows and a three-gabled mansard roof, it still stands on Mt. Victoria Road, near Christ Church. Surrounded by a wide expanse of field and woodland, cattle on every side, the prospect cannot be much altered from what it was in 1800.

Neale became a schoolmaster like his grandfather, teaching English literature and history for many years at Charlotte Hall School, an Episcopal school in All Faith Parish, just over the line in St. Mary's County. For many years he was a lay reader at the All Faith parish church, and eventually he took orders, becoming rector of All Faith about 1810. Both church and school still stand, neat, trim, and well maintained, exactly as they did in Neale's day.[6]

At the time Neale Shaw was ordained, the Episcopal Church of the United States was so sorely in need of rectors that the Bishop of Maryland expressed "no reluctance to dispense with a knowledge of the Greek and Latin languages" in Neale's case. These were traditional prerequisites for Anglican clerics. In a handful of letters preserved in the archives of the Maryland Episcopal Church in Baltimore, Neale apologizes profusely for his deficiency, blaming it on "the want of proper books, which my circumstances do not enable me to procure." He continues, "However, I have put my hand to the plough. I must use my best exertions, and such means as my temporal affairs will possibly admit, and if the Lord intend me to labour in his Vine-yard, I am sure he will assist me. And, Should I not succeed, I must be satisfied with the hope, that I endeavoured to discharge, what I thought to be my duty." This letter like most of the others closes with his elegant, flourished signature.

Neale Shaw officiated at All Faith church nearly until his death in 1831. It was a modest appointment; the parish had only forty-three communicants in 1822, half of them white, the other half black. Yet within his little sphere, Neale had the prestige of a gentleman.

Charlotte Hall School, All Faith Parish, St. Mary's County, Maryland. Neale H. Shaw taught English and history in this building in the first decades of the nineteenth century.

He taught his classes; he sorted out squabbles between pupils and teachers; he organized dancing parties, a literary society, and outings for the young gentlemen who boarded at the school. He conducted church services as well, and probably looked forward every June to the Episcopal Convention held in Baltimore. On one occasion, in the summer of 1819, he wrote to the bishop excusing himself from attending, for "Mrs. Shaw expects a little one daily, and we are both much indisposed at this time; bad colds, which are prevalent here."

In the same letter he describes a scandal within his congregation, asking the bishop for guidance "Respecting a Lady who has lately married her nephew.... She wishes to attend church again, and offer herself at the Holy communion,—I certainly refuse to let her commune—you will be kind enough to write to me on this subject—Your advice will ever be Thankfully received...." Such were the trials of the pastor at All Faith parish church.

Though Neale Shaw conducted his professional life in St. Mary's County, his wife's family, like the family he grew up in, had always worshipped at Christ Church in Charles County. The Neale Shaws seem to have kept up that connection as fully as they could. Long after his death, when his children or grandchildren commissioned a bronze plaque in remembrance of him, they had it placed at Christ Church. It can still be seen there, on the inner east wall. It reads:

A tribute of love to the memory of Charles Allison Ford, 1804–1881, and Neale Hamill, 1806–1882, sons of Rev. Neale Hamill Shaw, 1767–1831, and Ann Chandler Ford of Black Friars. They and their sisters Eliza Chandler, Kitty Hamill, and Mary Soph[ia] rest with their fathers to the fourth generation at Black Friars, Christ Church Parish.

Chandler, Hammill, Kitty, Neale. The names echo through the generations, reflecting the tightly knit, deeply traditional world of old Charles County.

PART III

PRINCE WILLIAM COUNTY, VIRGINIA

1778–1845

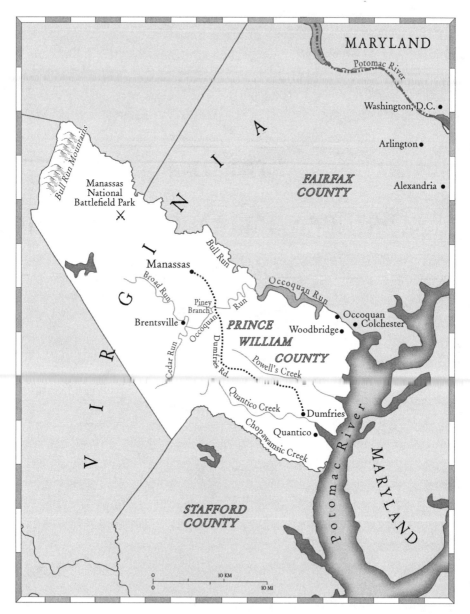

Prince William County, Virginia

II

Crossing the Potomac

———————— ❧ ————————

$\mathcal{P}$RINCE WILLIAM is one of Virginia's northernmost counties, and one of its oldest. It was created in 1730, with the Potomac River bounding it on the east and Chopawamsic Creek on the south. In 1740, Occoquan Run became the county's northern boundary when Fairfax County was formed on the north side of the run. In 1759, when Fauquier County was created, Bull Run Mountain became Prince William's western boundary. The county forms an irregular rectangle about thirty-five miles long and about eight miles wide at its western end, eighteen miles wide on the east. Its terrain descends gently southeast from Bull Run Mountain to the banks of the Potomac.

More or less in the county's center, Broad Run and Cedar Creek converge with Occoquan Run, dividing the county into two sectors: "upper," or western, and "lower," or eastern, Prince William. When Hugh Hammill took up residence in the county in the 1770s, the western or upper sector of the county was still lightly populated frontier country, though increasing numbers of planters were growing tobacco and wheat in the fertile, well-watered soils along Broad Run, Occoquan Run, and their tributaries.

Eastern, or lower, Prince William had begun to develop and then to boom in the third and fourth decades of the eighteenth century. When Hugh moved there, it was settled country whose history and politics were closely intertwined with those of the Maryland Tidewater and the cities of Baltimore and Alexandria. The town of Dumfries, on the Potomac shore in lower Prince William, lay eighteen or twenty miles from the village of Manassas in the upper sector of the county. It was a morning's ride on horseback or by carriage from one to the other, along roads that were often choked with dust or clogged with mud. Only the Potomac River separated Dumfries, on the Virginia side, from Budd's Ferry in Charles County, Maryland. In good weather, it was less than an hour's sail across those two miles of water. Families in lower Prince William had no trouble maintaining ties of marriage, kinship, and business with friends and relatives on the Maryland side of the Potomac.

In the colonial period and for a century after, lower Prince William's prosperity depended on its deep-water ports, situated where wide-mouthed creeks or runs poured from the hinterland into the Potomac. Colchester, at the edge of Fairfax County on the north side of Occoquan Run, was the earliest and shortest-lived of these. Dumfries, at the mouth of the Quantico, rivaled Boston and New York as a center of maritime commerce for several decades at the end of the eighteenth century. When Dumfries went the way of Colchester, the town of Occoquan boomed, until its port, too, silted up and became unnavigable some decades into the nineteenth century. These failures were the unintended consequence of deforestation and too-intensive tobacco and wheat cultivation along the creeks and rivers.

Today, all of Prince William County has been pulled willy-nilly into the vortex of development spinning south and west from Washington, D.C. The Occoquan-Woodbridge area, only thirty miles south of the nation's capital, is exploding with road construction, townhouse developments, shopping centers, and traffic. The expansion of I-95 and other gigantic projects obscure its natural landscape, but in Leesylvania State Park, located between Woodbridge and Dumfries on the Virginia side of the Potomac, one immediately recognizes western Charles County's woodsy, hilly terrain. In the park, at water's edge, the wide Potomac stretches eastward. Lilypads cluster in its shallows. On the horizon the Maryland shore hovers. For centuries, people canoed or sailed across those two miles of water, their possessions crowded around them, hanging onto their children. It was a short, pleasant trip, just a hop across a river.

Maryland entrepreneurs began their push to exploit the northern Virginia shore in the 1730s. Drawn by mature woodlands that could be harvested for blast-furnace fuel as well as by easy water transport, the industrialist John Tayloe looked from Maryland to Neabsco Creek, just north of the Quantico, and carried his iron works to the Virginia side in 1737. John Ballendine saw the potential of Occoquan Run as a source of waterpower, and in the 1750s built lumber and flour mills there, as well as an impressive fieldstone mansion that he called Rockledge. It still stands on the bluffs above the river. Tayloe bought out Ballendine in the 1760s and expanded his iron works along the Occoquan.

As international markets expanded, large proprietors set about cultivating tobacco and wheat along lower Prince William's creeks and runs. A flood of Scots fleeing political oppression poured into the area after 1745. They built wharves, warehouses, businesses, and homes, giving the name Dumfries to their settlement at the mouth of the Quantico. When, in 1761, Dumfries became the county seat, the town put up a substantial brick courthouse and several new taverns or inns, drawing more population along with a variety of trades.

Such activity was not lost on Edward Smoot of Charles County. Always alive to an opportunity, he purchased land in Prince William in May 1764, several years before buying the Rehoboth tract in Dorchester County, Maryland, where his son John Smoot and the Douglass brothers settled in 1768.[1]

Philip Shaw, Hugh Hammill's brother-in-law, moved to Prince William sometime in the 1760s. He purchased land in the upper district, near the confluence of Occoquan Run and Broad Run in the center of the county, and set about raising tobacco on those rich creek bottoms at the tobacco frontier. A chance deposition preserved in Prince William County court records suggests that he moved out of Charles County about 1766. He testified as an "aged & material witness" in a property dispute between William Tebbs and John Barron of Prince William County on 24 August 1796. In the deposition, Shaw gave his age as "62 or thereabouts," indicating that he was born about 1734. He stated that "upwards of 30 years ago," a certain chestnut oak was pointed out to him as a boundary tree for a disputed tract on the south side of Broad Run. So he had been living in Prince William County, on or near Broad Run, since at least 1766.[2]

Thomas Smoot waited until 1782, after his tour of duty in the Maryland militia, to settle in Prince William County. He leased land near Philip Shaw in the county's upper district, moving with his large family and several slaves to Bristoe's Tract, seventy-five hundred acres that had been confiscated from the loyalist Robert Bristow at the outbreak of the Revolution.[3]

And of course Hugh Hammill moved to Prince William, sometime between 1764 and 1778.[4] He settled in or near Dumfries, possibly to become overseer of his uncle's tobacco plantation on Powell's Creek. He would have supported himself and his family by leasing his Charles County tracts to tenant farmers. If he was an overseer, he also collected a salary, probably paid in tobacco as a cut of Edward Smoot's crop. It would be a fine thing to be able to prove that Hugh did this. At the moment, I cannot. No documents give the missing link, partly through an accident of history.

For the years between 1786, when Hugh Hammill appears for the last time in Charles County documents, and 1849, when his grandson, another Hugh, surfaces in Prince William County land records, information about the family is elusive. Within the family, two house fires in the late nineteenth century destroyed private documents and letters.[5] Public documents are also missing for the period. Crucial Virginia censuses of 1790 and 1800 were lost in transit to the National Archives a century ago, and no copies had been made or kept in the individual counties.[6]

Moreover, Prince William is one of several "burned counties" in Virginia. During the Civil War, Union armies burned and pillaged its courthouses, destroying records that went back to the early colonial period. I was at first shocked and then resigned when I encountered lines like the following one, from a register of Virginia wills: "No wills preserved for this time period and deeds 1759 and 1760 are missing." The Prince William County courthouse archivist told me that even now, after the year 2000, he receives the odd package of documents from a northern family who has discovered them in an attic—plunder squirreled away by a Union soldier.

The State of Virginia, in a dismal episode of its own, destroyed many records more. In 1895, a new library was opened in Richmond for the storage and protection of innumerable documents that had been accumulating in the Capitol archive for more than two hundred years. However, there was some miscommunication about which old documents ought to be saved:

> [T]he state authorities decided that much of this material was worthless and contracted with a junk dealer to haul it away. Chutes were constructed from the upper floor of the Capitol to facilitate the operation. Irreplaceable official papers going back many years and rare old volumes were catapulted into the junk wagons. The junk dealer was said to have complained that the ancient documents had so many wax seals on them that his men

had to spend time stripping them off, in preparing the papers for the mill. More than half a bushel of such seals were seen in a heap in the dealer's yard or scattered on the ground.[7]

The State of Virginia has done an exemplary job of retrieving and organizing the records that remain. The Library of Virginia hosts a superb Web site with digital access to most of what is available.

So destruction of records is one obstacle to reconstructing the Hammills' earliest decades in Virginia. Another is the simple absence of records. The Hammills did not own property in Prince William County until 1849. Between 1786 and 1849, they leased their homes and businesses, paid no land taxes, registered no deeds, and left no wills. A few mentions in court records, one land lease, and yearly personal property tax assessments from 1782 to 1845 provide the slender details I offer here and push the historian toward conjecture where facts are few. Let the reader be the judge of the results, and for those who are impatient, remember that after 1845 the historical fog lifts dramatically.

When Hugh Hammill left Charles County for Virginia in the mid-1770s, he was well into middle age, somewhere in his midforties. His wife, Elizabeth, was in her late thirties, their daughter Catherine probably in or near her teens. Personal property tax records suggest that one slave, Letty, or Lett for short, accompanied them to their new home—probably the same "negro girl Lety" that Hugh mortgaged to his brother-in-law John Shaw in 1773.

Tax records consistently locate Hugh in lower Prince William County, in or near the town of Dumfries. In 1782, the first year that Virginia levied a tax on personal property, officials divided the county into six parts and put a resident landowner in charge of canvassing each one. Hugh Hammill's name appears in the sixth district, in Burr Harrison's list. Harrison owned property in the far southeast of Prince William County, on Chopawamsic Run not far from Dumfries.[8]

After 1782, the county was divided into the familiar tax districts of upper and lower Prince William. Hugh was always assessed in the lower district, in the area of Dumfries. For example, in 1788, the tax collector called on Hugh Hammill on April 10, the same day he visited John Matthews, who leased property on the main road to Dumfries, William McDaniel, who ran an inn or ordinary right in town, and William Tebbs, whose elegant Georgian home was a Dumfries landmark. These were Hugh Hammill's neighbors. In the years before 1782, colonial court records also support the idea that Hugh Hammill lived in or near Dumfries.

On 5 October 1778, "Hugh Hammell" of Prince William County, Virginia, was issued a license "to Keep an Ordinary at his House, he having given Bond according to Law." Any public house must be located where there is demand for meals, drinks, and beds. Court days in Dumfries always brought crowds who needed or wanted to spend a night in town. Moreover, the stage road from Baltimore to Fredericksburg passed through Dumfries, and the Potomac Path, another important colonial thoroughfare, passed just east of it, along the river. The commerce of the area provided plenty of traffic.

That was even more the case in 1778, when the American Revolution was being waged on Dumfries's doorstep. Month in and month out, waves of prisoners, troops, supply trains, and wounded men moved through town or were transported to the Dumfries hospital camp. The officers in charge of these movements relied on ordinaries for accommodation—expeditionary maps of 1781 and 1782 indicate their locations as well as those of army camps and fortifications.[9]

Like his uncle Edward Smoot, Hugh Hammill kept his eye on opportunity. Perhaps he did not want to fight in the war, but he was happy to profit by it. If his family consisted only of himself, his wife, a half-grown daughter, and one woman slave who could do the heavy work, and if his house was located near to civilian and military traffic, an ordinary could be a shrewd business choice for him. He wouldn't need many rooms for his small family, and his wife and daughter could attend to the clientele.[10]

On 7 September 1779, Hugh appeared again in the records of the court, this time as the defendant in a case brought against him by the Reverend James Scott, rector of the Anglican church in the town of Dumfries. Predictably, Hugh Hammill lost the case:

> The Argument of the Parties by their Attornies being heard and by the Court fully Considered, Judgment is granted the Plaintiff Against the Said Defendant for Six hundred pounds of Crop Tobacco and his Costs by him in that behalf Expended.
>
> Ordered that the Reverend James Scott pay Richard Hewett Seventy Seven pounds of Tobacco for attending two days and Evidence for him Against Hugh Hammell and once coming and returning 9 miles to Stafford.[11]

Less than a year after receiving his business license, Hugh was hauled into court and fined for an offense against Scott that is not described. What could it have been? Aside from the mention quoted above, the records are silent. Did it have to do with the public house—trash in the alley beside the church, or noisy patrons at inconvenient hours? Was it an accident, like a fire or a runaway wagon, which destroyed some of Scott's property and for which Hugh was held responsible? Was it a squabble over property—Hugh mowing hay or felling trees that the Reverend considered his, perhaps? Whatever the details of the case, it locates Hugh in the Dumfries area. The glebe, or land set aside for the support of the Dumfries church and its rector, consisted of four hundred acres on Quantico Creek extending north along the Potomac to Dumfries.[12]

As to the lawsuit, the cards were stacked against Hugh from the start. It was not likely that he could prevail over Scott, a rich man, a gentleman raised and educated in Scotland, closely allied with the gentry of the county. He had been established there for decades, and his brother, the Reverend Alexander Scott, for decades before that. Scott did not even attend the court session in person, sending instead Richard Hewett, his man of business or perhaps an overseer. Scott remained in Stafford County, nine miles south, like a gentleman with more important things on his mind.

Shortly after the judgment, on 14 March 1780, Hugh signed a lease on two sizeable properties on Broad Run in upper Prince William. Tempting as it is to imagine that these three events are linked, that the ordinary caused the troubles with Scott, and the troubles with Scott resulted in the land lease, no connection can be proved. All that can be asserted is that Hugh wanted to increase his income, by opening an ordinary or by leasing tobacco land or by doing both. The ordinary was short-lived. Hugh's business license had lapsed by 1782, as that year he did not pay the fee to renew it.

There is no indication that Hugh Hammill left the Dumfries area to settle on his leased land in the center of the county. On the contrary—in May 1780, when a petition was raised to move the courthouse to a more central location in the county, Hugh signed the counterpetition, to leave the courthouse in Dumfries "where it now stands."[13] He lived in Dumfries as an absentee landlord, subleasing his Broad Run tracts to a tenant who saw to the cultivating of the land. By 1780, Hugh was collecting rents from leased properties on both sides of the Potomac.

Like the inventory of John Hammill's estate made thirteen years before it, Hugh Hammill's 1780 land lease is a touchstone in the family story. The lease names Hugh, his wife, Elizabeth, and their daughter, Catherine, the only time she is mentioned in any document. It places the family in their late-colonial social and economic context and shows how securely they were tied to the traditions of earlier centuries and to the British common law. It pins Hugh down like nothing else that remains of his history.

The lease is set "for and during the natural lives of the said Hugh Hammill, Elizabeth Hammill, and Catherine Hammill, his daughter, or the life of the longest liver of the three." It is a lease on three lives, just like those written in North Ayrshire, Scotland, two hundred years before. Hugh's daughter was apparently the youngest family member he could muster—he seems not to have had a grandchild to name.

In the lease, Hugh takes on "two certain lots or parcels of land containing one hundred and twenty eight acres in one lot, and one hundred sixty one acres in the other lot." The first lies "on the northwest side of the Piney Branch," a small tributary of Broad Run, and the second adjoins "the land of Col. Thomas Blackburn broad run."[14] Thomas Blackburn owned a lot of property in the county, some of it near Dumfries. He was the son of Richard Blackburn, who built Rippon Lodge on his large plantations bordering the Potomac. The lease specifies "the land of Col. Thomas Blackburn broad run" to distinguish it from the Potomac River tracts. So Hugh is leasing near Philip Shaw, in the center of Prince William. Hugh's property, like Philip's, fell in James Ewell Jr.'s district in the tax assessment of 1782. Hugh has followed Philip's lead, and has leased rich bottomland where tobacco and wheat thrive.

For the use of this land, Hugh is to pay yearly "the reasonable rent of one thousand pounds of crop tobacco … in one hogshead, together with the quitrents and tax." "Quitrents" are a true holdover from feudal times. They and the tax would be paid in silver, but the rent itself was, in 1780, still to be paid in tobacco. In addition, the lease obliges him to plant, or to have planted, two hundred peach trees and one hundred apple trees on each parcel of land within five years. This is another requirement typical in colonial leases. If Hugh defaults on the lease, or when the term is up, the landowner will profit from the trees. Until then, Hugh has the use of them. He also has the use of the "houses" or buildings already standing on the larger tract. On the second tract, he is required to build "a good dwelling house with other conveniences"—outbuildings, like a tobacco drying shed, a barn, perhaps a cabin for slaves to live in. To build them and to keep the place fenced and properly maintained, Hugh has the use of the plantation timber.

The lease's intent is clearly to encourage tenants to improve the land—to add value to it. Like the leases of the fifteenth and sixteenth centuries, the assumption is that Hugh will hold the land for the long term, perhaps even that, for a modest fee, his heirs will renew the lease when the last person named in it dies.

William Tebbs, that prominent citizen of Dumfries, owned the land, and he needed to do something with it. One parcel had belonged to William's brother James, who was deceased, and the other had been leased to James Graham, another gentleman of the county, who held it from 1777 to 1780, just three years.[15] Tebbs was looking for a more stable arrangement and has offered a generous lease to secure it. Often leases of the time prohibited tenants from harvesting plantation timber, and many contained a clause that prohibited subletting and insisted that the lessee live upon the land.[16] Hugh's lease does neither.

Now, what does it mean that Hugh was leasing land and not buying it? Or, put another way, what was the status of leaseholders in late colonial Virginia? Some historians seek to show that tenants were an exploited underclass both before and after the Revolution.[17] But that claim is too broad. True, some tenants struggled to make ends meet, cultivating their modest tracts with the help of their own families and a mule. Others, however, were prosperous men who did not labor on the land themselves. Subtenants and slaves did the work, and the leaseholder collected the rents. Many such men leased tracts in one county while owning land in another—like Hugh Hammill. In 1780, when he signed this lease, he still owned Promise with Baker's Addition and Ashbrooke's Rest, undoubtedly farmed by tenants who paid their rents to Hugh.

Moreover, his leased tracts amounted to 289 acres together, a considerable holding. The median Virginia leasehold contained only about ninety acres.[18] Hugh was not rich on the scale of Thomas

Blackburn or James Scott or William Tebbs—he did not own a mansion and thousands of acres cultivated by scores of slaves—but he was far from poor. He was a man of middling means or better, a solid citizen by the standards of his community. As a freeholder, he belonged to an exclusive group, the set of free white males who met certain age and property requirements and thus were entitled to the vote.

In colonial America as in late medieval Britain, the term *freeholder* did not signify the outright ownership of land. A Virginia statute of 1705 defines it like this: "[E]very person who hath an estate real for his own life, or the life of another, or any estate of greater dignity, shall be accounted a freeholder," as long as that person is free, white, and male and holds a minimum of twenty-five acres of improved land or a minimum of one hundred acres of unimproved woodland.[19] As it did centuries earlier, the lease on three lives conferred the privilege of the vote and the right to sell leases or improvements as the lessee saw fit.[20] Men like Hugh Hammill had much more in common with the "tacksmen" or "kindly tenants" or "heritors" of traditional Britain than with sharecroppers and small tradesmen who paid cash rents on short-term leases. Hugh Hammill, William Tebbs, and countless others lived by and continued the customs of their British heritage.

In the margin of the record book where this lease appears is a brief notation: "Exam'd and Delivered to Peter Smith by Hugh Hammill verbal order, October 1783." Peter Smith owned land adjoining Hugh's leasehold, and, unlike William Tebbs and many other landowners in the county, he lived on his property. County land records indicate that he often assisted absentee property owners in showing their land and delivering leases and other documents to tenants in the neighborhood.[21] Hugh Hammill and William Tebbs made their agreement in March 1780, and it was October 1783, three and a half years later, before the lease was written up and delivered to Hugh for his signature.

Delays like this were not unusual: "Frequently many years elapsed before a promised lease was put into writing: six years in the case of tenants on [some tracts]."[22] This could put tenants in a difficult position, especially the smaller ones who rented only one tract of ninety acres or less. Without a legal agreement, they were vulnerable to a landlord changing his mind, yet they needed to set about planting, harvesting, and building to meet the terms of their lease. In the case of Hugh Hammill, the three-year interval meant that by the time he held the lease in his hand, two of the lives it was written on had ended.

12

LIFE AND DEATH ON
REVOLUTION'S DOORSTEP

$\mathcal{T}$HOSE FIRST few years in Virginia must have been anything but tranquil, for Dumfries stood in the very corridors of war. In the spring of 1781, British ships harassed Potomac settlements between Dumfries and Alexandria. On 9 April, their men "Plundered the Houses of Messrs. Gerard Hooe, John Washington and many other persons of all their Furniture and other Valuable Effects and [took] off some Negroes."[1] The British targeted tobacco warehouses along the river, burning many before the American army could build defensive garrisons.

Later that year, the deputy commissary of Prince William County thought himself "authorized to take in beef cattle the tenth part of the number of each man's stock" to supply the American army. George Mason reported this to Thomas Jefferson, Virginia's governor, pointing out that "if the measure was to be executed ... every family would be left without beef, tallow, or leather for the ensuing year." Fortunately, the order was modified; Mason warned that were it "not timely prevented ... [it would] in many instances occasion lawsuits, and in some, most probably, violence."

American and French troops were quartered at the towns of Dumfries and Colchester, on both sides of the Occoquan. Troop movements between those towns destroyed much cropland and many fields of hay. On the tenth of September, on General Washington's orders, Col. Henry Lee set his men to building a new road and ford across the Occoquan at Wolf Run, west of Colchester, in a "fine fertile Country well improved with meadows" and "well supplied with forage." Washington urged Lee

> in very earnest terms ... to do this & to do it well. ... The baggage wagons of the French & American Armies, the Cavalry & beef cattle will all march by this route & may be expected in the course of a few days. ... I expect Count de Rochambeau, the Chevlr. De Chastellux & their respective suite at this place, tomorrow on their way to join the Army below. It would be a sad relief to them and their horses, and a mark of attention w'ch I am persuaded would be pleasing[.] [T]he Gentlemen of this state would assist them along in their carriages from stage to stage.

I imagine the gentlemen of the state did assist, quietly mourning the trampling of their fields and loss of their winter fodder. Smaller folk no doubt looked on, secured their animals and furniture as best they could, and waited in fear or excitement to see what would happen next.

When the war ended, in late summer of 1782, the victorious French and American troops marched north from Richmond, through Dumfries and Alexandria and on to Baltimore. At the camp in Alexandria, festivity reigned:

> The most elegant and handsome young ladies of the neighborhood danced with the officers on the turf ... the circle was

in great measure composed of soldiers who from the heat of the weather, had disengaged themselves from their clothes, retaining not an article of dress except their shirts, which in general were neither extremely long nor in the best condition; nor did this occasion the least embarrassment to the ladies, many of whom were of highly polished manners, and the most exquisite delicacy; or to their friends or parents; so whimsical and arbitrary are manners.[2]

Did Hugh, Elizabeth, and Catherine enjoy some of the fun before private misfortune overtook them? It may be that the political events of 1782 went scarcely noticed within the family. On 15 April 1783, the Charles County court recorded Hugh's sale of Promise with Baker's Addition, and for the first and only time in these transactions, Elizabeth did not acknowledge the sale. She could not; she had perished.[3]

Catherine, too, Hugh and Elizabeth's daughter, vanishes from the records and from all memory after her mention in the lease of 1780. In all likelihood, death took her with her mother, sometime between March 1780 and April 1783. And it took another of the Hammill family's intimate circle. Thomas Smoot, who only months earlier had assumed a leasehold in Bristoe's Tract, near Hugh's Broad Run land, signed his will on 20 May 1783. He died at forty-one, in the prime of life, leaving one married daughter, six sons, and his wife, Elizabeth Maddox Smoot, who was expecting their eighth child. Were these three deaths caused by the virulent influenza that raged worldwide in 1782 and 1783?[4] There is no way to know. All that can be said is that once more Hugh was a survivor—he and Thomas's widow. By early 1786, Hugh Hammill and Elizabeth Maddox Smoot had married.

I suppose it is not surprising that Hugh and Elizabeth Smoot should join forces after their spouses' deaths. They had known each other since they were children, sitting just a pew apart in Charles County's Christ Church all those years ago. Their lives had run at parallel for thirty years or longer, held there partly by their Smoot connection. But what an alteration his second marriage must have made in Hugh Hammill's existence! In just a handful of years, he went from being the only male in a family of three, to being a widower with no family at all, to becoming the stepfather of eight and probably a step-grandfather as well, for Elizabeth's daughter Mary had married in 1779 and had moved to Virginia with her husband, her parents, and, by 1782, maybe a child or two. Several of her younger brothers must have moved into Hugh's house upon their mother's second marriage. Baby Elizabeth was born some time after 20 May 1783. She would have been a child of three when her mother and Hugh set up housekeeping together.

And then, after her second marriage, Elizabeth Smoot Hammill produced two sons more—Hugh's sons, born when he was well past fifty. No birth date survives for Elizabeth Smoot, but, to have a married daughter in 1779, she herself could not have been born after 1749. She was certainly nearing forty in 1787, when the first son was born, and was probably over forty in 1789, at the birth of the second. Hugh named the boys following the Hammill tradition. The older was John, for his grandfather, and the younger was Stephen, for Hugh's brother.

If we members of the twenty-first century are tempted to believe that our lives are more complex than those of our forebears, this chronology should cure the illusion. From no children to eight and then to ten, practically overnight! In March 1786, after his second marriage, Hugh sold Ashbrooke's Rest, his last property in Charles County. As on every occasion but one in the past, the sale was acknowledged by Hugh's wife Elizabeth. This time, however, she was not Elizabeth Shaw, but Elizabeth Maddox Smoot.

The sale of Ashbrooke's Rest marks another of the transitions within the Hammill family just after the American Revolution. John Hammill had purchased it in 1736. It passed to John Jr., at his majority, then to Stephen, and then to Hugh after Stephen's death in 1765.

Fifty years after his father bought it, Hugh sold it to William Poston of Charles County. No doubt he needed the money. But that is only part of the story. William Poston was Hugh's nephew-in-law, the young husband of Stephen's daughter Sarah. The deal was all in the family.

On the back of the deed is this paragraph:

Memorandum, Charles County to wit on the 13th day of March 1786, Hugh Hamil party to the written Deed Entered upon the Tract of Land therein mentioned Ashbrook's Rest and delivered Seisin & possession of the Said Land to the Said William Poston therein mentioned by deliverying to the Said William Poston a twig & Turph upon the Said Land in the name of the whole Land aforesaid Called Ash Brook's Rest the Said Land with all the appurtenances thereto belonging. . . . in presents [presence] of us who were desired by the Said partys to Subscribe our names thereto as witnesses to the Said delivery and Seisin.

Signed Rich'd Barnes, Sam'l Hanson Jr.[5]

The physical delivery of twig and turf at the sale of land is an ancient practice under British common law. Many seventeenth-century colonial deeds mention the transfer of twig and turf, but by the late eighteenth century it was an anomaly, a throwback. The court recorder can't quite get the wording right; the legal phrase is "livery of seisin," but the clerk writes "deliverying" instead. This paragraph shows that Hugh and William enacted a kind of ceremony on the land itself, in the presence of witnesses, to commemorate the passing of family property from the old owner to the new. When Hugh passed a broken twig and a bit of turf to William, he represented the transfer of the whole parcel. It is the only time in the land records of the Hammill family that "twig & turph" is invoked. Hugh obviously attached a special significance to the transaction. What was it?

Certainly Hugh wished to remember and honor Stephen, his long-dead brother, and Stephen's daughter, Sarah Hammill Poston. But would he have made such a production of it had William Poston not been taking the place of Hugh's own son and heir? To my mind, this transaction proves that Hugh had no living sons by his first marriage. In March 1786, at the age of fifty-three, he in effect made William Poston his heir. He had no need to own land, for at the time he had no son to inherit it. His second marriage might bring him sons, but at his and Elizabeth Smoot's ages it probably seemed unlikely.

Even more pointedly, the ceremony of twig and turf shows Hugh's deep conservatism, his attachment to his British heritage. That same conservatism made him unwilling to sign his name to the Oath of Allegiance in 1778. In 1780, it led him to negotiate a land lease on three lives, the traditional gentleman's lease that seemed right and appropriate both to him and to the lessor, William Tebbs. Hugh and many other middle-aged and older men found themselves in an uncomfortable straddle after the Revolution. Through no doing of their own, they had become citizens of the new United States, but their identities were bound up in the old tradition, and it tugged at them inexorably. Their fathers, men of John Hammill's generation, fit securely into their culture as British colonials, and there they flourished. Hugh Hammill and others of his generation, especially those who were not at heart revolutionaries, must have felt themselves off balance for decades both before and after the war. I think some never regained a sense of balance, of belonging, in their new world. Did they flourish? Maybe yes, and maybe no.

The end of the war and his second marriage precipitated a further change in Hugh Hammill's life—an economic slide downward. Ten years of Virginia personal property tax records show his fortunes in steady decline.[6] In 1782, the first year a property tax was levied, his taxable household consisted of one free white male over sixteen—that's Hugh himself—two horses, two cows, and one slave over sixteen named Letty, or "Lett."[7] He paid no tax on luxury items like "wheels," then as now a valued status symbol, or a billiards table. In 1784 he paid no tax on cattle. By 1788, he no longer owned a slave. What happened to Letty? Perhaps Hugh sold her, or she may have died. The comfortably fixed young man who inherited all his father's land and goods has vanished. In his place is a man past his middle years, the head of a large family, forced to economize just when his needs were greatest. Hugh's reverses show in small the troubled state of the tobacco economy in late colonial times, and the bitter economic depression that followed the American Revolution.[8]

I always imagined that when the Revolution lifted the oppressor's thumb, the American economy burst into bloom—like a blue baby turning pink the minute the heart surgeon fixes that leaky valve. But historians say it was not so. In the Great Depression of 1929–33, real per capita gross national product declined by 48 percent. After the Revolution it fell by at least 46 percent, probably more, with similar consequences:

> [T]he net effect of the war was a sharp decline in individual income. The foreign sector was simply too central to the performance of the entire economy for its disruption to be suffered lightly.... Recovery, furthermore, was painfully slow ... it seems unlikely that the levels of income and wealth achieved in the early 1770s was attained again before the beginning of the nineteenth century.[9]

The colonial economy depended on transatlantic trade. The Revolution shattered that trade, and the naval blockades and battles of the Napoleonic Wars, which began in 1793, delayed its recovery.[10] It took time to establish new domestic industries and commercial relationships. In the Chesapeake, worn-out soils, escalating land prices of still-productive soils, and the flight of the young and energetic westward compounded every problem.[11] Thus the boom years that built John Hammill's livelihood contracted at the end of the eighteenth century for nearly everyone who stayed in the Tidewater. By 1787, only two-fifths of householders in Virginia's Northern Neck owned the land they farmed. Hugh and his family were typical; they leased their land, and, like most white people who stayed in the rural Chesapeake, they were "born in the region, and … descended from a long line of slaveholding freeholders."[12]

On 21 May 1792, "Hew Hamel" was once more assessed for the personal property tax, his eleventh such assessment. He never appears in the tax records after that. He was not excused from the tax, as an old and indigent man might have been. He simply disappears from the record. The best explanation is that he perished, sometime before the spring of 1793, at the age of fifty-nine or sixty. A misfortune for him, but a far greater one for his sons and for Elizabeth Smoot Hammill—widowed twice in a decade, with Stephen and John aged three and five, her daughter Elizabeth only eight years old, and two or three young sons more, still living at home. Who stepped in to provide for them all?

This is a perfect blank in the Hammill family history. Neither the widow nor her minor children became wards of the state, as happened when survivors were truly destitute. They found support somewhere, and it must have come from kin, probably piecemeal. If the widow renewed the lease for Hugh's Broad Run tracts, she would have those rents to live on. If Hugh lived on Edward Smoot's property in a house Smoot owned, Edward might have offered to keep his family there. Elizabeth's older children were rather distant kin to Edward, but Hugh's sons John and Stephen were his grand-nephews. The uncle outlived his nephew by a couple of years, dying in 1795 at the age of seventy-one. Perhaps his heirs extended their father's generosity to the Hammills until the children could manage on their own.

And perhaps Hugh's nephew John, Stephen Hammill's grown son, helped out. He appears to have followed his uncle from Charles

County to Prince William County about 1785, where he is attested in Prince William records on 7 August as surety for a Burroughs family bond.[13] Stephen's son John was born on 6 October 1763. In the summer of 1785 he would have been nearly twenty-two, old enough to sign such a document. A decade later, in 1795, a case in the Dumfries Land Causes mentions a surveying crew lineman by the name of Hammill.[14] Was it John Hammill? Possibly—a serendipitous connection to his grandfather, John Hammill the surveyor. A John Hammill paid personal property taxes in lower Prince William County yearly between 1795 and 1806, when he disappeared from those records. Was he the hero of the Hammill story after his Uncle Hugh died? I can only say, maybe.

And what of Elizabeth Smoot Hammill, Hugh's widow? However she managed, her methods were successful, fortunately for me. I am here writing this account because her son John, my three-times-great-grandfather, and his brother Stephen survived to adulthood, married, and eventually raised families of their own. Elizabeth Hammill is mentioned in Prince William County records as one of twenty-four witnesses to the death of Isaac Money on 5 December 1796.[15] This Elizabeth must be Hugh's widow, for her daughter Elizabeth was only thirteen on that date. In the census of 1810, neither she nor Hugh Hammill is named. Elizabeth Smoot Hammill could have died any time between 1796 and 1810. For her children's sake, I hope it was later rather than earlier in the first decade of the nineteenth century.

But county land records suggest that she might have died in the early part of 1800. Hugh's Broad Run parcel, the one that had originally belonged to James Tebbs, was re-leased on 6 November 1800, presumably after the death of Hugh's widow. It was then "in the ocupation of Thomas White," a subtenant, and was about to be leased to a new primary tenant, Charles Shaw. Charles also planned to sublet: "the aforesaid Charles Shaw his heirs or assigns is to be allowed to keep a Subtenant on said Land." One can hardly help wondering if this Thomas White had been Hugh's subtenant, and if Charles was the son of Philip Shaw. The new lease is written on just one life: "for and during the natural life of the aforesaid Willoughby Tebbs." How surprising that it is the life of the lessor, Willoughby Tebbs, not the lessee![16]

THE TWO decades that passed between 1792 and 1812 ushered the Hammill family into its third American generation. The nation underwent its own transition after the Revolution and before the War of 1812, as colonial modes of life and business mingled with and gradually yielded to the new American way. Tobacco as currency began to give way to plain American dollars. Indians who a century before had lived and prospered on the banks of the Occoquan returned, in 1801, to what they considered a sacred site, marked near the river with a cairn of stones. They staged a war dance, brandished their knives, whooped and yelled, and rounded out the event by consuming a keg of whiskey.[17] This was probably the last, certainly one of the last, times they did so.

13

THREE STORIES

***

Now the historian lays down her pen, stymied by the want of documentary evidence. The novelist is quite ready to pick it up, so intriguing are the hints that history has left dangling. In the first of these three stories, Elizabeth Maddox Smoot remembers her second husband, Hugh. In the next, Hugh's brother-in-law Philip Shaw explains some things about his sister, whom I nickname Bets. In the third, Hugh's "negro girl Lety" speaks of her years among the Hammills. How true are these fictions to the facts? As true as I can make them, given what little I know.

***

Elizabeth Remembers Her Second Husband, Hugh

It's an odd thing to live thirty years in an acquaintance with a man, and then suddenly find him at the center of your life. It's odd again when he disappears too soon, just as your life together takes form. Was he there at all? Do I remember him at all? Then his little boys come skipping in the door, with his hands, and his eyes, and of course he comes back into mind. I wonder if every twice-widowed woman feels like me, that she has two husbands but neither one at home. I talk to them both in my heart even yet.

Hugh was a tall man, and I was tall, too, with big Maddox bones. Healthy-grown, said my mother. Strong as an ox, said my father. Plain as porridge, said I, but to myself. I think it surprised Hugh when I stood at his side and the top of my head touched his nose. When we were alone, he would slip his arm around my waist and nuzzle my hair. "I never feel I might break you," he said.

We were both survivors, there was no doubt of that. How I and my children anguished when my first husband—that was Tom Smoot, of course—mustered up for the militia and marched out of sight, so trim in his blue coat, his musket on his back. How we rejoiced when he returned, thin and weary but no harm done, and how excited we were about our new Virginia life, and years more before us to stretch out and thrive. And then that influenza, and he was dead, and I was left with the children and a baby on the way—there is no understanding it.

That influenza made a shambles of Hugh's life, too. It carried off his pretty wife and half-grown girl before it ruined my family. Nothing could happen faster. Well one day, raging fever the next, wracking cough for three days more, and gone like that. We survivors left in the wreckage of our lives, wondering what to do next. Hugh came to me before I was delivered of Tommy's last child. He sat down in the kitchen and took off his hat and set my youngest on his knee, and he said, "Now, Lizy, I know it is too soon for you to think of your future, but when you come to it, I hope you will join your life to mine, for nothing would give me greater honor, and I believe there would be benefit to us both. And in the meantime, if you or your little ones should want for anything that I can give, you must call on me for it." From that day he came to see me every week, until my little boys watched for him and called out "Uncle Hugh!" when he rode up. When Elizabeth was born, he was the first man to take her in his big hands, gentle as ever a body could be. He was the only father she ever knew.

Hugh was not young when we married, not lively and trim and laughing like my Tom, and I missed that fun at first. His black coat and formal ways made him seem still older. He had his habits that he would not break, like his hour at the public house and his dinner-time pipe. Tom had hated pipes and snuff and all of that, though he made his living growing the leaf. Nor did Hugh much care to oversee his land or what his tenants were doing with the crop, so long as the rents were paid on time.

But he liked babies, and he would take the youngest on his lap and dandle it until it squealed with delight. When he was silent I learned to seek his eyes, where often I found amusement and not displeasure. I took up the Bible one Sunday not long after we were married, just when it was clear that his first child was in the making. I read a few verses out loud, choosing at random as had been my custom. The book fell open at Judges, the thirteenth chapter, and I stumbled over those Bible names.

"You could hardly have chosen better," he said, for the verses told of a childless man whose wife the Lord made to bear a son. "But you must say Ma-noah, not Manwa." He took the Bible from my hands and read the verses out again. "We must work on this," he said to me. "The children must read and write with the best, and you, too, for you are my wife as well as their mother."

That hurt me, though his eyes were kind, for I prided myself on how I read. He saw it, and he said, "A woman's mind is the equal of a man's, so my father taught me. My sister Kitty loved her book, and now look at her son, my nephew Neale, priming for the pulpit. You will read as well as he one day, if you wish it." He schooled us all, I would say patiently. For me, he brought home newspapers and such, and we read and talked them over almost man-to-man. "You have a good head on your shoulders, Lizy," he said. That pleased me, and when he passed on, I tried to teach his little boys what he taught me. It was a shame he did not live to do it himself.

In one thing we disagreed. He had little patience for religion, and none at all for church. A waste of a good morning, he called it. I don't believe he went with me above once or twice in the six years we were married, though he did not object when I dressed Tom's children in their best clothes and led them out the door. He stayed home and taught his little ones riddles and rhymes. John could reel off "The Grand Old Duke of York" by the time he was three. I came in one Sunday to find the boys stomping around the room, chanting, "When he was up, he was up! And when he was down, he was down! And when he was only halfway up, he was neither up nor down!" I thought it was sacrilege, being so rowdy on Sunday, but Hugh just smiled. "There were five of us boys at home," he said. "Let them be."

"But mama," said my daughter Mary, interrupting me one day as I rattled on with my stories. We were sitting outdoors under an apple tree, watching her children play. "But mama, did you love him? You couldn't have loved him like you did my daddy, or like I love my Sam."

That stopped me for a minute, I will admit. Did I love Hugh? What can love mean between a woman nearing forty and a man of fifty-three, with one marriage and several children behind each? My mind filled with the image of Hugh's long hands and tall figure, his dark coat and old-fashioned hat. I could see that from my daughter's point of view, he might seem hard to love. And then I remembered my children on his knee, and how he thanked me for his infant sons, as if they were gifts he had not dared to dream of. "Yes, I loved him," I said to Mary. "Have you asked yourself if he loved me?"

Prince William County, August 1798

❖

Philip Shaw Remembers Hugh, Husband of His Sister

WHO DID not know him, that tall, black-coated figure in the tricorn hat, gray-eyed and grim-faced until he smiled. I remarked on that grim look to my sister once, not so long before she died. "Are you not afraid of him, Bets?" I said. "He looks like he might bite." "No," said she. "You must look at his eyes. They're the same as when he came to fish the creek with you and Will, and I was a little girlie peeping round the door." That made me laugh, for well I recalled her pranks and Hugh's quick grin as he batted after her with his father's fishing net fastened on a pole.

So I sought to watch his eyes each time we met, which was not so often as I might have wished. Jane and I did not get into town above once in a month, so clotted with mud was the Dumfries road, unless of course it choked us with its dust. Nonetheless, I sought to watch his eyes. They were quick, I saw that. When they fell on my sister, they paused for just a breath. When they fell on Kitty with her bright hair and those long-fingered hands so like his own, his mouth would soften, then firm. But it was not easy to catch his glance. He was ever changing where he looked, or rather for the most part he looked nowhere, or everywhere—he looked past you, is what I want to say. Yet he seemed to see all. He noticed my study of him, at any rate. "What do you stare at, Philip?" he said one day. "Is there mud on my cheek, or do you admire my hat?" Then our eyes met, and I glimpsed what my sister meant. Gray they were, and full of light, not cold but observant, as if he watched for a sleek trout to dart out from the river weeds.

"Neither," said I. "But I wonder why you look so stern." "A grinning man looks like a fool," said he, swinging onto his big mare, "and one who stares looks much the same." But he waved his hat as he rode away, and I saw there was no hard feeling on his part. Nor on mine, as I thought of it. He was a proud man, and a conscious man, conscious of himself, I mean, the more as he grew older and his circumstances pinched. He cared for the world's respect, I suppose too much—more than Bets, and more than I, who was content to live in the countryside and see to my crop myself. After she died, and Kitty with her, he grew dour indeed, but then folk understood, or thought they did.

"A broken-hearted man," I heard behind him, "a disappointed man. Life has used him cruelly. He has no one but himself, you know." What wonder if at McDaniel's inn he took a bit more cider than was right, or passed whole afternoons and evenings there with the newspapers before him and his hat on a chair. Then his face would flush up, and he would kick out a seat for any comer, ready to argue on come what may. I took to passing an hour or two in his company whenever I could, first out of a grief for him and Bets, and my wife Jane's uneasiness about that tippling habit, but then because it pleased me. Bets died in December '82, when the war was not long over, and the papers and peoples' mouths were full of our victory. Hugh was glad enough the war had ended and the troops gone home, but he grunted when men glorified the Union, and if they persisted in it, he turned away.

"The British nation was two thousand years a-building, and we think we can match it in a day. Why, we are like the blue men prancing in the mist, we are at the dawn of our history. We shall miss our ties with Britain, you mark what I say." He would not speak so with just anyone, of course, but so he said to me, and time proved him right. These last fifteen years have been hard, very hard, naught but skimping, as Jane so often says.

I had a respect for the man, the more when he took me in his confidence about his plans. I believe it showed courage when he rode up to my gate—a long ride, mind you, near twenty miles—and asked for a word in private. We walked out to the river, midsummer it was, six or eight months after Bets's passing. Hot weather, fish leaping up for the insects that skimmed above the water. A beautiful day, you might call it.

"Philip," he said. "You have heard of the death of Thomas Smoot, of course." "Indeed," said I, "and have called upon the widow more than once, my wife as well." "I wish you to know that I mean to propose marriage to the widow, to Lizy Maddox that was. After a decent interval, you understand. Pray do not think that I have forgotten your sister. But it is no good for a man to be alone."

What did I feel? Surprise, I own, but also relief, for I was concerned for Hugh. And no hard feeling, much as I had loved my sister Bets. "Lord, Hugh!" I answered him. "You will be far from alone if you marry Lizy Smoot. She has children and to spare. No, man, you have my blessing if you want it, and I warrant Bets's, too, if she could give it. I congratulate you, for it seems to me there is little chance she will refuse your offer. Ah, we have known her since she was in pigtails, have we not?"

That was about the end of it, as far as words go, I mean. Off he rode, perhaps to see Lizy, for she did not live far from me. When I told Jane, she nodded. "He could have a child yet," she said. We did not speak of my sister's troubles in that line, but of course they were in both our minds. She bore him only three or four, and none lived but Kitty. When Kitty died right after Bets, none of us was surprised, exactly. My sister was a lovely thing, red-haired and nimble and full of life, but it seemed she could not be a mother.

What more is there to tell of Hugh? He and the widow Smoot were wed soon enough, and two little boys followed. They had Elizabeth and two or three of Tom's boys living with them, too, and Hugh's cottage was packed pretty tight. It had been plenty big for him and Bets and Kitty. Their means were cramped as well, but in that, they were no different from the rest of us. He kept up his evening hour at McDaniel's, I think to step outside the hubbub, for Hugh was not a young man, and this houseful by rights should have belonged to his son, and he the grandpapa, not the father.

It was a shock to me when Hugh died, at not quite sixty, and a worse one for Lizy. He had outlived so much, it seemed like he could outlive anything. But he went to bed one night and didn't wake in the morning, just walked off the stage without a bow or a farewell, so to say. I miss him yet, look for him yet as I round a corner in town near where he lived.

And was he happy in his last years? He had what he wanted, I think I can say that.

Prince William County, Septembrt 1798

❀

Letty Tells Her Story

MY NAME is Letty, but folks call me Lett, the white folks, leastways, because it's shorter for bossing me, I guess. My own folks called me Baby, on account of I was the last-born in my family, until old Mister Hammill he said one name was enough. What he meant was, enough for a negro, but you can be sure my mama held her tongue on that. So then I was Lett pretty much all around. My father and mother and us four children belonged to old Mister Hammill over on the Maryland side. I was born on their place called Promise, there on Pope's Creek, in Charles County, my father said it was. Until I was six or seven, life was happy enough, but then Mister and Missus both died in one year, and their children split us up, one or two to each. I went with Mister Hugh and Miz Elizabeth over to Durham Parish, and it might have killed me, but my mother and one brother were right nearby, and I saw them close to every day, one way or another.

The other thing that saved me was my master and my mistress's little baby girl, Miss Kitty was her name. I loved her, and she loved me, right from the start. Miz Elizabeth she showed me how to care for that baby, how to rock her and change her and button up her frock, and the baby would crow and put her arms up to me at five or six months old. I couldn't pick her up, because I was too small myself, but I could sit down to her cradle or down on the floor and talk to her and play with her by the hour. Miz Elizabeth didn't mind it, because then she had the time to fix her hair and put lace to her collars and do those lady things that my master enjoyed when he came in. When the baby slept, I had to hustle to get my other work done, but since it was just the three of them and one a baby, I managed all right.

But a dark day came, and that was in '73, when the white folks could not sell their crop, and the tobacco stood in hogsheads on the wharves or in the sheds for weeks and months on end. There was no trade, and that meant no credit, and my master lent me over to Mister John Shaw on a mortgage, he called it, to get some cash in hand. Miss Kitty and I both wailed and wept, but Mister Shaw carried me off on horseback nonetheless. Mister Hugh did try to comfort me, I reckon for his daughter's sake, and he said he hoped he could redeem me back one day, but that year I stayed with the Shaws was mighty long. Now I will say the Shaw children took to calling me Letty, but that was to sweet-talk me away from the chores their mama set me: "Letty, would you curl my hair," "Letty, would you mend this tear," "Letty, would you fix us your cherry shrub, would you, Letty, Letty?" Between Mistress Shaw and all those children, I was about run off my legs. When Mister Hugh came up one day and paid me off and carried me home, I was right glad.

Now it seemed we were going to move clean away from Charles County, across the big river, and well I remember clutching to Miss Kitty on that raft and both of us squealing and giggling, and the two of us were just all eyes, for it was such an adventure. We set up in Virginia, and Mister Hugh he did this and he did that, and the war came and it went. I grew some and filled out some, and one day Miz Elizabeth took a look at me and saw I wasn't a child anymore, and she didn't like it one little bit. Then she took to making my life a burden to me, in ways she didn't think her husband would see.

They had a rocking chair standing in the kitchen, and I had got an old flour bag and stuffed it with woolen scraps and then stitched up a cover in a pretty blue gingham that I pieced out of one of Miss Kitty's old frocks. I asked Miss Kitty for it, and she asked her mama, and Miz Elizabeth said all right, for she and Mister Hugh doted on that girl. I made a nice cushion to the chair, and it was about the kindliest seat in the house.

In the end, two creatures sat on that cushion, and none else, and one was Miz Elizabeth, and the other was her big white cat, Angelina by name. Well, one day I came in right weary from the wash and I don't know what all, and I set myself down on that cushion without a thought. In came Miz Elizabeth right behind me, and before I knew it I was down on the floor. "That chair is for Angelina before it's for you, and don't you forget it," she hollered. From there we went from bad to worse, and nothing Miss Kitty could say or do made a bit of difference.

Next thing that happened, and maybe it was the Lord above and maybe it was the Devil at his work, both Miss Kitty and Miz Elizabeth took sick and died, right like that. After the watchings and the buryings and the breakfasts and the suppers and the cleaning up and the clearing out, when the visitors went home and it got quiet and empty in the place, Mister Hugh called me to him and told me he had hired me out to Miz Tebbs at the big house down a street or two, more toward the river, for he could use the money and besides, it wouldn't do to have me stay and look after just him.

He said he had worked it around so I could come by each morning and fix his breakfast and leave his supper, and tidy up and take his linen back to do up with the rest at the Tebbs's, for they had a big establishment with five or six negroes in the house and plenty a-going every time you looked. So off I went, and I was not sorry, for I knew what Mister Hugh meant, that it wouldn't do. He meant folks would talk, me being young and a woman and all, and him alone. And besides, without Miss Kitty to look after, it was too quiet for me there by myself. I was right ready for some company of my own color.

So I went off with my bundle, and Angelina had that cushion to herself until she went out the door one day and never came back. Not enough doings for her either, I guess. At Miz Tebbs's I mostly helped the cook, and then I came to do the cooking myself, for I had a light hand with the biscuits, as they say, and people liked my cherry shrub that I learned to make from my mother way back at old Mister Hammill's when I was just a child. You need the cherries, and the loaf sugar, and ice if you can get it, and a drop of cherry cordial, that's the secret, or lemons, but they are mighty dear. The cordial's not enough to hurt the children but it tastes mighty fine. Of course you can put in more for the gents. They always want it, I find.

The Tebbses had a fine black man named Daniel who looked after the carriage and the horses and all their tack, and he took a liking to me, and I to him, and so at their place my life took a new and lucky turn. But that is my story, and not the Hammills', and I will not tell that here. I will say that when Mister Hugh married again, that tall Miz Lizy with all the boys and more to come, he brought me back to his place for maybe a year, but then Miz Tebbs asked to buy me outright, and Mister Hugh agreed, because of the expense of his new family, and he got good money for me, three hundred silver dollars. He wouldn't have that government paper money, no sir. I wouldn't either, in his place.

And I will say that Mister Hugh never laid a hand to me in any way, and I don't believe I had a hard word from him, for he loved Miss Kitty so, and he liked me for her sake. And I think he liked that blue cushion, too, because after his womenfolk died and Angelina left him, he sat on it whenever he was at home. I know, because it got worn, and his new missus wanted to put a new cover to it, but he wouldn't have it, because the stuff came from Miss Kitty's frock. He was a good master, as they go.

Prince William County, October 1798

14

THE SECOND JOHN HAMMILL, CITIZEN OF THE NEW REPUBLIC

———————— ❧ ————————

LIKE HIS father, Hugh, John Hammill of Prince William County is an elusive figure. Grandson of the Scots-Irish surveyor, schoolmaster, and planter for whom he was named, John was born in 1787, nearly one hundred years—two very long generations—after his grandfather's birth in 1692 or 1693. One can only speculate about his early life—where he lived, by whom he was raised, how well he was educated, whether he learned a trade. He seems to have passed most of his life in the Dumfries area, moving north to Occoquan perhaps around 1830. By 1833, his widow and children were living in Occoquan.[1]

John appears for the first time in Prince William County records on 3 April 1809, when he filed a marriage bond at the age of about twenty-two. His bride, Elizabeth McIntosh—yes, another Elizabeth—was about nineteen. This early marriage shows that he could already support a wife and family, whatever his means of livelihood.

I think he might have been a blacksmith. His sons Hugh, Stephen, and John all worked as blacksmiths for some part of their lives. Maybe they learned the trade from their father. John's mother, Elizabeth Smoot Hammill, might have apprenticed her youngest sons to a smith in Dumfries when they reached their early teens.

John served twice in the War of 1812, both times with the Dumfries, Virginia, militia. Those brief collisions with a sweeping historical event illuminate one corner of his personal story. Chesapeake Bay was a major theater of battle in that second war with Britain, for the British navy could get to it easily, and the American capital lay close by—a tempting plum. In 1812, Britain's great warships harassed farms and villages up and down the bay, seizing animals and crops, burning orchards and buildings, and capturing or sinking any American vessels they encountered. The British referred to the attacks as "frolics." America's undertrained and poorly supplied militias could do little to stop them.

John and Elizabeth Hammill and their neighbors in northeastern Virginia did not see these depredations firsthand, but they lived in terror that the British would finish off their plunder of the bay and then turn their ships toward the Potomac. John mustered up with the Dumfries militia in 1812 in anticipation of such an action, but it did not materialize. After a few days or weeks of waiting, the Dumfries militia broke up and went home. The war moved north and west, to the Great Lakes and Canada.

In August 1814, however, the British were back in the Chesapeake, determined to take Washington and win the war. While land forces marched on the town of Bladensburg and then on to the capital, Captain James Gordon of the British navy took his huge vessels into the mouth of the Potomac and with incredible labor and perseverance essentially dragged them upstream through shoaling water and against the wind to Washington. He and his men saw and rejoiced at the red-orange skies that signaled the destruction of Bladensburg and the burning of the capital. They saw Fort Washington, on the

Maryland side of the river, explode into flame as fleeing Americans destroyed it to prevent its capture. They ascended to the city of Alexandria and waited for instructions, only to be told they were not needed—the battle for the capital had been won days earlier.

So Gordon confiscated every American ship and all the stores of goods to be found in Alexandria. He did not burn property or harm civilians, for the town, completely undefended, surrendered to him at the instant of his arrival. Then Captain Gordon sailed laboriously back down the Potomac, slowed as before by treacherous shoals and unfavorable winds. This time, however, he was harried by American batteries that had been hastily assembled at several points along the river. One of these was at a place called the White House, near Mt. Vernon just below Alexandria. Another was at Indian Head, on the Maryland side of the river just opposite Dumfries. Both batteries inflicted significant damage on the British ships, but in the end Gordon was able to slip free and escape into the bay with only seven men dead and thirty-five injured.[2]

It may be that John Hammill took part in the action at the White House. He served for seven days, from 31 August to 7 September 1814, as one of eighteen men in an artillery company attached to the 36th Regiment of Virginia.[3] Those were precisely the days when Gordon's fleet was descending the Potomac. Whether he fought or not, certainly John and his family at home heard and saw the explosions of cannon, musketry, and rockets along the river. They saw the British ships both coming and going, watched the flames consuming Washington, and trembled with horror as Gordon sailed into Alexandria's harbor, not twenty miles north of Dumfries, with who knew what kind of destruction on his mind. Yet the Hammills escaped harm just as Gordon for the most part did. The war moved on to Baltimore, and at last to victory for the Americans.

How did John's young wife feel about his days or weeks with the militia? Unlike her father-in-law, Hugh, Elizabeth's father, William McIntosh, fought in the American Revolution, enlisting twice. At his death in 1846 he was buried with military honors in Mississippi, where he moved with his younger daughter Nancy and her husband around 1830. Between 1812 and 1814, William McIntosh still lived in Dumfries. Probably he encouraged his son-in-law John Hammill to do his part against the British. I imagine Elizabeth did the same, fearing for her husband's safety all the while.[4]

With all America, the Hammills exulted at the British defeat in 1814 and enjoyed the flood of prosperity that followed. Especially in the South, the resumption of international commerce without British interference meant plenty of consumer goods and, for most people, the money to purchase them.[5] That general prosperity would have been a boon to John and Elizabeth. However, even in good times, John Hammill was not an affluent man. He never owned land, hence never paid a land tax, and he left no will, for he had little to pass on to his wife and children. In 1810, just a year after his marriage, the federal census shows him as the owner of one slave. In the census of 1820 the slave has disappeared, and he never owned another. Indicators of wealth and status like stud horses and wheeled passenger vehicles played no part in his household. In 1816, a typical year, he paid a personal property tax of eighteen cents.

John's wealth lay in his family and nowhere else. By 1830, he and Elizabeth were the parents of nine living children ranging in age from twenty to four. Considering that all but one of his grandfather's children perished before they were thirty, and that his own father seems to have produced no surviving children until he was over fifty, this is an accomplishment. Later generations remembered that John and Elizabeth had ten children altogether, but they could come up with names for only eight of them. I think one might have died as an infant sometime between 1816 and 1820, where there is a gap in the family births. The other was a "free white male" who appeared twice in censuses of the Hammill household, the last time in 1840, when he was between fifteen and twenty. Then this son disappeared. He might have died, of course, or he might have gone west to California with his brother William in 1849. I will come back to that tantalizing possibility at the end of Part III.

The year 1831 was the last in which John Hammill appeared in the personal property tax lists for Prince William County. He paid no tax at all that spring. He was alive on 7 November 1831, when he purchased one black and white cow from the estate of his friend and neighbor William Selecman, who had died on 7 July.[6] He must have died himself not many months later, sometime between 7 November 1831 and 14 July 1832, when the tax assessments for the year were reported to the county.[7] He was only forty-five. No cause of death has survived for him, though he might have perished in the cholera epidemic of the early 1830s. The disease was particularly deadly in Baltimore and Alexandria.[8]

So it was that Elizabeth McIntosh Hammill raised her younger sons as a widow, just as her mother-in-law, Elizabeth Smoot Hammill, had done. However, she had two enormous advantages over her mother-in-law. First, she survived her husband by thirty-three years and so was able to watch her children grow to adulthood. Even more important, John and Elizabeth Hammill lived together for twenty-two years instead of five or six. John's children knew their father, and John saw his first grandchild before he died.

Though he could not have known much about his father and grandfather, John retained enough of the family naming traditions to call his first son Hugh and to name four other children Catherine, William, Stephen, and John. Did he feel the absence of his father and other Hammill kin as he grew up, or did the great web of Smoot half-brothers and half-cousins, of Shaw and Maddox first cousins, fill the void? Perhaps they did; John's daughter Margaret married Thomas Maddox of Charles County about 1835, showing that the Maddoxes and Hammills stayed in close touch.

The Hammills and the Shaws stayed in touch as well. Charles Shaw, probably the son of Philip Shaw, served along with John in the Dumfries militia. Decades after John died, Charles signed affidavits testifying to his wartime service. They entitled Elizabeth Hammill to receive John's veteran's bounty—a quarter-section of land in Iowa that she promptly sold.[9]

Two more observations might be made about the second John Hammill. His oldest son Hugh's death certificate indicates that Hugh was born on 5 February 1810. But in 1874, before a court of law, Hugh himself gave his birth date as 12 December.[10] The February date allows a respectable nine full months between John and Elizabeth's marriage and the birth of their first child. But I think a man should be trusted to know his own birth date. In all likelihood, Hugh was born on 12 December 1809. In other words, his parents were expecting him before their marriage. Propriety on the part of Hugh's children must have induced them to adjust the date for posterity.

The more interesting detail has to do with a "free colored woman" named Lizy Hammill whose death is mentioned in Prince William County vital records for the year 1857. Her death, at the age of eighty, was reported by a friend and neighbor named James Fair, who in the 1860 census was living in the county's lower district. Lizy Hammill thus lived in the vicinity of Occoquan, like the rest of the Hammills.[11]

Who was Lizy Hammill? No deed of manumission has survived to name her owner or the date of her release from slavery. Was she the slave listed in John Hammill's household in the census of 1810? Slaves were generally not freed at the peak of their working lives, and in 1810 Lizy would have been in her early to middle thirties. Still, it is not impossible. Was she a Hammill by blood, the child of Hugh and his slave Letty, or of Hugh's nephew John Hammill, who followed his uncle to Prince William about 1785?[12] It would not be at all surprising if this were the case, given the realities of slavery in the American South. Though these particular questions have no answers within the historical record, no storyteller could resist them. Lizy Hammill will come up again in the stories in chapter 15.

Now, a word about John's wife, Elizabeth McIntosh Hammill. She and her much younger sister Nancy were literate women who kept up a correspondence for decades after Nancy, her husband, and her father left Prince William for Noxubee County, Mississippi. One letter has been preserved, in which Nancy tells her sister of their father's death at the age of ninety-one:

Noxubee County, Miss., Nov. 9th, 1846

My dear Sister,

Once more I take up my pen to write to you but oh how different are my feelings to what they were when I wrote to you last. With an aching heart I must now tell you that our Father is gone. Oh my sister, I wish that you had been here with me to see him. Oh God, I hope he is happy. I have reason to hope. He only lived six days from the time he was taken sick. He was taken on Monday with an ague [chills and fever] and had one every other day until he died. He would not take any medicine at all. Two of our Town physicians came to see him. He suffered a great deal the last two days and nights but the last day he was calm and appeared to be easy until he left this world.

This has been a fatal year in our neighborhood, there have been ten or eleven deaths within a few short months and most of them old persons.

Several of my family have been very sick but they are all up at this time.

I must not forget to tell you that I have another little daughter about six months old, I call her for myself, Nancy.

I hope you will forgive me for not writing to you sooner, my heart is so full, I cannot write what I wish. My health is very bad at this time, I feel like I shall soon follow my Father. I feel thankful that I was spared to wait on him in his last hours. I hope these few lines will find you and your family in good health.

I almost forgot to tell you when our Father died. He left this world on the 25th. Of Oct. in the 91st year of his age and was buried on the next evening. He was carried by six persons to his grave and was followed by a large crowd of people. He was buried in the honors of War [as a veteran of the Revolution].

My dear sister, I must bid you farewell, I cannot write, my heart is too full. Prepare to meet me in Heaven where parting is no more. I am your affectionate sister until death,

Nancy [McIntosh] Liddell

This letter gives me hope that Elizabeth McIntosh Hammill taught her children to read and write as fluently as she and her sister did, maybe even that John Hammill could write an articulate letter when he chose to. Who would have educated him, other than his own mother, I cannot guess.

It has to be that, for the man himself, John Hammill's short life brimmed with excitement, fears, disappointments, and moments of pure happiness. For want of records, those who read about him now can only dimly visualize his four decades of earthly existence. But that dark age was supplanted by an age of light as John's son Hugh reached adulthood and took the stage in the family story.

The second Hugh Hammill appears for the first time in Prince William County personal property tax rolls in the year 1828, when he was only nineteen. He may still have been living with his parents, but he was already the proprietor of a blacksmith shop in Occoquan, and he owned two slaves. That year his father paid no property tax, but Hugh paid fifty cents. He was prosperous enough to marry on 30 December 1830. This marriage date is more evidence that his birthday was 12 December 1809. Had he been born on 5 February 1810, he would have been only twenty on his wedding day, and he would have needed his parents' consent to marry Jane Harley, who was herself just seventeen.

An early acquaintance with hard work and responsibility gave Hugh his head start in the climb to prosperity. He worked like a man from an early age, sharing with his father the duty of providing for his mother and eight younger siblings. In 1830, Hugh married; his oldest child, Hannah Ann, was born in 1831. One year later, his father died. Thus, at twenty-three Hugh was the head of a clan numbering eleven—his own wife and child, his mother, and his eight brothers and sisters, who ranged in age from twenty-two to six.

He reacted by expanding his blacksmithing business, building into vacant land behind his shop that had been platted out as a roadway but never improved. This information is given in a letter from Thomas L. Selecman, a business competitor of Hugh's. Selecman says, "I will give you a few facts about this old street. About 30 years ago Hugh Hammill built a blacksmith shop and wheelwright shop in it and know body [sic] complained. It was all right...."[13] So, sometime in the 1830s, Hugh turned a blurry legal situation to his advantage—maybe the first time in his business life, but not the last.

The letter also indicates that in the 1830s he was already building wagons as well as smithing. I imagine that in those same decades of the nineteenth century, his distant relatives, the Hammills of Northern Ireland, were building their coaches and blacksmithing just like him: "The Ballymagarry Hamills were well-known as blacksmiths for generations, and their blacksmith's shop with its entrance shaped in the form of a horseshoe were a familiar landmark locally."[14] Had some memory or mention of smithing as a family trade been passed along among the Virginia Hammills? It seems possible. The likelihood grows, it seems to me, that Hugh's father John had been a blacksmith too.

In 1834, Hugh Hammill took on an apprentice, Joseph Patton. This was a local youngster, probably the son of the William Patton who purchased a wood saw at William Selecman's 1831 estate sale. In 1836, Hugh added a second apprentice, Ben McPherson, and sold one of his slaves. Ben's father was also named in William Selecman's estate sale. Hugh seemed to prefer employing local youngsters to owning and working slaves. They may have been less expensive for him than grown men whom he had to feed, clothe, shelter, and care for in every way. The apprentices could sleep and eat some of their meals at home.

In 1836, by then the father of two, Hugh's personal property tax was forty-nine cents. That year it was assessed on the basis of three free males over sixteen: Hugh and his apprentices, as well as one slave and one taxable horse. By 1836, only thoroughbred or stud horses were taxed. No doubt he had other horses that were fit for the cart or plough. I imagine the slave was a woman who helped with the children and housekeeping. This was the case in 1850, when tax and census records provide such information.

But before the second Hugh's exuberant life buoys this history out of the first half of the nineteenth century and into the second, an adieu is in order, to the parents and grandparents who produced him out of the blur of the past. Three more stories close Part III in the chapter that follows.

15

THREE STORIES MORE

───────────────── ❦ ─────────────────

*T*HESE FICTIONS help to fill the holes in the historical record. In *Nobody's Secret*, Lizy Hammill, the free woman of color, answers Letty's story of chapter 13. In *A Letter to a Sister*, Elizabeth McIntosh Hammill speaks of her life with Lizy. Last, in *Letters Home*, John's son William Hammill describes his journey to California with his brother, the nameless free white male of the censuses of 1830 and 1840. The story mentions two Cornishmen, William and James Hammill. These men did in fact emigrate from Cornwall after 1830 to mine gold at the Empire Mine in Grass Valley, California. I do not know what became of the Virginia-born William Hammill or whether he ever found himself in Grass Valley.

Nobody's Secret

NOW THAT'S a pretty story my mama has told, about her young life and Mister Hugh and sweet Miss Kitty and all, but she has left out one little thing, just one itty bit of a thing, and what that is, is me. If you want to know why Miz Elizabeth took to shovin' my mama down on the floor and carryin' on like the red-haired witch she was, well then, you had best look to me for your explanation, for I am the answer to all of that. Mmhm, I am that answer.

Lizy Hammill is my name, and my mama Letty brought me into the world unexpected, you might say, in 1780 or thereabouts, just in the thick of the war. And Miz Elizabeth she believed her husband was my daddy and there was hell to pay until she and her sickly daughter fell out of the world both on the same day. If that ole Miz Elizabeth had lasted a couple years more, she would have seen with all the rest that Mister Hugh had nothin' to do with the making of me, for could he give a little black gal them bright blue eyes of mine, and dark hair streaked with gold, and skin like coffee with a lot of cream? Not him, with his red face and grizzly gray eyes and hair. No sir. All he gave me was my name, and a poor choice it was, for it brought Miz Elizabeth down on my mama like he done it to insult her. Sometimes that Mister Hugh just had no sense at all. It was his nephew John was my daddy, and my mama told me how it went when I plain made her, I was twelve and wiry strong, I took her arm and twisted it behind her back and made her say the truth, because she owed it to me.

I had guessed it anyway, because about the time I was twelve was when Mister John Hammill came over from Charles County for good, and one look at them blue eyes and that crooked grin was all I needed, that and the swat he gave me when no one was watchin' and I dished out his breakfast from the stove. "Li'l Lizy," he said, "seems to me I've seen you somewhere before, where'd you get them blue eyes, gal?" And him grinnin' fit to bust his jaw.

So I made my mama tell, for I wasn't going to be nobody's secret. I twisted her arm up good, and she cried out, and then she told how Mister Hugh's nephew John used to come over from time to time to get away from his sour-faced stepdaddy and his mama who couldn't stand up to the man, and how he would stay a week or two and follow his uncle Hugh around, and Mister Hugh would talk to him about his own real daddy, and that seemed to ease John's heart, my mama said. But then he got to be sixteen-seventeen, and good-looking, and wild to boot, and when he came over my mama didn't know whether to hide from him or give him a smile, and one thing led to another and then there was no going back because I was on the way.

Well, you got to remember she knew him from a child, because he was one of that pack of young'uns she worried over the year Mister Hugh mortgaged her to Mister John Shaw. Young John and his sister Sarah were Stephen Hammill's babies, and their mama Asinah brought them into the Shaw family when she married a second time, and bein' a Shaw set well enough with Sarah for she was a good, sweet child, but her brother John didn't take to his stepdaddy. No sir, for he was quick and lively like his own real father, and John Shaw was one of those slow, solemn fellows couldn't keep up with little John after he was five or six years old.

So my mama said they kinda made their own little clan, him and her and baby Ann Shaw, who thought the world of her half-brother John, and though my mama was black and they was white, and she was slave and they was free, and she was a couple years older than John, they made their own little clan because they was all on the outs one way or another with the rest of the Shaws, and they wasn't but children, like my mama kept saying. I reckon that's one reason why Mister John Shaw didn't object too much when Mister Hugh came to buy my mama back to work for him once more. Mister Shaw didn't like his baby Ann bein' too thick with my mama.

Mister Shaw got shut of John, too, quick as he could. He apprenticed him out when he was ten years old, to learn the smithing trade, and John he picked it up right handy because he was so quick, and he liked gadgets and tools of all sorts and working the bellows and so on. So he got a few days or a week now and then when work was slow, to go over to Virginny and visit.

But though my mama liked them blue eyes well enough in Mister John, she didn't care for them in me. They was an embarrassment to her, and I got in the way of her nursing that sickly Miss Kitty, and I made mama's life with Miz Elizabeth worse than it had been, and it went from bad to pretty near insupportable. It was a mercy to us both when she died, and Miss Kitty with her, and when mama went along to Miz Tebbs, I went too, because I was too little to be sold away. And when Mister Hugh brought that tall Miz Elizabeth to his home to be his second wife, he brought me back, and I was then about six or seven, and my mama Letty stayed with Miz Tebbs and I stayed with the Hammills.

So then there was two Lizy Hammills—little black Lizy, don't you see, and tall Miz Lizy with her passel of little boys to care for. But I reckon I wasn't much help at first. I was mighty angry with my daddy and with my mama for not giving me my due as their child, and one day after he come to Prince William to live, close by his uncle Hugh's place and right next door to the smithy where he hired out to work, my daddy John saw me in the street and he said to me, "Now Lizy, you got about as big a chip on your shoulder as I used to have on mine. Come on over here and let's have a talk."

So right there in the street I said to him, "Don't you be preachin' at me, you made your child a slave and that's a burden you ain't got and I ought not to have it neither." And he said, "I didn't make you a slave, the law done that, and I ain't got the means to buy you free." I knew both them things to be true, so I just made a face, and he said, "Lizy, I done wrong in my life, and I done right, and no life is all one way or the other, maybe you ain't thought about what I'm doing over here, movin' here when you was half-growed to help Miz Lizy get on with them little boys now her husband Hugh is dead. Come on along over here to the shop and let's us get this straight."

And I said I didn't care a lick why he come over, but I heard it was because he was a ne'er-do-well back home, and he was come to live off the leavings of his uncle Hugh, but I followed him into the shop, and he said, "You sit down and listen to me, child," and I did.

Well, it would be mighty long to tell you all that he told me, but in the end he said he just couldn't do to Hugh's little boys what had been done to him. He said, "I seen another John Hammill left alone in the world without his daddy, and a Stephen, too, named with my father's name, and it was too much to stomach, so I come over to do what I could. And maybe there's a blue-eyed gal hereabouts as well, who will know who her daddy is and what he can and cannot do, and when she sees him a-sweatin' at that forge all day, she can wipe the sweat off her own face with a better grace, and leave off that chip that's goin' to sink her like it almost done me."

Well I hated to admit it but all that talk did help, and I did leave off that chip one little bit at a time, and my daddy he stayed in Prince William till those little boys were pretty near growed, and brought up blacksmiths like him, and then he lit out to Kentucky like he planned before. But I never wanted to put myself in for the troubles of a man and a child in my life. I was Lizy Hammill the rest of my days, and them cousins of my daddy's became my family until they set me free, many long years later.

And you might ask what benefit I had of it, to be set free as a woman of thirty-five with another forty years of hard work before me, washing clothes and sewing for white folks and getting by doing the same as I did when I was in bondage. But I will say it was a comfort to me to know I would go to the Lord as a free woman and not no slave no more, and there I bested my mama, for she was a slave all her born days, and when I see her in heaven I will let her know it, you can be sure, and we'll see then how she feels about her blue-eyed black child Lizy.

Prince William County, August 1850

❖

A Letter to a Sister

March 31, 1857

My Dear Nancy,

We have had an event here in Occoquan that puts me in mind of the letter you sent after our dear Father's death, ten years ago and more, where you said your heart was so full of sorrow you did not think you could go on living. Yet you did live on, and your grief has eased, and you have the enjoyment of your children growing up and the comfort of your family's prosperity, and all is well with you in the riper days of your life.

I remind myself of this as my own heart is filled to bursting, and for a cause that seems so small compared to the death of our father and to my own husband's death so many, many years ago. But you will understand, for you are among the few who remember the days that have been brought back to me just now with such vividness. Lizy Hammill is gone, died this month in her little cabin in the shantytown outside Occoquan. She must have been getting on for eighty, and Mrs. Fair who attended her says she was very weak but alert nearly to the moment of her passing.

Now all that time is over, and none of it might have happened for all the world knows or cares today. I suppose a few town matrons might miss Lizy's lace cuffs and shirred bodices and all that smocking she did for their babies and grandbabies, but who is left to miss Lizy herself or even to know who she was?

It is strange that I am the one to mourn her, because when my husband John made her free it was altogether against my will, and against our father's too. You remember how the two of them had words over it, and father called my husband a damned fool without a care for money, and my husband said father cared for nothing but money and to the devil with him, and I wept with my arms around John's knees because we needed Lizy with all that brood of children coming to us in those years. But John would not hear a word of it, and he went to court and signed the papers to make her free though the magistrate himself said John was mad and would regret what he had done and it was an insult to the white race to add another free colored woman to that shantytown by the river.

Now I am grateful that he did it, and proud. Yet my husband did not free his slave out of any high principle. He did it for the man who stepped in to be his father, and saw to it that John and Stephen learned their trade as blacksmiths, and was a right hand to John and Stephen's mother when she was left a widow with little ones to raise.

It was a long time before my husband told me why his cousin John cared so about Lizy. I did not guess, and maybe you have not guessed, either. Some would say it's not the kind of thing nice people guess about, or even imagine. But the truth cannot be wished away. Lizy was cousin John's own child, the only one he had so far as any of us knew. Her mother was Letty, old Hugh's slave. When cousin John lay dying there in Kentucky, he sent my husband a note by the mail. I found it after my husband's death, under some old papers, folded small. It read, "I am not long for this world, they tell me. Do my soul a good turn and free Lizy if you can. You and Stephen were good boys. Farewell. John Hammill."

I suppose what overcomes me is not love of Lizy, for the ten years we kept her are long in the past, and she always belonged to my husband more than to me. No, it is sorrow for the fleetingness of life, that and a swell of love for my dead husband of the kind I have not felt since his passing. You will know how deeply I am affected when I tell you that I took out the blue-and-white tulip bowl that has been in my closet half my life, and walked to town, and bought a dozen red tulips in the bulb, and set the bowl of red blooms on the table, and then put my head down and wept over it, for my husband John gave me the very same on the day he asked me to be his wife. He had bought them at Riversdale, that fine house with such a splendid garden. It was on his route when he traveled to Baltimore to purchase iron for the smithy, you see.

I must close, this has rattled on far too long. I half doubt I should even send this letter. You will know your sister has a fond heart and a tender spot in it for you, my dear, though so many years and miles lie between us. Forgive my weakness and remember me in your prayers.

Your loving sister,
Elizabeth McIntosh Hammill

❧

Letters Home

To Mrs Elizabeth Hammill
c/o Mr Hugh Hammill, Occoquan Post Office, Virginia
From William Hammill, Sutter's Mill, California
June 9th 1850

Dear Ma,

I take my pen in hand to inform you that one son of yours is alive and in this world and that is me but Ma you got to know your other son that's Daniel Alexander, Ma he is not. And it wan't injuns nor bandits did him in tho we got plenty of both, but it was the bad water he drunk bad water two-three weeks back and he laid in a feaver two-three weeks and last night he passed with just a shed roof over his head and one blanket to warm him. Ma I done what I could for him but it wan't much it is a wild and rough place out here I couldn't find no doctor nor nobody to take an interest for such is happening out here every day and more than once in the day it is rough out here Ma.

And all along he was talkin' bout how he done wrong draggin' me out here and he sure would like to go home. I think there at the end he thot he was home for he was talkin' bout the river and them strawberries ole man Hanna has up in his field and he sure would like a plate of them strawberries. I was givin' him boiled water in a spoon but it wan't no strawberries and then he passed. Me and a coupla other fellows wrapped him up as good as we could in the blanket and we buried him this morning and put a stone on the place to keep the animals off but I don't know Ma. And we said what bible verses we could recall because most any fellow can bring a few to mind if he trys, and we did try and we did the best we could, and now I am setting here wonderin' what I ought to do next for it is mighty lonesome bein' out here without Danny.

And now I will close and Ma I sure hope you get this letter I will write another soon as I can I will post it up to Sutter's Mill where they got some kind of post office bout a day or two's ride from here. It is rough out here you would not credit it Ma anything rough there is to see you see it here, I seen it all Ma but I ain't seen any gold but a lot of mud and dirt and I am thinkin' what to do next.

Your loving son William

November 20th 1850

Dear Ma,

There ain't no way you can reach me with a letter because I am always movin' on and in these little places with names like Murderer's Bar and Dead Man's Butte it ain't no wonder they don't get mail or nothing else hardly, these places are just a coupla shacks and mountains of what we call tailings which is the dirt they throw up digging for gold, and a few skinny horses and fellows with a crazy look in their eyes some of them, they are so mad to find that gold. Well I'll tell you Ma I am blacksmithing as I go and they always need me wherever I go for someone's horse has always throwd a shoe or their shovel or pick is busted or their wagon or what have you. The trick is to get paid and now I get paid ahead even if it is a hatful of flour or an Injun blanket, and I don't do no digging. That is rough work Ma. My tools is my pillow and thank the Lord I brought them out here they are my salvation and I sleep on top of them so they don't get stole. And the other thing, the fellows think it's mighty amusin' but any water I drink I boil it first, some gent in a black coat told us that when Danny and me was coming out this way, and we didn't do it and he got sick. But now I keep a can of it boiled and ready and that's what I drink or make coffee out of it.

And I am headin' north along these rivers we got so many of, but they ain't like our big rivers back home but mountain streams is what they are, round about them it can be grassy and nice and there is getting to be a handful of farming folk in these meadows and they are more settled folks and not running mad like these miners which I had about enough of. There is one little place folks call it Grass Valley it's a mighty nice name I'm headed that way, its between two of these little rivers, the Bear and the Yuba, some fellow told me about it the other day down to Sacramento where I was buyin' me some boots. You got to have boots out here and a horse, or you ain't goin' to do nothing but shrivel up and perish, I'm tellin' you Ma. This fellow he said there's a big mine up there but some farming and grazing too, and that might mean good work for me. So I close for now and I pray you get my letter,

Your loving son William

June 21st 1851

Dear Ma,

I take my pen in hand to do my duty and let you know how I am getting along now I been gone from home two years just about exactly, and I have the chance to post you a letter since I am down to Sacramento buying supplies. I been up at Grass Valley bout five-six months now and I am doin' all right up there but it ain't Virginny and I sure do miss all you folks but it's a long way back and I reckon I'll stick out here now things are goin' better and I ain't fightin' for my life which is what I was doin' before what with these rough fellows and no decent food or nothing.

Now Ma you won't hardly credit this but here is what happened to me up to Grass Valley just about the day I got there. I rode on up to a little store or trading post that was all I could see besides a few cabins and such, because the mining operation is hid behind a butte or hill, and I

went in and asked the gent behind the counter did he have any blacksmithing, and I had my tools right on my back for I do not leave them away
from me for one minute. And he said could I fix a busted axle on a wagon,
and I said yes, if he had the iron, and he said "Son let's see what you can
do, for if you can do some smithing you'll be an asset to our little community here." Which was mighty amusin' since there ain't what you might
call a community but just a few shacks, like I said I couldn't see the mine.
So I set up and fixed his wagon and he said, "Son, what's your name?" and
I said "William Hammill from Virginny at your service."

And he stood back and crossed his arms and he said, "Now Son you
tell me who you are right smart for I can't give you work if you're a-hidin'
something," and I said "William Hammill is my name and been a name in
my fam'ly time out of mind and don't you suggest it ain't my name or who
I am." And he said, "But we got a William Hammill already, and he don't
look or talk like you." "Well show me this man," says I, "and we'll see who's
a-hiding something because it ain't me."

So right then the door opens and in comes a little black-haired fellow
not half my size hardly, and the storekeeper says "Now Mr. Hammill you
tell this young man who you are," and he says "William Hammill late of
Cornwall, England come over on a boat with my brother James. We mined
the tin back home and now we mine the gold and the two are much the
same, for down is down and dark is dark and min'ral is min'ral," says he,
"but the money is better here and so is the land, and how does it concern
this young gent, will you kindly tell me?"

Well I did not knock him down for it would have come too easy, him
bein' so little and such a foreigner with that way of talking I could hardly
follow at first, so we shook hands on our name and agreed it was good
enough for two, though neither one of us can fathom how we come to
share it. Folks call us Big Bill and Little Bill and we take it since we can't
change it and it's all right. I smith for all who needs it out here and lend
a hand with the equipment at the mine there where him and James work,
which is run like a real company and not so much of these wild crazy fellows goin' on drunks each night and stealin' each other blind every chance

they get. James has got a wife he brought from home and she feeds me meat pies once or twice a week that are mighty tasty, pasties they call them, and I see to the repairs on their place for her trouble, and William is a lot of fun, he sure does like to talk.

I can't hardly hold this pen for one more minute and my paper is about out too, but in closing I will say that it's all right Ma, things are all right for me now, and Ma write to me and let me know any news I sure hope you all are well and no misfortune come to you since I been away. You can write me c/o the Empire Mine, Grass Valley, California, USA, and I will get it because the other fellows do. It's a big operation out here, like I said.

Your loving son William

PART IV

PRINCE WILLIAM COUNTY, VIRGINIA

1845–1896

The Chesapeake Region

16

THE SECOND HUGH HAMMILL,
A KEEN, SHREWD MAN

A CLEAR AND verifiable portrait of the second Hugh Hammill emerges about 1845 and remains intact until his death in the last decade of the nineteenth century. No fictional stories are needed to flesh out this irascible character, for real, documented voices produce plenty of dissonance, complexity of view, and drama.

A handful of sources provide the illumination. First is simple remembrance. Hugh's grandchildren, grandnieces, and grandnephews described him and something of his way of life to their children, and they in turn to theirs. No photographs seem to have survived for Hugh Hammill, but family memory renders him as a tall man, six feet or more in stature, and powerfully built, as blacksmiths tended to be. He had big feet, too, and wore a size twelve boot—the kind of detail a wife or daughter would not forget, because of the inconvenience it created in knitting stockings that fit.[1]

And then there are court and land records that document his doings, and a cache of letters that capture his voice. The bonanza, however, is Hugh Hammill's approved claim under the Southern Claims Commission Act of 1871. The 158 manuscript pages of this claim detail the minutiae of Hugh's business and family, dramatize the impact of the Civil War in Prince William County, and convey enough in Hugh's own words and those of his neighbors to convey a solid idea of the man's habits and personality. Here, briefly, is where that claim came from.

On 3 March 1871, seven years after the end of the Civil War, the U.S. Congress passed an act that offered reparations to U.S. citizens who had lived in a seceding state, could prove loss of property to Union armies, and could convince a board of three commissioners that they had been loyal to the United States throughout the course of the war.[2] Congress appointed House Republican Asa Owen Aldis of Vermont as chief commissioner, and James B. Howell of Iowa and Orange Ferris of New York State, also House Republicans, as subcommissioners, to hear and evaluate all the claims made under the act. Congress estimated that the act would remain in effect for about two years, but the commission was so overwhelmed by southern response that it could not be dissolved until 1879. About twenty-two thousand claims were made, for an amount that exceeded sixty million dollars. Most claims were denied, but the commissioners approved about a third to go before Congress, which voted on the compensation to be offered. Few claims were paid in full. Most claimants received about a third of what they asked for, including Hugh Hammill.

Like a great many government programs, the Southern Claims Commission Act was easier to pass than to administer. Loyalty was difficult both to prove and to disprove. The commissioners expended their energy on that question, while the claimants wanted to talk about the specifics of their losses. A list of blanket questions was prepared for claimants and witnesses to answer. Special investigators collected depositions on each claim for weeks or months. Then the claim was heard, in a congressional hearing room in the capitol building in Washington, D.C. Hearings, too, could last days and weeks, generating a mountain of paperwork, since every word spoken in the hearing room was taken down in shorthand by a court reporter and then transcribed into longhand for the record.

In the end, Congress became custodian of thousands of pages of transcriptions generated by the Southern Claims Commission Act. Stored in the National Archives in Washington, D.C., they have only recently been microfilmed. Hugh Hammill's claim, number 18565, was entered on 25 March 1874. He asked for $1,517.50 to reimburse him for the loss of livestock—five horses, nine hogs, a cow, and a bull—and goods that included an iron axle wagon, two tons of iron bars and scraps, two anvils, and odds and ends like two saddles and bridles and a load of hay and straw. Two years of depositions and court hearings followed, and then a delay of two more years. Congress finally approved the claim on 13 December 1878. Sometime after that date, Hugh received his payment of $580, about ten thousand dollars in today's money.[3]

For Hugh Hammill, who spent four years of his life traveling, testifying, defending, and waiting on the claim, that result might have been disappointing. For the historian, the claim itself is the reward. Its only shortcoming is that it portrays a man in later life, in his fifties and sixties, as Hugh was between 1860 and 1874. Fortunately, court and land records of the 1840s and 1850s and an exchange of business letters from 1858 present a younger Hugh who was occupied in transforming himself from a blacksmith and wheelwright working from a cobbled-together shop into the man of property who in 1874 made the claim that is the heart of the chapters to come.

I take up the story in the year 1845. Hugh Hammill was thirty-five years old that year, in the prime of his young manhood, already embarked on his rise to prosperity as a successful tradesman in Occoquan. The state of Virginia, however, was not in its prime, neither economically nor in terms of moral leadership. Powerful as a colony, Virginia lost momentum steadily after 1800. Its population dwindled as the young and vital headed out of state toward the southern and western frontiers. Growth passed it by; it was slow to build canals, slow to develop roads, bridges, and railroads, slow to adopt a program of public education. Henry Ruffner, president of Washington College, bluntly summed up the state's situation in a famous address of 1847: "evident signs of stagnation or of positive decay—a sparse population—a slovenly cultivation spread over vast fields that are wearing out, among others already worn out and desolate; villages and towns 'few and far between,' rarely growing, often decaying, sometimes mere remnants of what they were ... generally no manufactures, not even trades, except the indispensable few ... instead of the stir and bustle of industry, a dull and dreamy stillness..."[4]

Slavery was no small part of the problem. As early as 1830, for a variety of reasons including soil exhaustion, tobacco cultivation had given way to wheat, fruit, and vegetable crops in Maryland and northern Virginia. Labor-intensive tobacco, rice, and cotton moved further south, and the need for slaves moved with them. Many slave owners began selling slaves "downriver," to Alabama, Mississippi, and other states that could use their labor, to rid themselves of the financial liability their bondsmen had become. For intermittent labor, they hired their neighbors' slaves, freeing themselves of any responsibility for their long-term support or well-being. The status of slaves had always been abysmal; in the 1830s and 1840s it degenerated further as increasing numbers of slave families were torn apart and their members shipped downriver in dreadful conditions or marched, chained at the ankle, hundreds of miles to their new owners. Many died en route; many others died soon after their arrival. Runaways became ever more frequent and more cruelly punished. The reputation of the South fell lower with every incident of inhumanity that was picked up by the Abolitionist press, and states like Virginia became belligerently defensive in attitude as well as brutal in practice.

Amid these troubles and reflecting them, eastern Prince William County was electrified by two gruesome murders and then an execution in a slave-and-master drama that unfolded between 1845 and 1850. Two of the victims were slave women, and one was their owner—none other than Gerard Mason, grandson of George Mason, the famous Revolutionary War–era lawyer and statesman. The murders occurred at Mason's Neck, just north of the town of Occoquan. Court records show that Hugh Hammill, with several of his neighbors, played a bit part in the story.

Gerard Mason had a long history of violence, drunkenness, and brutality toward his slaves. Local newspaper advertisements show that Mason's men Will and Bill ran away in the winter of 1822–23, then ran away again, Will in 1828 and Bill in 1840.[5] In the fall of 1845, Mason assaulted his bondswoman Katy with such violence that she died of her injuries, and the Prince William County coroner called for an inquest. On 29 October, several of Mason's neighbors and peers gave evidence against him. What they reported was horrifying:

Wm Johnson—On last Wednesday week was hauling wood by Gerard Mason's house—entering saw Mr. Mason at the quarters where Katy was, apparently in a violent rage—threw a stick at a negro boy & a stone at a little negro girl—then ran into the quarters where Katy was & threw out a box & some bed clothes then into the cabin where he made a great noise as if thumping or knocking people about—witness went on—returning by same place from making next load at about 11 o'clock a.m. saw negro Katy lying in the yard in the quarters, seemed to be in great pain as if from a beating—just breathing, just talking not able to turn about.

Jas. Foster Jr.—Knows nothing of any beating received recently by Katy—saw Gerard Mason stomp Katy in his yard at his dwelling, late in the summer or early fall of 1844.

Wm. Bates—Has been in Gerard Mason's neighborhood
for about two months past—When he first came, Katy was
unable to walk about & has continued so ever since, has seen her
crawling about her cabin & when crawling would sometimes fall
some—has been in her cabin three times.

Henry Duvall—Went to Gerard Mason during last harvest
to sell wood—saw Mason beat Katy with a large stick at the
home, drove her back to the field, pursued & beat her a second
time—knocked her down and left her lying on the ground.
A few days after saw Katy get another beating from Mason in
which he seemed to strike with anything he could get hold of.

After this testimony, the twelve jurors, "good and lawful men of
the county aforesaid," swore on their oaths that

One Gerard Mason, yeoman, late of the said County of Prince
William not having the fear of God before his eyes, but being
moved and seduced by the instigation of the devil, a short time
before the death of his negro woman slave Katy or Kate aforesaid, which occurred on the 23rd day of the present month,
with force and arms at a cabin on the farm of said Gerard
Mason ... voluntarily made an assault [on] the aforesaid Katy
or Kate in and upon the head ... violently struck and cut and
gave to the said slave Katy or Kate ... several severe wounds ...
of which said wounds the aforesaid Katy or Kate shortly after
their infliction died.[6]

Mason was charged with murder at the inquest and was imprisoned in the county jail for a week, until he could be tried. Yet he
seems to have been acquitted, for four years later he was at his sav-
agery again. On 19 December 1849, Mason assaulted his slave woman
Agnes, climbing up from his house to the slave quarters before dawn.
She got the better of him in the short run, knocking his brains out

with an axe because, she said, Mason had tried to shoot her. At the inquest, one young man testified that Mason had been drunk. Other witnesses maintained that he had attempted to rape Agnes. The case raised a furor throughout the state. Governor John Buchanan Floyd received numerous petitions both for clemency and for the death penalty for Agnes. In the end, the state executed her and "paid $450 to the executors of the deceased's estate to reimburse the valuation placed upon his slave."[7]

This was the reality of slavery. One admires the coroner, who by insisting on an inquest at Katy's death forced the issue into the open, and also the white men who testified against Mason at the inquest. Yet it is clear from the court transcript that the community had known of and tolerated Mason's crimes for years. Among the twelve jurors at Katy's inquest were William Selecman, Charles Shaw, Hugh Hammill, and others whose names resonate in this account. Several of them, including Hugh, also signed petitions for clemency toward Agnes. Yet the census of 1850 shows that each of these charitable white men owned at least one slave at the time. Hugh's was a black woman, age forty-five. How he reconciled his ideas of clemency with those of bondage, I cannot say.[8]

Running counter to these disturbing events and the "dull and dreamy stillness" of Virginia's sagging economy, on 1 May 1849 Hugh Hammill took the ambitious step of purchasing 150 acres east of Occoquan and moving his family out of town, to a district called Marumsco. That Dogue Indian word is said to mean "the end of the waters," indicating the place where Occoquan Run empties into the Potomac, at Belmont Bay. Marumsco's low-lying soils had been exhausted by a hundred years of tobacco cultivation, and its hills, wooded with pine, hickory, chestnut, and black and white oak, discouraged agriculture. In the late 1840s, local owners were ready to sell their acreage cheap. Hugh was able to purchase the land from Rebecca and John Richard Spinks for three hundred dollars, or two dollars an acre, a very low price even in the 1840s.[9] Fast-flowing

Marumsco Creek cut across those hilly woodlands, and where the Spinks family saw waste property, Hugh saw the potential for a sawmill as well as plenty of timber to keep the mill supplied.

The next year, on 1 July 1850, he bought eighty-seven acres on Occoquan Run west of town, from Isaiah Fisher. The total cost was seventy-four dollars—river frontage for less than a dollar an acre! That purchase was a speculation, a successful one. Eight years later, in March 1858, Hugh sold those eighty-seven acres to Joseph Janney for two hundred dollars, nearly tripling his money.

In June 1854, Hugh purchased another tract in Marumsco, this time fifty-one acres on Occoquan Run between Swann's Point and Belmont Bay. For that prime river frontage he paid ten dollars an acre, gaining a desirable tract for a big new home. Far more important, the river frontage provided him with water transport for the

Site of the Hammill gristmill and sawmill, Marumsco Creek, Prince William County, Virginia. The creek is much diminished from its size in the mid- to late nineteenth century.

products of his blacksmith business as well as for his manufactured wagons and milled lumber, so he could expand into Alexandria and Washington, D.C., even into Baltimore and other cities around the Chesapeake. On Belmont Bay, his immediate neighbors included Joseph Janney, the Quaker proprietor of the Occoquan cotton mill and owner of many Occoquan lots and buildings, and William H. Tayloe, owner of Deep Hole farm and fishery and hundreds of acres more in the area. Hugh was becoming one of the prosperous businessmen of his community.[10]

In the years that followed, Hugh continued to buy and sell land and town lots as speculations. But for forty years, the family lived on the Marumsco tracts. There they farmed, blacksmithed, and built wagons. Soon after 1850, they began to mill lumber and grain.[11] They sent lumber and other goods up and down the Potomac to city markets in their own small ships. One of these was the *Martha Washington*, a sleek longboat ideal for transporting lumber, rigged like a schooner—that is, it had three masts. There were one or two smaller boats as well, for Hugh's six daughters and their mother and grandmother preferred to sail up and do their shopping in Alexandria.

Sometime around 1850, Hugh built a fine new house overlooking Belmont Bay. He called it River View.[12] It had fourteen chimneys, one in every room, a picture window in a front parlor that eventually held a grand piano, a spacious dining room for entertaining guests, and a wide porch or veranda typical of well-to-do southern households.

In this big, comfortable house lived fifteen people. By 1858, the Hammill family included Hugh and his wife, Jane; five unmarried daughters ranging in age from twenty-two to four; Hugh's long-widowed mother and a widowed daughter, Hannah Ann, with her three children, John, Jennie, and Izzie (Hezekiah) West; two sons, Rueben and William; and the hired man, Redmon Mills. Hugh and Jane's oldest son, Edward, was already married and a father, living with his family in Occoquan. Between 1846 and 1850, the family had included a fourth son, born on Christmas Day 1846 and named John Hugh after his grandfather and father. This son drowned in Occoquan Run as a four-year-old.

With the expansive house and large family went good whiskey, fine horses, and southern sociability. In the course of his Civil War claim, Hugh calls himself "a pretty good judge of liquor," especially rye whiskey. He describes "pretty good times" with friends and neighbors, and horses "as fine … as a man ever throwed a leg over." Relatives mention a "very fine" dun horse, a dark bay thoroughbred, and a pair of "very fine" colts worth more than six hundred dollars—ten or twelve thousand dollars in today's money. His friends thought well of him, commenting that he was as a man of "considerable property" and "a shrewd business man" as well as "a worthy, good man" and "very kind." By 1858, as he approached the age of fifty, Hugh Hammill had achieved the status that as a young man he had dreamed of.

Two letters preserved by chance in the Tayloe family archives give a close-up look at Hugh's business manner and his clientele as the 1850s drew to a close.[13] By 1858, the date of these letters, William H. Tayloe was planting cotton in Alabama and leasing his Prince William acreage, including Deep Hole Farm, right next to Hugh. But he still liked to do business with Hugh Hammill.

To Hugh Hammill Esq
Occoquan, Va

Dear Sir,

I send you my check for One Hundred & twenty five dollars which my Brother wrote I owe you for my two Horse Waggon. That is a big price but I hope you have made one worth the money. If as good as the others I will be satisfied. They are good yet.

I wrote you for your Bill but you did not answer my letter, as you might have had the money long ago—it has been in the

Fredericksburg Bank, idle since last spring. I [never] heard your charge till my Brothers last letter. The waggon may be yet at Baltimore.

Such a good Builder of Waggons should not stay about Occoquan, but go to some city like Baltimore or Richmond, where you could ship your work readily to any of the states.

Wishing you well

Yrs Friendly, Wm. H. Tayloe

March 17, 1858

Near Morristown
Perry County
Alabama
Ocoquan
Mr. William H. Tayloe

Dear Sir,

Your kind favour of 6 March is now at hand & I hasten to reply. As soon as I received your direction where to send the wagon I sent it to Alexandria to Mr. G. Washington & went up my self & inquired of him if there was any vesel expected to sail for Mobile in a short time. He informed me there was not. I immediately went to Washington to see your brother Ogle & there I met with your son. He said he could not inform me what to do. I went to Baltimore & saw Mrs Chapman & Guimer [Mr. Tayloe's sisters, I believe]. They informed me there was a vesel loading at that time & would leave that week. I immediately rote to Mr. G. Washington to send the wagon on the railroad to Baltimore as there was a vesel going to leave that week & sent the necessary directions about the wagon.

You said in your letter you thought the price high. Mr. W. H. Tayloe, I can assure you when you have received the wagon if you

do not say it is the best one you ever saw you may set your own
price on it, which I think will be more than mine. I can assure
you there is not twenty dollars difference in the one at $150 and
the one at $125. You can hitch four horses for a long time until the
[tongue?] is worn thin. If there is any of your neighbours wishing
one, I would thank you kindly to use your influence in getting
me a job. I can assure you I can get it to Baltimore in three days
notice. I received your check for one hundred and twenty five
dollars. It brings [payment] in ful of all demands. You omitted
to sign your name to the check but I suppose if I send the letter
Rec'd Hugh Hammill 17 March 1858 $125 for a waggon.

I suppose you would like to hear something of your ole farm
Deep Hole.

Mr. Ole Quaker has dismissed the best overseer that has been
there for many years & employed a northern one. He is putting
up som[e] new buildings at the marsh fishing. At this time the
sluices is in bad order; most all have washed away. Confident[ial]
ly speaking, I am afraid the ole Quaker will not repair the shanty.
He intends to fish Deep Hole this spring. I do not [k]now how you
get along with him but I can say for myself we get along badly. I
am doing a great deal of sawing for his new buildings. I hope you
will soon visit the ole farm & if you do you must certinly call, as
I would be glad to see you in our country onst [once] more. You
must excuse both speling & righting as my education is limited &
my eyesight verry bad. I am yours verry Respectfully,

Hugh Hammill

The schoolmarm in me can only remark that education in the
family has nosedived between 1726 and 1858. Yet Hugh is literate, I
would say articulate, and he clearly enjoys communicating verbally.
His "speling & righting" seem to falter most just at the moment
when he mentions his limitations. Failure of nerve may be as much

to blame as poor eyesight and skimpy schooling. Still, a vast educational as well as social gulf divides the men. William H., like several generations of Tayloe males, was Harvard-educated. He lived as a southern planter of the first rank, at the Deep Hole property near Hugh, and then at his plantations in Alabama, where slaves and cotton maintained his wealth. But the two men were obviously well acquainted, and though Tayloe condescends to Hugh, his business advice was both freely given and excellent.

To move into a bigger position as a manufacturer, Hugh would almost certainly need to relocate to a city like Richmond or Baltimore. And he would need to run his affairs more efficiently—no more waiting months and months on outstanding debts, no more running around personally from household to household, looking for shipping instructions. Hugh's excited response shows that Tayloe's suggestions have fallen on deaf ears. Hugh feels he has already taken that step into the big time. He can ship by rail, or by boat from his wharf on Belmont Bay if his customer prefers water transport.

Besides, Hugh enjoys transacting his business in person and calling on customers at their homes. He does not want to rush anyone. He operates on an old-fashioned model of "business between gentlemen," perhaps almost a colonial model, where tobacco planters felt it was undignified to inquire where merchants sold their crop and at what price. That mode of doing business brought many a planter to ruin during tobacco depressions, and it can hardly help Hugh in the long run. But he doesn't see it. He just wants Tayloe to send him more business, which he will transact the old-fashioned way, crafting excellent wagons in the neighborhood where he grew up.

These letters confirm that by 1858 Hugh had been milling lumber for some years. They also show that he loved to run about town, visit, and gossip. He told Tayloe that he did not care for "Mr. Ole Quaker," Joseph Janney, assuming that Tayloe will not be offended by this opinion. Relative newcomers to Prince William, the Janneys opposed slavery, as Quakers were obliged to do. They owned about half of Occoquan, and Janney hired a northern overseer who was not attending to the sluices at the fishery. All might antagonize county old-timers. But Hugh also said he was "doing a great deal of sawing" for Janney's new buildings. Whatever Hugh disliked about the old Quaker, it did not get in the way of business.

This was Hugh Hammill as he approached the age of fifty, his prosperity and confidence intact. Just two years later, in 1860, a half-comic, half-ominous train of events disturbed the peace in Prince William County and gave a small taste of what would soon come. The trigger was Virginia's presidential primary election, held in the spring of 1860. To most Virginia voters, Republicans Abraham Lincoln and his running mate, Hannibal Hamlin, were anathema. Virginians supported John C. Breckinridge, a Southern Democrat who passionately supported states' rights and the institution of slavery, or John Bell, the Whig candidate, who defended the Union and the Constitution while taking no stand on slavery. But in Prince William County, fifty-five men voted the Lincoln-Hamlin ticket in the primary. And all of them lived in the vicinity of Occoquan. Among them were Joseph Janney, the old Quaker, and Hugh Hammill's brother, Stephen Hammill, thirteen years younger than Hugh. Their secession-minded neighbors called them Black Republicans.

On 4 July 1860, the Black Republicans raised a flagpole on Janney's land and flew the Union flag from it, as well as a pennant carrying the names of Lincoln and Hamlin. Their more conservative neighbors went wild, but were prevented from pulling down the pole by musket-carrying Republicans who defended it night and day. A flurry of newspaper articles, letters, and editorials followed. The story was covered all month in the *New York Times* and the *Washington Post* as well as many smaller papers. Eventually, on 27 July, the Prince William Cavalry under Captain William W. Thornton marched onto Janney's property and chopped down the flagpole amid jeers, insults, and fistfights.[14] A year before Fort Sumter, the citizens of

Prince William County had learned to distrust and repudiate their neighbors over the issues of slavery and secession.

In November 1860, all fifty-five of Occoquan's Black Republicans voted for Lincoln in the Presidential election. After Lincoln's victory, and as secession began to appear imminent for Virginia, most of these men moved out of harm's way, to Washington, D.C., Maryland, and elsewhere in the winter and spring of 1861. Joseph Janney moved to Alexandria. Stephen Hammill left his family in Occoquan and went up to Washington to serve as a blacksmith for the Union army. Stephen had named his first son Zachariah, possibly for Zachariah Chandler, the abolitionist Congressman from Michigan. Stephen must have been something of a firebrand, opinionated and ready to act on his convictions.

And where did Hugh stand politically? In his claim, he described himself as "an old Henry Clay Whig," a member of the party that strongly supported the Union but kept silent on the divisive issue of slavery. There must have been many older men like Hugh who had joined the Whig party in its heyday, in the 1830s and 1840s, and twenty years later found that Henry Clay was no longer admired but condemned for his compromises regarding slavery and his appeal to "business interests," the upper middle class and those who aspired to it. In the election of 1860, the Whig party was doomed.

Hugh's response to the Whig defeat was to withdraw from the political process altogether. After the primary, he stopped voting: "I never voted for secession. I never voted for Jeff Davis at the regular Presidential election, and I didn't go near the polls" after the Whig delegates to the national convention were defeated. He seems to have hoped that he could remain neutral and thus invisible in his home county while he pursued his business as usual. He stayed in Prince William County after the first shot was fired at Fort Sumter on 14 April 1861, and he stayed after Virginia seceded from the Union three days later. In his Civil War claim, he explained why: "I had my all there—everything that I had worked for all my life-time was there."

He could not bring himself to leave his home and livelihood even though, if he professed his views, the Confederate authorities would surely see him as an enemy, perhaps arrest him or seize his property or persecute him in other ways. He might have to prevaricate, to pretend a sympathy for the secessionist cause that he did not feel, but that risk weighed little against the possibility of losing all he had built up in five decades of tireless striving. He could not abandon his possessions or leave them in the hands of his wife and family to seek refuge himself in a Union state.

Hugh is the third Hammill in this account whose pursuit of material well-being was brought up short by war. Two generations earlier, his grandfather, Hugh the first, signed Maryland's Oath of Fidelity with an X to protect his property yet not betray his convictions during the upheavals of the American Revolution. Almost a century before that, in the aftermath of England's Glorious Revolution, William Hammill mourned his brother's ruin and his own in his 1701 pamphlet, *A View of the Danger and Folly of Being Publich-Spirited, and Sincerely Loving One's Country*. William says he "spent and laid out above 4000 £, which was his All; not doubting in the least but that a Debt of so much Merit, ... would ... have been Justly and Honourably Paid." The debt was not paid, and William died penniless in Newgate Gaol.

The second Hugh used the same language to express his decision as the American Civil War loomed. He stayed where he had his "all," despite what that might mean for his family's safety and his own. Was it the best choice? Such a question can only be asked from the security of a warm house and a comfortable livelihood unthreatened by outside turmoil. Staying on the land where he had his all was the only choice Hugh felt he could make.

17

THE CIVIL WAR COMES TO
PRINCE WILLIAM COUNTY

*E*VENTS MOVED rapidly after war commenced in April 1861.
Both Union and Confederate authorities recognized the
necessity of controlling eastern Prince William's waterways, especially Occoquan Run and the Potomac, as they acted as highways
rather than barriers to troops and supplies moving in and out of
Washington, D.C. Early in May, the Union army created the Potomac Flotilla and positioned gunships in that river with their cannons trained on Alexandria and other prime targets. Among these
ships was the USS *Resolute.* Confederate troops took up positions
on the south side of the Occoquan, turning the river into a major
line of defense, and began building batteries along the Virginia side
of the Potomac from Dumfries to Mathias Point in King George
County to the south. Their purpose was to harass the Potomac Flotilla and interfere with Union shipping into the capital. Then, on 12
June 1861, in an action devastating for local residents, the Albemarle

Light Horse Cavalry of Virginia was ordered to "seize all flats, scows, boats and barges on the Occoquan and block navigation within" the river to restrict access and prevent Union sympathizers—those Black Republicans and their friends—from aiding the enemy in any fashion.[1]

One casualty was Hugh's "bran-new" longboat, the *Martha Washington*. Its captain, Hugh's employee Luther Swann, explained what happened in his deposition of 1 January 1876.[2] Swann said that he had loaded the boat with lumber and was just setting out from Belmont Bay when "Mr. Hammill came down to the mouth of the bay and hollered to me from there and told me to take the boat back to Ocquicon and unload her, and said that orders were for no boat to leave the Creek." Swann continued, "I took her back to Ocquicon and unloaded her, put her in shallow water, board a hole in her bottom and sunk her, according to his [Hugh Hammill's] orders, to keep her from being used by any Federal troops to cross the Creek."

Swann said he did not recollect whether Hugh's instruction to sink the boat was a response to orders made by Confederate officers. He did recollect that "there was a little union flag in the boat, and Mr. Hammill told me to be very careful and not let them see that flag, as it would make trouble and they might burn his mill or other property. He seemed at that time to be very fearful they might burn his property.... At the time Mr. Hammill came down to the mouth of the Bay and hollered to me from the shore and told me to take the boat back to Ocquicon, there were others on the shore with him. I should think half a dozen persons. I did not know who they were, but learned afterwards that one of them was William Selecman, who was a rampant secessionist. I do not know but that some of them might have been Confederate officers and do not know that any of them were."

So Hugh told his longboat captain to sink that valuable ship as a gesture to stay on good terms with his secessionist neighbors. He may also have felt that sinking it in shallow water with one hole to the bottom was preferable to leaving it in the bay, where Union troops could commandeer it or Confederates could fire it, or vice versa. If the ship lay intact on the river floor, one day it could be raised, cleaned, and put into service once more. In the meantime, Hugh could avoid retribution from Rebel sympathizers by pretending that he was following Confederate orders to clear the Occoquan of traffic. In the first weeks of the war, he had already engaged himself in a complex game of protecting his interests and hiding his allegiances from the Rebels around him.

The sinking of his longboat in June 1861 was just the beginning of Hugh's wartime troubles. Before December of that year, the Confederates had arrested him three times. One of these arrests occurred very early in the war—Hugh comments that he was "the first Union man arrested in our country." It must have been about the time of the longboat incident, maybe even before it. The arresting officer was Captain William W. Thornton of the Prince William County Cavalry, the very one who had chopped down Joseph Janney's flagpole the summer before.

Thornton knew Hugh personally, and described him in his deposition of 18 January 1878 as a "worthy, good citizen" who nevertheless had to be monitored closely: "It was reported that Mr. Hamill was a man not above suspicion as a Union man, & one likely to communicate with the enemy: & I was instructed to watch his movements." Thornton's pickets arrested Hugh and his neighbor, Samuel Troth, for going through the Confederate lines "contrary to my orders." But since Thornton knew Hugh and "as he was an old man with a large family," the Captain released him on his promise "to stay at home and attend to his business."

A few months later, Hugh was arrested again. Two newspapers, the *Washington Star* and the Fairfax County *Local News*, reported that on 26 November 1861, Hugh Hammill, Samuel Troth, Henry Smoot, and several others were stopped and detained for "returning the salute of the Federal troops who came down opposite Occoquan

Creek."[3] That return salute was not taken kindly by Rebel authorities, but there seems to have been no long-term consequence for Hugh and the others. That was not the case when Hugh was arrested in early July 1861, two or three weeks before the first battle of Manassas—or Bull Run, as the Union forces called it.

The Confederacy was then struggling to recruit, train, and transport troops to protect the railroad junctions at Manassas and Fairfax Station, both within thirty or forty miles of Washington, D.C. They were anticipating attack at every moment, and tensions ran high. General Wade Hampton had brought up his Hampton Legion from South Carolina, and it was encamped within a mile of Hugh Hammill's home. Virginia regiments were encamped at Fairfax Station, and two North Carolina regiments, the 6th and the 12th, mostly made up of raw, untrained men, took positions between Manassas and Occoquan. A contingent from one of these regiments, egged on by Hugh's Confederate neighbors, arrested him as he traveled between Occoquan and Alexandria. Hugh gave his account of what happened in his first hearing, held 25 March 1874:

> I had been coming up to Alexandria (I had a pass to go backwards and forwards), and a parcel of them in Occoquan told them that my brother [Stephen] came up and joined the union army, and when I came back with this pass (I had been to Alexandria to get a note renewed that I had indorsed)—the bridge was burned then, and I had to swim my horse over, and when I got back one of these Colonels says "Who is that fellow?", and a man says "he has a brother who has run off to Lincoln, and he is an enemy of his country"; and when I got over they demanded my pass, and I showed it to them, and they turned it over and fooled with it a long time and I was waiting for it and I finally took it out of his hand (he was a North Carolina Colonel, I don't recollect his name, I don't know that I ever heard it) but I just took the pass out of his hand. Then a man named Hanna said

to me "old man, there is a great excitement about you running
up and down to town, and you had better go home," and I went
home, and about five of them came and dragged me off without
any coat and it was in a pouring down rain, and I had no coat
on, and there I staid until morning, (they had two guards over
me)—until nine o'clock in the morning. I hadn't anything to
eat, and I was soaking wet, and I asked them to let me go home
and get something to eat and to put dry clothes on, and one of
them said "I will give you something to eat when I get ready." &
I said "I wouldn't eat a damned mouthful you have if I was to
starve to death," and he told them to send me to Capt Adams,
and they did so. Captain Adams knew me: he used to come up
to my house where I had some fine rye, and we used to have a
drink together, and we had pretty good times together, and when
Capt. Adams saw me he said "you just go on home; this is a bad
set here, and they had just as lief shoot you as anything else and
you had better go home, and come back this evening," which
I did. They sent me at first, you know, to Manassas, and from
what they told me, Beauregard said it was just such a pass as
anybody would require coming into their lines and wanting to go
out again; that it was no impropriety in having the pass, and he
turned me loose.

But the worst of the incident was that Hugh's oldest son, Edward,
as well as several other men were with Hugh when the soldiers seized
him at his home. Edward was a healthy young fellow of twenty-five.
The Rebels wanted him: "They said if he didn't go into the army that
they were going to arrest all of us." Under this pressure, Hugh told
Edward to go with them, and offered him a horse: "I had a horse,
and I just gave him the horse, and said 'you can go if you want to,
and if you can get off, why do so.'"

So Edward went off with the regiment, and he served with the
Confederates for two or three weeks, in a ragtag company headed

by a Captain Davis. Hugh said, "They just rode around there, they didn't have any arms; they had nothing but some old sabres, and some had shotguns." When asked if Edward had been "regularly enlisted," Hugh replied, "No sir: he just joined Captain Davis' company, and after the battle of Manassas when they fell back, he was helping get a cannon out, and got mashed and ruptured, and they discharged him, and he was never in the army afterwards, and then he went backwards and forwards to Alexandria all the time during the war & carried rags" for use as bandages in army hospitals. This commerce in rags was apparently Edward's chief livelihood until the war was over.

For the commissioners, the question was whether that gift of a horse represented a disloyal act. In the end, they decided that it had not been disloyal but rather "an act springing from fear & duress, as he had been arrested just before he let his son have the horse." But the issue came up several times in the course of the hearing, finally prompting a heated exchange between Commissioner Aldis and Hugh Hammill:

Q When your oldest son went into the rebel army you furnished him a horse?
A Yes sir.
Q Did you do that for the purpose of aiding the rebel cause?
A I certainly did not, and I will put my hand on the Book now—
Q Well, stop there . . .
A —For I was a union man, and they all called me an abolitionist, and all that kind of thing, and when they arrrested me they said, 'now they have got the old abolitionist—'
Q Stop! You didn't do that to aid the rebel cause in any way?
A I certainly did not.
Q Did you do it to prevent harm & injury to your family?
A Certainly. He said: 'I ain't going to stay long,' and I thought it would keep them off of me. I had my all there—everything that I had worked for all my life-time was there—

Q If you had been free to act in that regard what would have been
your action?
A He never would have gone.
Q You would have kept him out?
A Yes sir. He was acquainted with a great many young men—
Q Don't talk so much.

Ouch! The commissioners were impatient because Hugh insisted
on describing his losses to the Confederate army, and by definition
his claim could have nothing to do with that. But Hugh was determined to have his moment in court, to tell his story in his own way.
This painful moment set the pattern for many more to come. Hugh
could not have enjoyed it, but the court reporter did. He carefully
punctuated to dramatize the exchange. Who can blame him? Many
of these hearings must have been dull to the last degree.

As the first year of the war unfolded, further calamities befell the
Hammills at the hands of the Confederates, who occupied Prince
William County between May 1861 and March 1862. Texas Rangers
passing through took cattle and hogs and skinned them in Hugh's
field one day while he was watching. When Hugh protested, they
answered, "[D]amn you I will skin you if you don't get out of that
field … if you don't get out of that field we will skin you pretty damn
quick."

But General Wade Hampton and his Hampton Legion were
responsible for most of Hugh's early losses. Hugh mentioned these
in his first hearing and elaborated in his second, held 27 October
1875. Hampton's troops "took all my corn, hay, and oats and used
them up, and they killed nine head of my cattle there one day, and
if ever I got even an ounce of their tallow I do not know it … They
just came there & put their sick in my house with the measles and
mumps, and their broken legs, and once in a while Hampton would
come in to see how things were coming on, and then he would ride
off about his business.…"

Everything of value that he possessed went to support the Confederate army. "[T]hey took all my post and rail fence, and took my buildings down to make coffins out of, and I never got a ten cent piece from them." Then they destroyed his trade as a blacksmith. They "took my tools and cleaned my shop out—I was doing jobs and I hired men to work in the shop and they just cleaned the shop out, and I had nothing to do then."

Even worse were the human injuries and losses of that first year. Edward Hammill never fully recovered from being "mashed and ruptured" by the cannon at Manassas. He had been raised to blacksmith, like his father and two of his uncles, but after his injuries he worked at less physically strenuous jobs, after the war as a hotelkeeper in Occoquan. Stephen Hammill, Hugh's abolitionist brother, succumbed to smallpox on 18 February 1862 at the age of thirty-nine, while in the service of the Union army. He left a widow, several young children, and an older brother who believed he was "one of the best blacksmiths in this country." I don't suppose it helped Hugh to remind himself that Stephen had followed his convictions and served in the army of the side he believed in.

The Confederate line was pushed south to Fredericksburg in March 1862, but the war was far from over and neither were Hugh Hammill's troubles. Former Virginia governor Henry H. Wells, in his testimony given 21 May 1875, characterized the Occoquan area during the three years between March 1862 and May 1865 as "a sort of neutral ground.... Sometimes we had a force that occupied the place, you know, and then, again, for a long period, it would be open." This neutrality was punctuated by horrible surprises whenever troops moved through. Hugh was astonished and then outraged when Union forces were no kinder to him and his property than the Confederates had been. His defense attorney, Richard McAllister, Esq., summed up Hugh's position admirably in that May hearing: "You were between two fires, as it were?" Hugh answered, "Yes sir, certainly. First one side in, and then the other."

In his October 1875 testimony, Hugh said he fed men from the 17th Pennsylvania who camped for three weeks at his sawmill—"nine of them that were camped there, and I never got a cent for that." When they broke camp and moved on, these men slaughtered nine of Hugh's hogs and two head of cattle for fresh meat. They were among the animals that Hugh claimed as losses twelve years later. Hugh gave the details in March 1874, for his friend and neighbor, a man named Allen, had caught the troops in the very act:

> This man Allen sent word to me, he says 'old man, come down here as quick as you can; they are shooting your cattle, and skinning your hogs.' I went down there, and I had a Durham cow ... and they had skinned her, and they had taken my bull and cut a steak off his hind quarters and left him there kicking—he wasn't dead, but there he was alive when I went down there, and they gathered up the skins and carried the skins away with the cow.

The commissioners were incredulous at this; one of them asked, "You don't mean that they had skinned the bull alive?" Hugh answered, "Yes sir, skinned him down as far as they needed to cut a steak off him, and then left him there a-kicking." One of the offending soldiers half-apologized to Hugh: "I know there is a good deal of pork and meat in the camp, but we wanted fresh beef; and we haven't been paid off or else we would club together and pay you."

So Hugh got a receipt for the slaughtered animals from the officer in charge, and showed it to General Meigs to see if the government would reimburse him. Meigs understood that his troops had behaved badly. He told Hugh, "those scamps just took them for fresh meat; they had plenty to eat," or in Hugh's words, "a plenty of pork, barrels of pork." But in the end Meigs said, "old man, if the government was to pay for all such depredations as this, it would break the government up ... you are living in a rebellious state, and if you have got anything to do you had better go home and do it."

Ironically enough, since Head Commissioner Asa O. Aldis was also a Vermonter, Hugh's most painful experiences with Union forces involved the 13th Vermont, especially their commanding officer, Colonel Francis Voltaire Randall.[4] A first lieutenant named Albert Clarke wrote a history of the 13th Vermont that gives context to Hugh Hammill's somewhat confusing account of the winter of 1862–63. Clarke explains that in late October 1862, three Vermont regiments under the command of Colonel Randall set up their winter camp near Alexandria, Virginia. They called themselves the Vermont Brigade, and their camp was called Camp Vermont.[5]

The 13th Vermont soon moved out of camp to Bull Run, where the troops spent several weeks in makeshift quarters, guarding the railroad "in constant readiness for an expected encounter with Confederate cavalry." The weather was miserably cold and wet. On 5 December, when the attack had still not come, the Vermont troops made their way back to Alexandria "on flat cars in a heavy, damp snow storm. When they reached camp in the evening it was still snowing, their tents had not arrived and they were without food, fuel or water. A few found shelter in neighboring buildings, but the greater number were taken in by the other regiments of the brigade. Many, however, took colds and some of them never recovered."

In late January 1863, the 13th Vermont with other regiments moved their camp south ten or twenty miles to Wolf Run Shoals, a fording place on the Occoquan just west of town. There it remained until 2 April, when it moved several miles downstream, building "Camp Carusi" on the north side of the river, just across from the Hammills. They were truly in Hugh's backyard all that winter. Clarke goes on:

> Detachments were sent thence to guard the ferry at Occo-
> quan and several fords above.... On the morning of May 14,
> a wagon train from the regiment, on its way to Fairfax Station
> for supplies, though more than a mile in rear of the picket line,
> was attacked by a small body of Moseby's men and the drivers,

guards and mules were captured. The men, seven in all, were treated to a bareback ride of twenty-seven miles on mules and were then paroled and allowed to return on foot. News of the capture soon reached the camp and the regiment started upon a run to intercept the captors at the nearest ford, but arrived a few minutes too late.

Shortly after this, the Vermont Brigade moved north toward Gettysburg, Pennsylvania.

Hugh Hammill remembered that wet December snow very well. Some Vermont troops sought shelter from the storm at his house. In his first hearing, 25 March 1874, he described having "taken them all in out of the snow-storm and given them a clean bed and suppers, breakfasts and lodging and never charged them a quarter of a cent for it." And how did these men repay him for his hospitality? They seized four of his best horses and rode off on them.

> **Commissioner Aldis:** You charge in your petition, I see, four horses taken in December 1863.[6]
> A Yes sir.
> Q Did you see the Union soldiers take this property?
> A Yes sir: they grabbed me, and came very near breaking my neck when they—
> Q That is no sort of consequence: direct your attention to the horses.
> A Well, I was on one of them when they took it. . . . I rode ahead of one of them, and he just grabbed me and pulled me backwards in the snow. He said, "I want to buy this horse, and if you will come to Occoquan I will give you $250;" and when they got me halfway, they grabbed me and jerked me off, and away they went. They left one horse, a nice four year old colt, branded "U.S.", and a bran new saddle and saddlebags and bridle, and I got on this horse and turned to go after them and I met some of the

other fellows a short distance off, and these other two had gone
as fast as they could go. I said to one of these I met, "my friend,
that is very bad treatment to an old man," and he says, "they are
just going to have a little race; they are not going to take your
horse." I followed them up to Wolf Run Shoals, and came up
with them, and said, "gentlemen, don't take possession of those
horses if you please, I have just lost four & have only one to haul
for my family of six daughters; just leave me something to haul
[with]"; and one of them said, "we are ordered to take horses
wherever we find them, and ours are run down, and the government will pay you," and so they started off again. I had this
young colt and I started after them. I thought I would meet more
soldiers in the road and get them to assist me about the horses,
but they got away up on the hill, and they saw me coming along
behind on this colt and they just drew up their horses and came
back to me on a full spring and said "you damned old scoundrel;
if you value your horses more than your brains, you just follow
us. If you follow us up we will blow your brains out: you just
go home," and I thought likely they might do so so I went back
home. . . . I was so completely tore up about losing the horses
that I went to bed . . . and that was the last I ever saw of the
horses.

Q So much for 2 horses: now what have you to say as to the other
two? . . .

A Well I will tell you about the other 2 now. I ought to have
commenced at those two first. When Colonel Randall came there
and stationed himself about Occoquan about a mile and a half
on the left [on the north side of Occoquan Creek; the army had a
pontoon ferry there], he had about a thousand soldiers with him
and he was acquainted with a gentleman in Occoquan named
Gregg, and he [Randall] used to come across there and knock
about with him, and finally there was a young lady who used to
come over in the camp there and knock around, & he [Randall]

starts off a whole lot of teams up to Lee's station for provisions, and he started no guard or scout with them, and when the rebels [Moseby's men, in Clarke's account] up there about Charles Runnell's saw those wagons coming without any guard, they just fired into the drivers and they jumped off and ran, and they took out his mule teams six mules to a team, and carried them off. I was up here in Washington with a boat load of wood at that very time, and he just sends over to my house, and he takes four out of the plow, and he took the last one I had, and he sends over to an old man named Harrison . . . and takes his colt, four or five years old, and he took several horses and made up his team, and he took these two Morgan colts of mine and one of those he rode himself, and the other one this young lady rode about with him.

Q What was that man's name?

A Randall of the 13th Vermont . . .

Q Randall took the 2 horses, did he? . . .

A Yes sir. . . .

Commissioner Howell: Who was this young lady you speak of?

A She was a young lady who lived in Occoquan. . . . and he had a side saddle that he borrowed, and they would ride about together. . . .

Comm. Aldis: Did you ever ask this Randall for a receipt?

A I went over after my horses—

Q Answer the question.

A No sir, I did not . . . but I will tell you what I did do. When I came back with this load of wood from Washington (I was in Washington at the time) a man named Allen was fishing down there, and he said "old man, they have got every one of your horses." I said "goodness alive! Don't tell me so." And he said "Randall has been to your house and got every horse you have." I didn't even wait to go home; I went right to the camp, and the fellow who let me come across the ferry went over with me, and when Randall saw me he said to this man who had brought me

over "you damned scoundrel, if you ever bring another man over
here on such business I will shoot you. . . . if you ever let this
man across that ferry again, I will shoot you and him too. Take
him and just walk him back home; you can't get any of those
horses."

Q That is all the answer you got from the officer when you asked
for the horses?

A Yes sir, and then after that I had to come to Alexandria and
tote my bacon and luggage on my back, and when I came back
to Occoquan he and this woman were there on these 2 colts, and
they just rode ahead of me and tantalized me all the way, and
there I had to tote my stuff from Alexandria on my back. I hadn't
a horse—not one for my family or myself. Then when I got over
there he says "you shall not cross [via the ferry] across the creek;
your pass only says to Occoquan, it doesn't say across the creek,"
and he said "move yourself back to town." I said "great goodness,
Colonel, I have walked with this luggage until I can hardly drag
one foot after another"; and he said "you shall not come." So I
had to go above [where the creek was narrow and shallow enough
to ford] and cross in water up to my waist and when I got home
I was completely busted up. I was fearful some of them would
see me hurrying across and I would be shot, and I was laid up for
about 3 days after I got home.

Their reactions suggest that some of what Hugh described embar-
rassed Aldis and the other commissioners. Down on the ground, in
the communities where it was fought, the war had been raw, mean,
and unscrupulous. The troops did behave like scamps or scoundrels,
and their officers were hardly better. Randall either took pleasure
in antagonizing Hugh Hammill, whom he regarded as an old troublemaker of no consequence, or he was oblivious to the injury he
inflicted—even more demeaning to Hugh.

But that embarrassment did not go far. The idea that Hugh Hammill, Colonel Randall, and Commissioner Aldis were all gentlemen who should behave honorably to each other was laughable in the Northerners' view. Hugh was just an old man living in a rebellious state, and if he pushed his interests too vigorously, Yankees would toss him into a snowbank or forbid him from the ferry or deny his claim. It seems to me that Hugh came off as the more generous man, the more gentlemanly man, in his dealings with these Vermonters.

Moreover, he was honest with them and with himself. He has examined his own reactions to the theft of his horses and sums them up forthrightly in the hearing room:

[W]hen this man took my horses, you know, and took everything—the government I had stuck to, you know, to strip me of everything & leave me nothing in the world . . . it soured me, you know, and it seemed to me I didn't care two straws which was the best man. . . . I thought to myself if I could only get Randall off that colt of mine . . . and he a-tantalizing of me, you know, with this pretty woman he had ahead—I just thought if I had him off, you know, and could just get a twist on him, it would do me good to give him a little kind of a rubbing. Let everybody strip you of everything & it will make you feel a little sour at times.

18

A Virginian in a Yankee Court

Commissioners Aldis, Howell, and Ferris were very busy men, probably far busier than they had expected to be when they were appointed to hear the claims made under the Southern Claims Commission Act. Yet in the hearing room, their stance toward Hugh Hammill went beyond impatience. They were primed to distrust him by the activities of Special Agent George Tucker, who spent many hours before and after each hearing in collecting depositions from neighbors, employees, and acquaintances who might reasonably remember whether Hugh Hammill had been pro-Union or pro-Confederacy in the war. The commissioners read those depositions and concluded, with Tucker, that Hugh Hammill sympathized with the South during the war, whatever he said afterward.

Redmon Mills, Hugh's hired farm hand who lived in the family home before, during, and after the war, on 21 May 1875 deposed to Agent Tucker on his oath that Hugh never spoke in favor of the South or of the North in Mills's hearing. But then Mills commented that Mr. Hammill "was gone from home a great deal of the time during the war, driving about in his buggy." When questioned about this, Mills said that Hugh often went to Richmond, Alexandria, and elsewhere for supplies. Special Agent Tucker saw his behavior as suspicious. Perhaps Hugh was passing information to the enemy.

The same day, Henry Selecman told Tucker that he and Hugh "grew up boys together," and went on, "I talked in favor of the South at that time, although I did not feel that way." Yet he was not sure the same was true of Hugh: "I cannot [say] but that he talked contrary to his own feelings also, but I thought he really was in favor" of the South. Another neighbor, A. P. Lynn, stated, "I have been acquainted with Mr. Hugh Hammill over 40 years," and continued, "I was in favor of the South and he always agreed with me on the subject."

In a deposition given 30 December 1875, W. H. Rolls, like Hugh a Union sympathizer, told Tucker that "most of the people who had expressed union sentiments here before the war commenced left at the commencement of the war." The presumption was that those who remained in the county were loyal to the Confederacy. Rolls also said that "[p]eople in this vicinity were very careful about talking on that subject [i.e., their political loyalties] after the war commenced." Hugh had apparently been more than careful—he had actively misled the Rebels who lived around him. Or else he was lying to the commissioners. Hugh vehemently denied this in his first hearing: "I never did anything in any way, shape, or form during the war—in no way, shape, or form was I connected with it or had anything to do with it!" But his passion fed their suspicions instead of quenching them.

Time and again the questioning came back to Hugh's trips to Richmond in the early part of the war. The commissioners suspected that he went as a spy for the Confederates. Hugh maintained that, on the contrary, Union authorities in Alexandria asked him to inform for them, but he declined. In March 1874, he testified: "They wanted me to go to Fredericksburg and knock around there to see how the army was settled, and I told them 'No, if they got me down there they would know I had no business there and I would go up the spout, and I could not do it.'" But Aldis and the others were not satisfied. It did not help that Hugh had no memory for battle names and dates and no aptitude for the cool, brief, matter-of-fact answers the commissioners preferred:

Comm. Aldis: Now the question is, during that winter preceding May 1864, did you go to Richmond?

A No sir. I never was in Richmond after that battle.

Q I do not say <u>after</u> the battle . . . You told me a little while ago when I asked you the question, that you went to Richmond some six or nine months before the Southern army fell back.

A Yes sir, I guess it was about that time.

Q Was it six or nine months before the battle of the Wilderness?

A It was early in the Spring, and the roads were awful . . .

Q Now if General Grant started for the battle of the Wilderness on the 5th of May 1864—if it was in the spring of 1864, why it would have been within one or two months.

A Well, here, just let me understand you better.

Q You will understand me if you pay attention to the question.

A Well, you want to know of me what time I went there, don't you?

Q You pay attention to me and hear my question!

A Well then, just go on, and I will answer: certainly.

Q Now, as I told you, the battle of the Wilderness was in the early part of May 1864 . . . now you have been telling that the last time you went to Richmond was in the Spring?

A Yes sir—in the Spring.

Q And you say the roads were miry?

A Yes sir.

Q And that you had an old horse?

A Yes sir.

Q And that you recollect it was in the spring?

A Yes sir.

Q Now was it in the spring of 1864 ... was it that spring? ...

A No sir. . . The Southern army fell back to Fredericksburg in the winter didn't they?

Q Do you mean that they fell back to Fredericksburg?

A Yes sir, I do. When did McClellan march on them to start to go to Manassas? I cannot recollect, I have been so bothered, and broken up, and torn up. Well, sir, I was not in Richmond for two years before that battle was fought. . . .

Q You do not mean two years before the battle of the Wilderness?

A Yes sir, I do mean that . . .

Once again, Hugh has defeated the commissioners. He made that trip to Richmond in the spring of 1862, when the roads were so miry as to be nearly impassable. He apologized for his inability to remember dates—"I cannot keep these things in my head"—but it is quite true that he resisted giving the whole truth about his visits to Richmond. At length, during his second hearing in October 1875, the examiners badgered some information out of him.

Several of those trips had to do with a business deal Hugh made with a man named John Payne. Payne was licensed to deal in liquor in Prince William County. Hugh said Payne approached him with a scheme to purchase whiskey and brandy in Richmond and sell it in Prince William County. Hugh would transport it to Manassas Junction by train ("on the cars"), then haul it by wagon to supply any who had money to spend:

"Well, I was doing nothing in the world ... I had nothing to do; my wood was burned up, and this man [Payne] said, 'I am going to buy a large lot of liquor, and I will pay your expenses down there if you will pick out a large lot of liquor for me.... you take it up there, and you sell it to [the soldiers]—I will give you a permit to sell it—and we will divide the profits.'" But then "[w]e had some falling out. He put water in his whiskey and I didn't water mine, and they [his customers] all quit him and came to me…. And then he got jealous of me—got mad … and then I went on my own hook."

The commissioners were skeptical of Hugh's assertion that, as a Union man, he had no trouble crossing the Confederate lines into or out of Richmond when he went to purchase the liquor. John Payne was also skeptical when he was deposed late in 1875.[1]

Payne told Agent Tucker: "During the first year of the war Mr. Hammill went frequently to Richmond and bought goods there. He went several times with me, and always represented himself as a good Confederate. He could not have made those trips to Richmond if he had not been considered a good Confederate."

But Hugh maintained he never had to show a pass or sign a certificate of loyalty to cross the lines. Once he had trouble getting on a train to Richmond, but the problem was simply that all the trains had been requisitioned by the army: "It was a special train, and they were carrying soldiers, and they were not letting anybody but soldiers go, and I just sat right down on a seat with my head hanging right down in this way (indicating)—on the hind part of the steps, and went to Richmond in that way."

The court recorder was so caught up in the story that he conveyed Hugh's very gestures in the transcript. The commissioners saw only glib prevarication. Payne's deposition supported them: "No, sir, I never had a falling out with Mr. Hammill…. I never was in partnership with him in any way…. I helped him about buying his liquor and about getting transportation for it." Who was telling the truth?

In trusting John Payne's statements over Hugh Hammill's, the commissioners followed Special Agent George Tucker's lead. Tucker's opinion against Hugh never wavered. In fact, it became more forceful as the hearings went on and he collected more information about Hugh's activities during the war. Hugh's trips to Richmond were suspicious. The doings clustered around the sinking of his longboat, the *Martha Washington*, were more so. W. H. Rolls put Tucker on that trail when he deposed as follows:

> I was a prisoner at Dumfries at the time of the Confederate built Batteries at Quantico. I was a prisoner of the Confederates at that time and we were told that we were arrested on suspicion that we might be union men and carry information to the Federals of the building of the batteries. I saw Mr. Hugh Hammill at his house on the day I was arrested. I passed by his house in charge of the Captain and squad of men. Captain Wilson was the captain. We all stop[p]ed at Mr. Hammill's house a few moments. Whilst we were at Mr. Hammill's house there was something said about Mr. Hammill's Boat. I understood Captain Wilson to ask him how much he wanted for his boat. There was something said about the price but I can not tell what it was, but the Captain seemed to think it was too much. Whilst I remained a prisoner at Dumfries, the boat was taken around into Quantico Creek. Mr. Hammill was not a prisoner at this time that I was aware of, and I think I should have known it if he had been. I think I was a prisoner there about seven weeks, and about a week before I was released I saw Mr. Hammill's boat in Quantico Creek.

John Payne's deposition continued the story:

> The last time I saw him in Richmond he was there to get pay for a boat of his which was sunk in Quantico Creek whilst in possession of the Confederates. He came to me and talked with me about getting pay for the boat. . . . I understood before he left town that he got $2800 for his boat. I think he told me so himself. I also understood that he changed the Confederate money which he obtained for it into State Bank notes, and payed off an indebtedness in Baltimore.

When Tucker confronted him with these details, Hugh was eva-
sive: "He said he did not remember how much he got" for his boat.
Tucker felt there was only one possible conclusion, which he summarized in his report of 3 January 1876:

> All these things put together ... amount almost to a
> demonstration that he voluntarily sold [the Confederates] the
> boat. First he orders the boat back into the Creek and within
> the control of the Rebels, when it was loaded with wood for
> Washington, and so far out into the bay that no blaim [blame]
> could have fallen upon him if he had not gone down there three
> or four miles to order it back. 2nd, shortly after that, he is heard
> talking to a Confederate Captain about a price for his boat. 3rd
> when his friends are suddenly compelled to fall back and to
> burn their naval armament in Quantico Creek he follows them
> to Richmond and they promptly pay him a liberal price for this
> boat.... That he had a purchase voucher for the boat and a
> certificate of loyalty to the Confederate cause, would not be a
> violent presumption.

A published account of the Confederate blockade of Washington, D.C., corrects one detail of Agent Tucker's exposition. The Federals, not the Confederates, fired the *Martha Washington*:

> One of the Navy's most daring exploits occurred on October 11,
> 1861. The rebels had been fitting out a large schooner, the *Martha
> Washington*, in Quantico Creek.... Lieutenant Commanding
> Abram D. Harrell with his gig and two other launches entered
> the mouth of Quantico Creek as quietly as possible at 2:30 a.m.
> on October 11th.... The sailors boarded the schooner, piled the
> cabin furniture and watched as Acting Master Amos P. Foster of
> the [USS] *Resolute* applied the torch that doomed the ship.[2]

Luther Swann clarified further. The Washington newspapers had reported that a boat from the Federal flotilla had entered Quantico Creek and fired what was identified as a schooner, but that was not correct: "It was published as a schooner at the time, but it was not, it was a very nice long boat, schooner rigged." Swann continued, "After the close of the war Mr. Hammill raised the hull of his boat in Quantico Creek and rebuilt her, and I was in charge of her again until he sold her."

Did Hugh sell his longboat to the Confederates, as Agent Tucker believed? He certainly knew they wanted it. Whether they bought it or appropriated it, the Confederates raised the boat after Swann sank it, took it to Quantico Creek, and set about refitting it as a warship. At the last moment, the Federals fired it and sank it again. Hugh collected his money anyway, for the Confederates had taken the boat even if they hadn't used it. After the war he raised the hull and ran his boat once more, for the Confederacy was extinct and could make no claim to ownership.

Hugh unquestionably withheld information about the *Martha Washington* from Tucker and the commissioners. It does not follow, however, that he provided the *Martha Washington* to the Confederates to support their cause or that he was able to travel to Richmond because he carried a certificate of loyalty to the Confederacy. He knew that his activities regarding the boat did not make him look good in Union eyes, and that is why he volunteered so little about it. Maybe he even felt a bit guilty.

But I am certain he would defend what he had done with his last breath. He wanted a return on his investment in that boat, and he was willing to play a few games to get it, even to pose as a Confederate sympathizer if that would protect his property and livelihood. At every juncture, he made sure he got his money. It was no wonder that his friends considered him a good bargainer, a "keen, shrewd" businessman. The same motives explain why he made his claim and endured the drawn-out and sometimes humiliating proceedings it entailed. He had lost property to the U.S. government, and he wanted as much of its value back as he could get.

Over the course of many depositions and much testimony, Hugh's attorneys, Mr. Richard McAllister and his son, Richard McAllister Jr., gradually forced a turn in the tide against Hugh. Their strategy was to produce an unending stream of influential individuals to write letters or speak in Hugh's favor. On 21 May 1875, Wilmer McLean, a prominent farmer and sugar broker to the Confederacy during the war, told the commissioners that Hugh "was violently opposed to secession and has been ever since I have known him." Lewis McKenzie, mayor of Alexandria from 1861 to 1863, agreed: "Mr. Hammill I have always considered a loyal man." W. W. Winship, assistant provost-marshal at Alexandria under Henry H. Wells, commented that Hugh Hammill "had the reputation of being a shrewd business man, & sometimes people would say he was taking out stuff to sell, but we never could establish that.... we were never able to detect him in anything that was improper.... We gave him all the privileges that we would to a person whom we regarded as being union."

Even more impressive, the former governor of Virginia, Henry H. Wells, was ready to vouch for Hugh: "Mr. Hammill is quarrelsome and sometimes out of temper, and used to blow us up considerably at the office, but I never had any occasion to doubt his fidelity or his loyalty."

Wells had been provost-marshal for the city of Alexandria in 1862 and 1863 and provost-marshal-general for the entire Union army from 1863 until the war ended. In 1868 and 1869, he served as Virginia's provisional governor. He came to know Hugh Hammill because the provost-marshal's office issued passes to civilians who needed to cross military lines, and Hugh Hammill had been a frequent visitor.

When Hugh mentioned his acquaintance with Wells in his first testimony, the commissioners could hardly believe that such an important man had dealings with the likes of Hugh Hammill. They were also bewildered by Hugh's explanation of why he needed passes. He needed them to get on with another of his side businesses—conveying refugees from the Confederate states by boat across Occoquan Run, into Alexandria, and to the provost-marshal's office and safety behind Union lines:

A Colonel Wells knows all about it.

Q What Colonel Wells?

A The Wells who was provost-marshal at Alexandria for 2 years.

Q Governor Wells?

A Yes sir.

Q Does Governor Wells know you personally?

A Yes sir; he has known me for a long time. I was going there all the time to get passes.

Q Do you say that you can refer to Govr Wells to prove your loyalty?

A Yes sir....

Q You say you brought up refugees to Gov. Wells?

A Yes sir, I expect at least a thousand; that was my business. That was the only support I had. Sometimes I would keep them a week and not get a cent for it.

Q These were persons escaping from the Confederacy?

A Yes sir.

Q You knew that fact?

A Yes sir. We had but little to aid them, but I gave them all I could.

Q You brought up a thousand of those refugees?

A Yes sir, to Col. Wells, and he measured their height, and examined their teeth and everything about them, and passed them on. Some of them were from Alexandria, and there they took the oath [of loyalty to the Union], and there things staid.

Perplexed and incredulous, the commissioners summoned former Governor Wells to testify. When he arrived at the capitol hearing room on 21 May 1875, the examination in progress was suspended to allow him to give his testimony:

Comm. Aldis: Mr Hamill the claimant in this case alleges that he was well-known to you as a union man. What do you say as to that?

Gov. Wells: Yes sir: he was. He was in my office as often as once or twice a week, and I frequently gave him passes for himself and occasionally permits to take out supplies. He quarreled with me sometimes when I would not give him all he asked.

Q He speaks of bringing in loads of refugees from time to time, from the enemy.

A Yes sir, he did it very frequently. . . .

Q What was this business of bringing in refugees: I don't understand it exactly.

A Well, Mr. Hamill was living down there near Occoquan, and people were very anxious to get within our lines—some to go North, and some to come and live, and some for one reason, and some for another, and they were generally people in great distress, and ordinarily without any means of conveyance. Mr. Hamill was commonly in the habit of bringing these people in: I suppose they paid him what they could for it, on those occasions.

Claimant: —And very frequently nothing.

Wells went on to say that he believed this business of transporting refugees "was a service which no one but a loyal man would have rendered." Wells's clout went a long way in that hearing room—when the commissioners finally approved Hugh's claim, on 13 December 1878, they quoted Wells verbatim in their summary.

A bit more can be added on the topic of the refugees. Samuel Gedney, a steamboat pilot on the Potomac during the war and superintendent of the Potomac Ferry Company afterward, explained what he knew in the second hearing, 27 October 1875:

A ... During the war I was running a boat at the time and Mr. Hamill came up there very often with refugees ... and I talked with these refugees and they said he had fed them for weeks and weeks, and their families also, and they said that they could not stay there and that he was kind enough to bring them away at his own expense, and loss: that is, everybody down there was "spotted" who did anything for the Union people. Three or four times a month he would come up with a load, and I would take them up free.

Q Your boat ran between what points?

A Between Washington and Alexandria.

Q He would bring them to Alexandria, and you would bring them up here?

A Yes sir. And they had no money, and I talked with them, and this happened, probably, two or three times a month. I would sometimes meet him [Hugh], and say "you have got a good many groceries," and he would say "the people down there are starving to death, and their husbands dare not come home, and I will feed them as long as I can, and when I can not I will give it up." I knew everybody living in that section of the country, and that is the way I came to know anything about it.—it was my natural observation, being Captain of a steamboat. I suppose he brought in 15 or 20 loads of people that I brought up free.

Hugh did not elaborate on who these refugees were, though the testimony offers some hints. Samuel Gedney indicated that many were women whose husbands dared not come home, probably because they were avoiding conscription into the Confederate army. The ones whose teeth were examined and whose height was taken at the provost-marshal's office would have been slaves escaping from the South. These escapees were known as "contraband," and many thousands of them converged on Alexandria and Washington, D.C., where they were held in prisons and then in specially built barracks until the war was over. They could not have paid Hugh for taking them out of harm's way, and probably few of the fleeing white women could pay him, either.

Other refugees were better fixed, among them former Mississippi senator Henry Stuart Foote and his wife, Rachael Foote. Though he served in the Confederate House of Representatives through most of the war, Foote was passionately against secession. Early in 1865, he and his wife attempted to flee the Confederacy to Alexandria. W. W. Winship explained that the Footes took refuge at Hugh Hammill's house, hoping to be carried to Alexandria in one of Hugh's boats. However, high water on the Occoquan delayed them too long.[3] "[T]he rebel cavalry overtook him at his [Hugh's] house and carried him back to Richmond, but left his wife, and Mr. Hamill brought his wife in." Certainly the Footes paid him well for that service and for their keep at his house, and there must have been others who did the same.

Those refugees help to explain why Hugh needed so many groceries, so many supplies, and why he ran back and forth to whatever town was available to make purchases. As always, he was going after two birds with one stone. A thousand people were safe behind Union lines through his efforts, yet he might not have made those trips if no passengers ever paid him for his trouble. How far did his generosity and concern extended beyond business? Hugh would object to posing the question in that way. He sought a win-win situation whenever he could, and very often, he found it.

19

NOTHING TO DO AND NOTHING TO DO IT WITH— THE WAR'S LAST YEARS

ﾞ

ONE OF the most difficult aspects of the Civil War for Hugh Hammill, and probably for every other male civilian who endured it, was how little he could find to do with his time when his usual business was interrupted. Idleness drew him into danger on several occasions. When General Hampton's men ransacked his blacksmith shop and burned his lumber during their 1862 retreat, Hugh retaliated by confiscating tents and some iron pots and tent posts they left behind. He thought he might be able to sell those goods, or use them himself to continue his trade, to give himself something to do.

Unfortunately for him, his friend Henry Selecman saw him collecting the tents. To hide his real purpose, Hugh fibbed to Selecman: "[H]e said to me, that I must not take any thing from there that was worth any thing, for the reason that Gen'l Hampton had left orders with him to take charge of every thing there." That deposition made trouble for Hugh in the hearing room, and he never did get to sell the tents. He told the commissioners in October 1875 that "a man from Alexandria named Bright came down and took everything that I had picked up from the place" for the use of the Union army. So that scheme of Hugh's fell flat. He made no money and still had no iron to use in his blacksmith shop. Soon after, he went into the liquor business with John Payne, explaining, "Well, I was doing nothing in the world … I had nothing to do." More than once, Confederate and Union officers told him that he was endangering himself by interfering in their business, but it tortured him to have nothing to do.

He did better at protecting his three sons from the dangers of war and frantic idleness. Edward, the oldest, was twenty-five and married when the war began, the father of two small children. He lived in Occoquan and worked in his father's blacksmith shop until he was "mashed and ruptured" by that cannon after the First Manassas.[1] Exactly what happened to him isn't clear, but he was hurt badly enough that the Confederates did not conscript him when he recovered. Hugh's second son, Rueben, was twenty-one when war broke out. He was saved from the Confederate army because he worked as a miller of wheat and corn in his father's mill. Neither soldiers nor civilians could live without flour, so milling was considered an essential occupation in both North and South. In March 1875, Hugh told the commissioners that Rueben "was anxious to go" with the Rebels like many of his friends, but his father managed to stop him from volunteering and to keep him busy in the mill and on the farm, through threats or persuasion or both.

Hugh seemed surprised when the commissioners asked him about his youngest son, William. He told them the boy was too young to serve in the army: "He was I reckon, about 12 or 13." He spent his time taking care of the mill and farm along with Rueben. But in fact William was seventeen in 1861. Was Hugh hiding William's age from the commissioners? There was no reason for him to do so, as the war was long over. Hugh simply forgot his youngest son's age. He had a way of muddling dates badly.

So Hugh kept his sons employed and took the burden of idleness onto his own shoulders, along with that of providing for the family as well as he could. What did he do for his wife and daughters? When the war began in 1861, there were nine girls and women in his household, spread across four generations. His mother was about seventy, his wife, Jane, in her late forties, and his widowed daughter Hannah Ann thirty or thirty-one. The younger daughters ranged in age from twenty-two to five. They were Elizabeth, named for her grandmother Elizabeth McIntosh Hammill; Jane, called Jennie, named for her mother, Jane; Margaret, named for Hugh's sister Margaret; then Catherine, who carried a time-honored Hammill given name but was called Kate rather than Kitty. Last came Ellen, called Nellie. And Hannah Ann had a little girl, Jane or Jennie West, who was six in 1861.

Hugh felt a keen responsibility to keep these women busy "doing," to give them the wherewithal for "doing." It was humiliating as well as exhausting for him when Colonel Randall took every one of his horses and forced him to "tote [his] bacon and luggage" on his back all the way home from Alexandria. But it was far worse for his womenfolk when he had no way to haul provisions or provide transportation for them. He told the commissioners in his first testimony, "They had nothing to do, and there was nothing to do it with."

A moment's thought shows how true this must have been. Only the most rudimentary cooking and baking would be possible without molasses, sugar, salt, and leavening from town. No coffee either, or tea; little in the way of meat, fruit, or vegetables after a regiment came through. They probably lived on bacon and cornbread, with greens from the woods or garden thrown in. Sewing and knitting—again, not possible without yarn, fabric, thread, pins and needles, ribbon, all the paraphernalia of a woman's sewing basket. Children outgrow their clothing; adults wear out their aprons, shirts, and skirts. Patching may have been about the only sewing that circumstances permitted, a sore trial for everyone as the war dragged on.

Magazines and newspapers, toys for the younger children, schoolbooks—out of the question for the women at home if they had no conveyance and no one could get out to town. And think how the girls would have been confined. Young women could not roam a neighborhood where a thousand soldiers were encamped. They probably stayed indoors for days on end. With no horse to draw a buggy or wagon, they could not go visiting. Friendships must have languished, and boredom mixed with anxiety must have shadowed all their hours.

William A. Gaskins, who like Hugh was in the milling business, remarked in his testimony of 27 October 1875 that Hugh's habit of traveling across military lines worried his wife terribly. On at least one occasion she "begged him not to go," but he wouldn't hear of it: "He said he was ruined if he didn't get [some money] changed." Even when Hugh brought home gifts—he described purchasing two silk dresses for his wife in Richmond on one occasion—there must have been fear in the household every time he stepped out the door.

But illness damaged the family more deeply than warfare or idleness. Stephen Hammill perished of smallpox in 1862. In 1864, in the last dreadful year of conflict, three more members of the family lost their lives. Hugh's mother, Elizabeth McIntosh Hammill, died in the spring of that year at the age of seventy-four. Virginia death records give "old age and exhaustion" as the cause. It may be that sorrow exhausted her more than the passing of years. In February 1864 her great-granddaughter Jennie West, age ten, succumbed to typhoid fever. A month later, in March, her grandson Rueben Hammill also died of typhoid. He was twenty-four, at the peak of his youth and vitality. "A friend" by the name of John Hammill reported

Jennie's death to the authorities.[2] He was her great-uncle, Hugh's youngest brother. In 1864, fighting for the Confederate army, he had narrowly escaped death from typhoid himself.[3]

So much sorrow and loss must have marked each surviving family member as the war dragged to a close. Throughout his claim, commissioners, witnesses, and deposers refer to Hugh as "old man." He refers to himself the same way. However, in 1861, when hostilities commenced, he was only fifty-one or fifty-two, not old by today's standards.

Did his bad eyes affect his appearance? He mentioned poor vision in his 1858 letter to William H. Tayloe, and again when the commissioners asked about his means of livelihood. On 25 March 1874 he said, "I was a blacksmith but my eyes got bad and I am furnishing timber now for the Govt." Of course, trouble with one's eyes is a matter of degree. For a wheelwright and blacksmith who relied on keen short-range vision, as a machinist must do, ordinary aging of the eyes might have been his problem. He certainly saw well enough to drive a buggy or wagon and travel from one end of the county to the other on errands of all sorts.

In his first court appearance, he overstated his age by five or six years, declaring before the examiners, "I was 70 the 12th of last December." If he had turned seventy on that date, his birth year would have been 1803. However, his parents were not married until April 1809, and his death certificate and family records give his birth date as 5 February 1810. I think Hugh gave the day of his birth correctly, as 12 December. But he forgot his birth year, which was 1809. A birth date of 12 December 1809 has the advantage of showing that Hugh had reached the age of 21 before he was married, on 30 December 1830, and could take a wife without his parents' consent. He put the six years onto his birth date that he removed from his son William's. Could Hugh's memory for dates have been as bad as that? Apparently the answer is yes. Though he turned sixty-five late in 1873, he easily passed for seventy. He must have looked every day of it.

Hugh Hammill's testimony shows that his concerns, like those of most men and women, centered on his immediate family. Political loyalties were secondary to their well-being. His claim also shows that he was a contentious man who tended to be as overbearing in personality as he was in stature. He was inventive, even an opportunist, where his livelihood was concerned, relentless in pursuing his advantage and completely undone if, after all his efforts, he did not gain his aims. Twice he took to his bed after exhausting himself trying to protect his property as the war raged around him. When he could not carry on his usual businesses, he cobbled together new ones, carrying refugees to safety, buying and selling liquor to soldiers and civilians, confiscating gear that the army left behind.

He had a restless energy that kept him on the move even as an older man. By buggy, on horseback, by boat, or on foot, he traveled ceaselessly across Confederate and Union lines to change Confederate to Union currency, endorse and pay off promissory notes, buy supplies, and seek reimbursement for his losses. He was insistent on what he believed to be his rights, and argumentative, even quarrelsome, when he did not get what he wanted.

Yet Hugh had a kind heart and a deep belief in courtesy to strangers. The range of depositions in his case suggests that he was acquainted with many, many people of every social class and political conviction. He fed and sheltered any who came his way, whether they were refugees or soldiers. In May 1875, Wilmer McLean described him as truthful and reliable—"none more so"—and commented rather poetically, "He would let no man go from his house hungry." In his testimony, the last of the case, Confederate Captain William W. Thornton described him on 18 November 1878 as "a very kind man," "a worthy, good citizen," yet also "a man who talks very freely, & is outspoken in his sentiments."

Thornton understood Hugh very well. Hugh Hammill was a man who loved to talk. He gossiped with William H. Tayloe in his letter about the wagon. His testimony abounds in loquacious narrative and slangy turns of phrase. A natural dramatist, he told stories elaborately and could engulf both friends and strangers in a sea of words. No doubt he gained his way in many instances through sheer listener fatigue. His volubility drove the commissioners crazy, and it is true that a congressional hearing room was not the ideal setting for a display of his verbal gifts. But the court reporters who took down his testimony seem to have enjoyed every word he said, and, in reading the transcript, so did I.

When the war ended, of course Hugh's life went on, and so did the lives of his surviving family members. The full impact of the Confederate defeat did not hit them immediately. Initially there would have been relief at the end of hostilities, and a burst of activity directed at fixing or replacing what had been damaged or destroyed. In that period Hugh raised the hull of his longboat and had it rebuilt. He took advantage of army auctions to replace his lost farm wagons. A Captain H. F. Hammill purchased several decommissioned navy steamboats at a Maryland auction in late February 1866, for the very large sum of $19,200, plus another $5,000 for the boiler of a defunct ship.[4] Was that Hugh?[5] He and his son Edward ran steamers on the Occoquan and the Potomac in the 1870s, so maybe it was—but what did the F. stand for in his name, and how did he come by all that money so soon after the war?

The first question is a stumper, as no other record gives Hugh a middle name or initial. I can suggest an answer to the second question, though I can't begin to prove it. On 9 February 1866, Hugh's half-brother-in-law John Athey signed his will and died. John was a well-loved relative who maintained close ties with the Hammills even after he moved to Washington, D.C., sometime after 1850. In his last illness, he came back to Prince William County to be nursed and cared for by his half-sister, Hugh's wife, Jane. At the end, he was too weak to sign his name to his will—he made his "mark" instead.

John Athey left modest sums of cash and personal items like his pocket watches to his half-sisters, nieces, and nephews. The whole remainder of his estate he left to Hugh Hammill, some of it in cash.[6] Was it enough cash to finance Hugh's purchase of those steamboats? It somehow seems unlikely—unless Hugh bought them mostly on credit, sold off a good many of them, and kept just one or two. Hugh Hammill might well have done that.

There is more to say about John Athey and his relations with the Hammills. John was born in 1804, the third of five children of his mother's first marriage, to James Birch Athey. The family lived just across Occoquan Run, near Lorton in Fairfax County. John had a younger brother, William, to whom he was very close, and three half-sisters, Jane, Caroline, and Pauline Harley, born of his mother's second marriage to William Harley when John was a young teen. He maintained close ties to all three half-sisters, but perhaps most of all to Jane. When Jane married Hugh Hammill at the tender age of seventeen, John accompanied the couple to Washington, D.C., where he signed the register of marriages for her, as she was still a minor. He gave her name as Jane Athey, forgetting for the moment that she was the child of a different father. His slip shows how close he felt the bond with her to be.[7]

John Athey never married and had no children of his own. He made a good living as a merchant and businessman, first in Prince William County and then in Washington, D.C. He lived there with his half-sister Caroline and her husband, Henry Haislip. The men owned a lumber business together. In the 1860 census, the Haislips were sharing their home not only with John Athey but with Jennie Hammill, Hugh's eleven-year-old daughter. The families were tightly knit.

John seems to have been a sensitive man, perhaps to a fault. When his brother William died on 15 October 1843, he was devastated. Family legend describes how he followed the hearse to the cemetery, stumbling on foot through muck and mud, hands over his face to hide his tears. Another legend has it that as a youth he courted a girl, presented her with a ring, and was rebuffed. So John Athey slipped the ring onto a twig of some tree in the woods and walked away, never reclaiming the ring, never venturing another proposal.

Yet he was a shrewd businessman with an eye for opportunity. In 1835 he purchased a three-story brick building in the town of Occoquan from a man named Silas Beach. Beach had purchased the building from Joseph and John H. Janney a few years earlier.[8] The Janney brothers seem to have built it on one of their vacant town lots as a speculation around 1830.[9] It may be that Athey hoped to raise a family there someday. Instead, he moved to Washington, and the brick building went into some kind of receivership. For many years, its taxes were paid by the estate of Robert White, an Alexandria financier.[10] Perhaps Athey and White had been in business together. One way or another, the building ended up in John Athey's estate at his death.

Hugh inherited this big brick building, and he immediately set about refurbishing it.[11] It opened about 1868, providing Hugh with a useful supplementary income and giving employment to his son Edward, who operated it day to day and finally owned it. In 1877, the hotel was called Commercial House.[12] At some point, it became simply the Hammill Hotel. Edward ran it for several decades, well into the twentieth century.

The hotel was not John Athey's only gift to the Hammill family. When he still lived in the Occoquan area, he saw to it that the Hammill youngsters received an education, sparing them the embarrassment that Hugh felt about his spelling, writing, and grammar. He paid the salary of a tutor who taught them at home in the traditional southern way, so that all of them were comfortable with pen, ink, and paper. They read for pleasure, too, and could sum up their figures and keep neat accounts and hold their own with other well-schooled young people in their community.

It may also be that John Athey brought Hugh and Jane Hammill into the Methodist church, after untold generations of Episcopal worship in both the old country and the new. The Atheys and their kin, the Cranfords and the Plasketts, were instrumental in establishing Cranford Methodist Church in Lorton. John Athey and his brother were both buried there in the Lewis Chapel. No evidence indicates that the Hammills were Methodists before Hugh's generation, but all of them seem to have been afterward.

And John Athey left the family money. It was probably Athey's money that enabled Hugh to make his last substantial land purchase. On 16 May 1868 Hugh acquired two parcels from the estate of Joseph Janney Sr., father of the "ole Quaker." Twenty-nine of these acres lay along Marumsco Creek, and one hundred more lay between Belmont Bay and the creek's mouth.[13] That purchase gave Hugh 376 acres of Prince William farm and woodland, almost exactly what his great grandfather John had owned four generations earlier in Charles County, Maryland. Hugh and his children owed a debt of deepest gratitude to Jane Hammill's half-brother, John Athey.

Another acquaintance, this one a woman, also compelled a good deal of attention from Hugh Hammill in the first decade after the war. She was Sophie Cooke Tayloe Snyder, the widowed daughter of William H. Tayloe. Hugh seems to have befriended Sophie, almost to have acted as a father to her after Tayloe died in 1871. Their association shows yet another side of Hugh.

Sophie, born in 1831, was the same age as Hugh's oldest daughter, Hannah Ann. When her father and brothers moved to plantations in Alabama and Richmond County, Virginia, around 1854, she was already married. She stayed behind in Georgetown with her husband, Dr. John Marshall Snyder. The Snyders were the parents of two sons, Arthur Augustine and William Tayloe, and possibly other children when Dr. Snyder died in 1863. Sophie lived on in the big house in Georgetown through the war and its aftermath. Again like Hannah Ann, she raised her children as a widow. When her father died, she no doubt assumed that her inheritance would ensure a secure and easy life for herself and her family. Instead, at least initially, it brought her nothing but trouble.[14]

The Tayloe family holdings included 835 acres of agricultural land in Prince William County, all of it leased to tenants. In addition to the land was Deep Hole fishery, a superbly productive fishing bed in the Potomac near Mason's Neck that had provided significant income to the Tayloes for several generations. By the late 1850s, the family was renting Deep Hole fishery to sportsmen on holiday as well as fishing it commercially. Sophie's father seems to have left these properties to her. She lived nearby and could attend to them with the help of her attorneys, brothers, and other agents, and he wanted to provide comfortably for his widowed daughter and grandchildren.

Sophie's difficulties began with the failure of Deep Hole fishery. Early in 1873, the Virginia corps of engineers dredged out the Occoquan and the Potomac south of Washington, D.C., to facilitate commercial shipping, and the operation dumped tons of mud into Deep Hole. The catch dwindled immediately, and so did Sophie's income from that source.

Soon after, in August 1874, she began to receive very disagreeable notices from the Prince William County tax collector advising her that she owed back taxes on her properties in the county. In 1878 came disappointing news regarding the claim that her father had made to the U.S. Congress under the Southern Claims Act. Tayloe had sought $1,875 in payment for fifteen hundred bushels of corn that had been appropriated by the Union army at the end of the war. The claim was entered on 14 December 1871, immediately after the act became law—Tayloe wanted to be at the head of the line when the money was dished out.

But the claim was denied, partly because the Tayloes had been vocal secessionists and partly because the Confederate army had originally appropriated the corn, paying for it in Confederate money. The South surrendered before the corn could be used, and when the Union troops came through Alabama, they seized it from the railroad yard where it stood, shelled and sacked, and fed it to their mules. Commissioner Howell, who heard the claim, commented drily, "Then as I understand, having received pay for the corn already from the Confederate Government, they [the Tayloes] propose to get paid a second time, by the Government of the United States, for the same corn."[15] The rejection was predictable, but it must have dismayed Sophie.

Sophie Snyder came from a large family. She had brothers, a brother-in-law, and male cousins she could ask for advice, and she was surrounded by her father's men of business—their names come up in passing throughout her papers. Yet between 1872 and 1875, she turned most frequently to Hugh Hammill for help in managing her father's properties in Prince William County.

Hugh, ever the busybody, made Tayloe's business his own as soon as he heard of the man's death. In June 1872, he wrote to Tayloe's nephew, Edward Thornton (1829–81), who lived in Hale County, Alabama, notifying him that tenants on the Branmell tract in Prince William were cutting wood without authorization. He warned, "I think you had better give it your early attention." Eighteen months later, on 9 December 1873, Hugh wrote to Sophie's brother Henry Augustine (1836–1908), who lived at Mt. Airy in Richmond County, Virginia. This time Hugh's concern was Deep Hole fishery, generally rented out to sportsmen in the spring: "I think it will be better to rent the Fishing share for cash in advance, & if they should leave before the season is over there will be no trouble about the money."

Hugh continued, "I am going to Washington this week & will call to see your Sisters [Sophie Snyder and Emma Munford], & will let them have some money just as soon as I can get it. The RR Company owes me $500, which I expect to get very soon, & I will attend to it." Could it be that Hugh was acting as banker for Sophie and her sister, to help them out of a situation where cash was short and indebtedness pressing? The word *let* implies that his giving the money was voluntary. Whatever the details, Hugh was clearly in close contact and on familiar terms with Sophie and her siblings.

The winter of 1875 produced several more letters. Here is the first, dated 22 January 1875:

Mrs Snyder

Dear Madam

Enclosed you will find the receipt which we had such a look for. I had left it at home. I am going to Brentsville on Monday next—Court day—and will see the commissioners and let you know by letter or in person about the balance of the Taxes & will settle them and take a receipt; Hoping this is satisfactory. I am Yours

Very Respectfully

Hugh Hammill

And the second:

Office of the Chief of Engineers,
Washington, D.C. Feby. 25, 1875.
Mr. H. Hammill,
Occoquan P.O.
Prince William Co., Va.

Sir:

Your letter of the 11th inst. complaining of damage done the fishing at "Deep Hole Farm" near the Occoquan River by a deposit of mud excavated by the Contractor for the Occoquan River &c. has been received.

Your letter was referred to the officer charged with the improvement at Occoquan at the time the dredging referred to was executed and a copy of his report thereon is enclosed for your information.

By command of Brig. Gen'l Humphreys

Very respectfully
Your Obt. Serv't.

John G. Parke
Major of Engineers

The letters show that Hugh was interceding on Sophie's behalf regarding her tax difficulties and the damaged fishery. He was her messenger to and from the tax office at the county courthouse in Brentsville, delivering tax monies to the collector and carrying the receipts back to Georgetown. Several receipts preserved in the archives carry notes such as this one: "Received of Mrs. Sophia C. Snyder through the hands of Mr. Hugh Hammill, sixty dol[lar]s on her taxes for the year of 1874. Jan[uar]y 2nd 1875, Mr. W. Tansill, Coll[ector]."

As to the fishery, Hugh and his neighbor Henry Selecman swore an affidavit against the Engineers Department in Washington, D.C., certifying that "the damage done to the fishing at Deep Hole farm, in Prince William County, Virginia, in consequence of dredging in the year 1873 is at <u>least one thousand dollars</u>, the same being permanent and irreparable from the filling in of matter excavated. The rent of the fishing has in consequence been reduced some hundreds of dollars annually." In answer, Sophie received a polite letter from the Chief Engineer "regretting extremely" the damage, but explaining that nothing could be done about it.

One would think that Sophie paid Hugh some kind of honorarium for all this running around. The archive containing her papers bursts with odds and ends that many would have consigned to the wastebasket, including envelopes for letters and old tax stubs marked "paid." But there are no invoices in it from Hugh to Sophie, no cancelled checks from Sophie payable to Hugh. Of course she might have passed him a bank note from time to time—but it is also possible that he regarded these errands as favors and that she accepted them as such.

When Sophie decided to sell the land in Prince William, she consulted on every detail with Hugh. She wrote to her agent, "If I can make a cash sale I will take $12 an acre, the conveyance at the cost of the purchaser. If I have to sell on time, I must ask $15 an acre. I am assured by Mr. Hugh Hammill that the place is cheap at the latter price." He apparently advised her well, for she soon found a buyer and sold out. Her papers show no further correspondence with Hugh Hammill after 1875, though I imagine he continued to call on her when he visited Georgetown.

What should be made of this unlikely relationship between the patrician widow and a country farmer and businessman much older than she? The novelist Anthony Trollope, that genius at portraying nineteenth-century relationships of every sort, asks rhetorically in a short piece in his book *An Editor's Tales*, "Where is the man of fifty, who in the course of his life has not learned to love some woman simply because it has come in his way to help her, and to be good to her in her struggles?"[16] Perhaps that observation could be applied to Sophie Snyder and Hugh Hammill.

Hugh was not fifty but sixty-six in 1875, and Sophie was not eighteen, like Mary Gresley, but forty-four. But she had neither father nor husband, and she might have been lovely or at least elegant. Hugh's concern for her went past duty to his old patron's daughter. It held some value for him personally, as a man, to be of service to such a woman, to be the individual she looked to for guidance and concern. And from Sophie's point of view? Perhaps Hugh was simply of use to her—I cannot say.

This association brings to mind the relationship between Hugh Hammill, proprietor of Ballyatwood House in County Down, Ireland, and his patroness, Lady Alice Hamilton. One hundred fifty years before Hugh Hammill of Prince William County came to Sophie Snyder's aid, that earlier Hugh had acted as agent and confidant to a temperamental beauty embroiled in an ugly lawsuit of her own making. What was it about these Hughs that made women in difficulty seek them out? Apparently they inspired confidence and showed patience with a lady's concerns. Or maybe they liked to be satellites of women of high status. One possibility seems admirable, the other, not so much.

20

HUGH TAKES CARE OF
HIS CHILDREN

———————————— ⤜ ————————————

*T*HE MOST immediate and most damaging consequence of the
Civil War for the Hammills was unquestionably the death of
three family members in 1864. As the decade of the 1870s progressed,
another consequence slowly emerged. In 1873, when she was twenty,
Hugh and Jane's next-youngest daughter, Catherine, married a
young man named David Cofrode. David was a native of Philadelphia who came to work in Prince William County after the war. The
next year, in 1874, Hugh and Jane's son William married Lucretia
Soule, from Rockingham County in western Virginia. He was thirty,
she was twenty-eight. After those marriages, no others took place
in the family. Hannah Ann never remarried, and Elizabeth, Jennie,
Margaret, and Nellie lived single all their lives. They had no pros-
pects for marriage, for too many young men had died in the war, and
too many of the survivors left the South as soon as they could. The

South was a desolate place for a young woman if she hoped for a husband and children of her own.

Still, throughout that decade the Hammills remained prosperous. In the 1870 census, Hugh Hammill's real estate was valued at eleven thousand dollars and his personal property at five thousand dollars, giving him a net worth of about $240,000 in today's money. Such comparisons are elusive, but certainly the family led a comfortable middle-class life. The household included two female domestic servants, Julia Cole, mulatto, age forty, and Catherine Winters, black, age eighteen, to look after Hugh and Jane, their son William, five grown daughters, and Hannah Ann's sons, John and Izzie West. William continued to operate the mills, and Hugh encouraged his older son Edward to expand his hotel business, catering to tourists who could be transported by steamer on day or overnight trips to and from Alexandria and Occoquan. On at least one occasion, in January 1870, the Hammills' steamer *Prince William* struck another boat in the Potomac, causing some minor damage but no injuries or deaths. Maybe, after that, Captain Edward took some lessons in navigation or hired a captain to run his boat for him.

As his children settled into adulthood and his own financial situation reached its zenith in the later 1870s, Hugh turned his attention to securing the futures of his sons and daughters to the extent that he could. On 10 August 1875 he purchased thirty-two and a half acres of land from the Barbee family, putting it in trust for his newly married daughter Catherine for her "sole, separate and exclusive use and benefit … free from the debts and control of her husband."[1] He wanted Catherine to have something of her own to fall back on, should she need it someday. I don't know what became of that property. Maybe Catherine sold it when she and David left Virginia to move back to Philadelphia around 1876.

On 16 July 1878, Hugh sold the family hotel to Edward to get that valuable asset into Edward's name. Edward paid his father three hundred dollars for it, though for nearly thirty years the hotel had been valued in property tax records at twelve to fifteen hundred dollars.[2] It was a sweetheart deal, or rather Edward's patrimony, and he repaid his father by running the hotel profitably into the twentieth century. Edward and his wife, Lucy Ashby, raised a family of ten children very comfortably on the income.[3]

On 24 August 1881, Hugh made another significant gift, this time to his four unmarried daughters, who still lived with their parents on the old home place. The deed reads in part:

> whereas the parties of the second part have since the close of
> the war, done and performed the various domestic duties of
> the family of the party of the first part, which services would
> have cost the said party of the first part the annual sum of two
> hundred dollars, which amount he hereby acknowledges he is
> justly indebted to the parties of the second part ... for and in
> consideration of the services herein set forth, and in liquidation
> of the aforesaid indebtedness, the part[y] of the first part has
> granted, bargained and sold ... two pieces or parcels of land ...
> the first being the tract of land which the party of the first
> part purchased of Rebecca and J R Spin[ks]; and upon which
> the party of the first part now resides ... the second being an
> adjacent tract purchased of Thomas L. Selecman.[4]

Hugh was deeding the home place, the land he originally purchased in 1849 and 1854, to his daughters. He set up the transaction as the repayment of a debt he owed them for housekeeping and other domestic duties they provided to the family over the years since the war. It was an ingenious strategy for getting the property into their hands without their having to pay for it.

And what about William Harrison Hammill, Hugh's youngest son? What did Hugh provide to this young man when he married in 1874, or when he announced he was moving out west with his wife and family in 1878? For the moment, it appears that William did his father a good turn in removing himself, his wife, and their two children from the household, reducing expense for his parents and thinning out the crowd of people at home. Maybe William did not need his father's help to make a life for himself.

The census of 1880 does not value a household's possessions, but in that year the Hammills did not employ a domestic servant. By then, the daughters were doing the household work. The family was smaller by 1880. William and Catherine were married and gone. So were John and Izzie West, Hannah Ann's sons. In 1880, the household consisted of Hugh and Jane, who were seventy or nearly, five adult daughters, and thirty-five-year-old James Tanner, Hugh and Jane's nephew, who had taken over the work of the family mills when William moved away.

But it may be that Hugh's financial circumstances were slipping by 1880 or even earlier, another delayed consequence of the Civil War. On 1 December 1878, he secured a debt to May & McCormick, an Alexandria farm supply company from which he purchased animal feed, fertilizers, farm implements, and seeds. He pledged fifty tons of hay, fifteen head of cattle, fifty bushels of wheat, and his entire fall wheat crop against his outstanding balance of $378.26.[5] It is hard to know whether this was simply business as usual for Hugh—in his Civil War claim, he frequently mentioned redeeming or transferring notes—but this is the only time I know of that he pledged commodities against a debt. The economic depression that followed the war was tightening its grip on the South. Hugh was running short of money, and no amount of skillful borrowing and redeeming of notes could fix the problem. In the end, he may have been able to clear the debt without losing his whole farm income for the year. Or maybe not.

The census of 1880 shows the Hammill family intact, with both parents and all five daughters still living at home. That quickly changed in the decade that followed. Hannah Ann died on 11 May 1882. Family members said she died "of a severe headache," but Virginia vital statistics give the cause of death as cancer.[6] Possibly she suffered from a brain tumor. She was fifty-one at her death.

Then Jane Hammill, Hugh's wife, perished, on 12 March 1885. She and Hugh had been married for fifty-five years. At some point in that decade, Elizabeth, Jennie, Margaret, and Nellie picked up and moved into Washington, D.C., where they lived together and operated a small hotel or boarding house into the twentieth century.[7] Perhaps they waited until Hannah Ann died to make their move, for she must have required their nursing care until her passing. It seems unlikely that they would have left their father alone on the farm after Jane Hammill died. Most likely they moved into town between the two deaths, and Hugh must have encouraged their decision. The U.S. census of 1920 indicates that their boarding house was a rental property, but even if they did not own it, they would have required capital to set up their business. I imagine Hugh furnished at least part of the money, perhaps selling off some property to do so. He did not sell the home place, for he continued to live there for a few years, apparently alone.

On 13 July 1889, this ad ran in the *Washington Post*:

For Sale or Exchange—For City property, a fine farm near Woodbridge station; a new house, saw mill, large orchard. For particulars, address Hugh Hammill, Occoquan, Va.[8]

The house was new because the old one had burned down some years earlier. The large orchard is enticing—but Hugh has decided to sell out. He was seventy-nine or eighty, and probably his daughters were pressing him to come live with them in the city.

A few weeks later, the local Prince William newspaper carried the following notice:

SUIT—PUBLIC SALE of valuable land by virtue of decree entered at October term 1888 in Circuit Court of Prince William

Co. in Chancery Cause of Poole and Hunt versus Hammill, will on Monday 5 August 1889 in front of the courthouse at Brentsville, Virginia offer for sale:

First tract—250 acres located near Occoquan, Prince William Co., being the same land now occupied by Hugh Hammill. This land has a grist mill and a sawmill, a dwelling house, and necessary out-buildings on it.

Second tract—Containing 126 acres and located near the first, iswoodland.[9]

The chancery court of Prince William County was forcing Hugh's hand. He owed money to a company called Poole & Hunt, an engineering firm located in Baltimore whose specialty was the Poole-Leffel turbine waterwheel. In the 1880s, this was the most modern driving assembly on the market for water-powered mills.[10] At some point, Hugh must have purchased such a turbine, and in October 1888 he had been put on notice that he had to clear the debt. At the last moment, realizing that he could not delay any longer, he tried to sell his property to raise the money. But it was too late. The auction went forward, and a man named Bubb ended up with both tracts, no doubt at a bargain price. He ran a dairy farm on the land until after World War I.

At about the time the auction took place, Hugh moved out of Prince William County into Washington, D.C., where he lived with his daughters at their boarding house in the city. He died on 20 May 1896, at the age of eighty-six or eighty-seven. His death certificate gives his occupation as "machinist" and the cause of death as "old age and exhaustion." He did not die in debt; he did his children a last service by settling his affairs so they did not have to settle them for him. But he was probably sorely disappointed that after such a long lifetime of unremitting work and several decades of solid prosperity, he had neither property nor money to leave them.

THE TOWN of Woodbridge, Virginia, has grown up just east of the village of Occoquan, where the bluffs along Occoquan Run yield to flatter land that can accommodate more buildings, traffic, and people. I drove to Woodbridge one Sunday afternoon in April, taking I-95 from Reagan International Airport in Washington, D.C. That drive was a nightmare. It represented a very special hell we humans have created for ourselves from gasoline engines and asphalt. The traffic was bumper-to-bumper, creeping, poking. Drivers honked. Other drivers honked at the honkers. Windows rolled down. People rested their arms on their car doors, staring, sometimes smoking. The warm spring air and sunshine poured over us. Someone had two canoes on top of his SUV. Someone else had a mattress. Where were we getting to? Nowhere fast. I worked my way to an exit and found myself on Old Colchester Road, two lanes, southbound through Fairfax County. That was more like it! I rolled down my windows and turned off the AC. Not many cars were on this road. I saw wooded hillsides, some built up and some quite empty. Small streams crisscrossed the rolling terrain. It looked a lot like Charles County, Maryland. I began to relax.

Then, suddenly, I came to a stoplight. I was back in traffic on Highway 1. How did that happen? It didn't matter; I was in Prince William County, my destination. I was crossing Occoquan Run into Woodbridge. There was Marumsco Plaza, a small strip mall; across the road was Marumsco Village, a rather seedy apartment complex. A sign announced that I was approaching Marumsco Creek. I slowed down, aggravating all the drivers behind me, and craned to the right to get a look. Um, was that an open sewer? You couldn't run a mill on that trickle.

People behind me began to honk. I sped up and began the adventure of finding my motel. Luck guided me the first time. Huge, new, and spiffy, it stood in the heart of Potomac Mills, the most gigantic shopping center I have ever seen. There were acres of parking lot, acres of automobiles. New, spindly trees had been planted to take the edge off the pavement. They were faintly successful, better than nothing.

My room was big, clean, and comfortable. The screened windows opened easily, and the spring air flowed in. So did the sound of traffic passing on I-95, just a few hundred yards to the east. Between me and the trucks on the expressway were a grassy berm and a narrow strip of woods. From my windows, I could read the green traffic sign through the trees: South/Richmond. The sound was like the ocean, not so much loud as unceasing.

In my room, as I fell asleep or woke in the early dawn, I watched the stream of headlights moving northbound at a stately pace, southbound a bit more briskly. One morning I woke to the memory of the radio beacon that lit my bedroom when I was small. On top of Rocky Butte in Portland, Oregon, about as far from Woodbridge as a person can get in the continental USA, the beacon turned around and around, tracing its red light across the wall all night long. My brother liked it, and slept in the top bunk to get a better view. I liked the bottom bunk and darkness.

It was very hard to stay off I-95 in Woodbridge. My most frustrating moments were spent trying to stay out of lanes that were exiting onto the expressway. Often I failed, and made a big patient loop around the perimeter of the shopping center to try once more. There's a knack to finding the side streets, I told myself. I can learn how to do this. But detours and road construction complicated the task. Many times I simply could not get where I wanted to be. Swann's Point? A private marina made it inaccessible. Belmont Bay? Deep Hole? They both eluded me. I did find the vast Potomac, off a cul-de-sac marked NO THROUGH TRAFFIC, with a fence and gate posted NO TRESPASSING in case a visitor might be tempted to walk down to the water. McMansions stood along the shore.

The village of Occoquan was less daunting, once I figured out how to get to it. Clearly it had been a forgotten backwater not many years past. Today it has been refurbished for tourists, with a history walk, gift shops, and plenty of cafés. The Hammill Hotel still stands, big, square, solid, built of red brick, on the corner of Union and Commerce streets. It is an apartment house now. I visited the clapboard storefront on Mill Street where Hugh Hammill's brother John ran a dry goods business after the Civil War and saw what was left of Joseph Janney's mill—not much, just the miller's stone cottage. The rest burned in a fire decades past.

No Hammill homes are left, either—fire destroyed all of them at one time or another in the last century. Rockledge, the fieldstone mansion built by John Ballendine in 1757, looked well kept, though Christmas wreaths tied with red bows still hung in its windows. Nobody lives there now. Above the village, townhouse developments loomed from the bluffs. I-95 arced across the river, dwarfing boats and buildings below. Road equipment roared above my head—the I-95 bridge was being widened to accommodate more traffic. What would its former citizens think of their town now? They couldn't miss the fact that it is booming, along with most of eastern Prince William County.

Another day, back in Woodbridge, I went in search of Hammill Mill Park. I had been startled to find it listed on the Prince William County visitors' Web site as I was planning my trip. The Web site said it had a swimming pool, a children's playground, and picnic tables with barbecue facilities. I found it also had some beautiful flowering crabapple and cherry trees, and a roofed shelter overlooking Marumsco Creek. Maybe that was the site of the mill, though no sign said so, nor was there any exhibit or plaque that explained what kind of mill it was or who built and ran it. The flow of water in the creek nowadays couldn't begin to turn a millwheel. But a blue heron was happy with it. I watched it wade along, stabbing now and then for snails and tiny fish. The heron and I were the only visitors that Monday morning.

I explored on pathways and then a dirt access road that wound uphill through brush and woods to a wire fence marking off the park boundary. Beyond the fence was a big green sign for I-95. Once more I heard and saw the flood of traffic. The expressway was built right across Hugh's property. He did live along a kind of highway between Richmond and Washington, D.C. Today's road builders found the route as desirable as it had been all those generations ago.

Back at the Hammill Mill Park playground, I looked across the street. A water tower loomed over the modest 1950s-era homes like a gigantic Martian lander, a bulbous body perched on long green legs. As I turned to admire the park sign, road equipment rumbled down the dirt track beside me. "They're taking down that water tower," said a man's voice at my shoulder. "Doesn't do the job anymore." A stocky fellow in a baseball cap, I guessed in his late fifties, had joined me on the sidewalk to watch the action. He was a retired postman, friendly and conversational, ready to tell me all about the neighborhood. He was not happy with it; too many foreigners coming in, Hispanics and Asians.

I understood. There were so few affordable homes in the Woodbridge area, so few places for working people to live—this dead-end street in an out of the way corner of town, with hummocky lawns and overgrown shrubbery around the houses and a park next door, was a godsend for families who made their livings in the mall businesses surrounding us. But they were edging out the old-timers. This man lived next door to his nephew, had lived there for years. I told him my great-great-grandfather once owned this land. He sold out in 1889 to a man named Bubb, who ran a dairy farm on it.

"Bubb!" said the postman. "Why, old Mrs. Bubb still lives here, in that brick house with the wood porch in front." But he hadn't heard of the Hammills.

I left Woodbridge on a Friday. A sprinkle of rain drifted down, turning the pavement black. As I crossed Occoquan Run into Fairfax County on the giant expressway bridge, a sign caught my eye: Occoquan Regional Park. There wasn't much traffic at ten in the morning; I made the exit easily, and found myself descending toward the

Potomac on a narrow, winding road lined with flowering trees and shrubs. Yellow forsythia bent into the roadway, their flowers luminous on that rainy day. Pink and rose-colored plum and cherry blossoms dropped their petals onto the windshield.

I parked in an empty lot at the bottom of the hill and walked back up the road to an overlook I'd passed. A blue heron stalked along, going my way on the other side of the pavement. The overlook gave a great view of Occoquan Run, and of the old river town. Could this have been the site of Colchester, that first port settlement in the northeast corner of Prince William? There was no sign to explain. But I couldn't linger in any case—I had a plane to catch.

When the story behind Occoquan Regional Park emerged months later, my visit there seemed almost prophetic. One of Prince William's oldest cemeteries was located on that site. Revolutionary War soldiers had been buried in it, along with a good many of the county's early residents. In 1911, the authorities in charge of Washington, D.C.,'s penal system decided the old graveyard was an ideal place to build a prison workhouse and brickyard. The protests of local citizens delayed construction for a couple of years, but in the end, up it went.

Wade Hampton Hammill was one of those who protested. His complaint was published in the local newspaper: "See here, you cannot disturb these graves. Everyone around here has relatives buried in this graveyard, and I have ancestors buried here."[11] Wade was one of Edward Hammill's sons, a grandson to Hugh Hammill. Apparently Edward had forgotten how much damage General Hampton's troops had inflicted on Hammill property during the war, or he wouldn't have given his son that name.

As to the brickyard, time proved Wade Hammill right—it never should have been built. It operated for a few decades, providing employment to men of the area who worked as prison guards, and then was closed. The property lay abandoned for some years. Finally Occoquan Regional Park was put on top of it. Under that paved parking lot lie the graves of Elizabeth McIntosh Hammill and her husband, John. Hugh and Jane Hammill, Stephen and Rueben Hammill, Jennie and Hannah Ann West are buried there. Possibly the first Hugh Hammill is as well, with his wives Elizabeth Shaw and Elizabeth Smoot and his daughter Catherine, with all the information their gravestones might have held for researchers like me. It is a pity—a great pity.

And yet I did walk there. I did see the beautiful spring morning there where the Occoquan flows into the Potomac and so much history—Hammill history and the nation's history—has been enacted. Maybe that should be enough.

PART V

THE HAMMILL FAMILY
IN THE FAR NORTHWEST
1880–1928

Washington State

21

A VIRGINIAN WEIGHS HIS OPTIONS

———————— ❧ ————————

*A*S IN the Chesapeake region and the areas of Scotland and Ireland that border the Irish Sea, water and land vie for dominance in western Washington State. The vast strait of Juan de Fuca extends nearly one hundred miles along Washington's northern border, cutting the Olympic Peninsula away from Canada. Puget Sound carries Pacific waters deeply inland to Seattle, Tacoma, Olympia, and other cities. Willapa Bay and Gray's Harbor carve into Washington's west coast. To the south, the wide Columbia separates Washington and Oregon for a distance of three hundred miles, historically providing a major transportation route between the inland Columbia Plateau and the Pacific.

Smaller rivers and streams crisscross western Washington. The Chehalis, Newaukum, Skookumchuck, Cowlitz, and many other rivers named for and by Native Americans fostered white settlement along their banks. In the late nineteenth and early twentieth centuries, riverboat traffic from Portland and Oregon City traveled north and east up the Columbia and then the Cowlitz to the town of Toledo. There, at the Cowlitz Landing, cargo and passengers en route to Puget Sound continued their journey overland along the Cowlitz Trail by coach, wagon, or on foot. Goods and people bound east along the Cowlitz could travel by small shallow-draft steamers to other landings some miles further upriver, as far as the whitewater rapids of the Mayfield Chasm.

About 1882, William Hammill, a native of Virginia, took out a land claim in central Lewis County, Washington Territory, on the Cowlitz River just below the Mayfield Chasm. The claim was hilly and heavily timbered, with some rich bottomland for pasturage and crops. Better still, from William's point of view, was the twenty-five-foot waterfall on Salkum Creek less than a mile from the point where the creek joined the Cowlitz. His father had built a mill on Marumsco Creek in Prince William County, Virginia; William planned to build one on Salkum Creek in Lewis County, Washington. Like generations of his family before him, he established himself in a new land-and-waterscape that was very similar to the one he had left behind.

William lived nearly fifty years in the Northwest, and he died there in 1928 at the age of eighty-four. His experiences as a frontier settler form the heart of the chapters to come. But though his story ends in the Pacific Northwest, it does not begin there. Like his two-times-great-grandfather John, who was in his thirties when he left Northern Ireland to begin a new life in Maryland Colony, and his great-grandfather Hugh, who was in his forties when he moved from Maryland to Virginia, William was well into adulthood when he left his southern home. More than three decades of personal history, including the traumatic years of the Civil War, anchored him in Virginia even as he helped his wife and two small children aboard the westbound train that carried them to Topeka, Kansas. The year was 1878. William's farewells, spoken in a soft Virginia drawl, showed he was a southerner through and through.

Born 26 April 1844, William Harrison Hammill was the fifth child and third son of Hugh and Jane Hammill of Prince William County. Unlike his father and grandfather, who were the oldest children in their families, he had five older siblings to protect his growing up and five siblings more who were younger than he. His four-year-old younger brother drowned in about 1850, and then William became the youngest male in a family of six daughters and three sons. Sheltered and probably dominated by his older siblings and with four younger sisters to compete with, William, or Billy as he was called at home, grew up quiet and hardworking. His lifetime habits of silent observation and private amusement were probably formed at the family dinner table, where twelve individuals vied noisily for a share in the conversation.

Rueben, William's next older brother, was a precocious child much petted in the family for his ability to memorize and recite prodigious numbers of Bible verses by the time he was three. Hannah Ann, the oldest child, was thirteen years William's senior. She must have been something of a second mother to him, probably a bossy one. Hannah Ann was married briefly; when she was widowed, she returned to her parents and siblings with three young children of her own. For several years thereafter, the family consisted of fifteen people representing every life stage. Hannah Ann, her mother, and her grandmother formed a female triumvirate whose authority came second only to that of the head of the household, the voluble, opinionated Hugh Hammill. I don't want to say that William was lost in the family shuffle, but so many assertive individuals ahead of him must have encouraged him to observe, reflect, and keep his opinions to himself.

As soon as they were old enough to help, Hugh brought his sons into the family businesses. Edward, the oldest son, became a blacksmith like his father. Rueben learned to run the family milling operation. William helped Rueben in the mill, and he did a good deal of farm work as well. He grew up to be a big, powerfully built man like his father, over six feet tall and about 225 pounds, broad-shouldered, with his father's large feet. Yet within the family he was regarded as the kid brother. His father underestimated his age at the outbreak of the Civil War, telling the commissioners in the course of his court testimony that William had been "about 12 or 13."

In fact, William was seventeen when the war commenced. Many men served who were far younger than he. But William was a kid in his father's eyes until the last year of the war, when, in the space of three months, three family members lost their lives. Elizabeth McIntosh Hammill, William's grandmother, died in April 1864 at the age of seventy-four. Hannah Ann's daughter Jennie died of typhoid at the age of ten, in February of that year. But the devastating death was Rueben's, also from typhoid, in March 1864, when he was twenty-four or twenty-five.

At once William became the second son in the family and the only one at home, for Edward had married just before the war and lived with his wife and two children in Occoquan. William was no longer the kid brother, the family backup for mill and farm work. Now he was his father's right hand, especially at the mill. He took his new status very seriously, determined to fill his brother's shoes and probably missing Rueben desperately as he did so.

Unlike his father and grandfather, who married soon after they came of age, William devoted the decade of his twenties to helping his father repair the family livelihood after the war. He became a master miller and a devout Methodist, committing himself to the family trade and to its faith with a zeal that may have surprised his parents. Perhaps they worried that he was too hardworking, too dedicated to his religion. Or perhaps they were simply proud of him.

The events of William's later life convince me that throughout his years at home, the Methodist fellowship provided by local congregations and preachers was his primary diversion and source of social contact outside the family. I am sure he traveled to Alexandria, Washington, D.C., and other cities in a wide radius around Occoquan to hear new preachers on the circuit and to take part in the revival meetings that were such an important aspect of Methodist worship. They were the rock concerts of the era, with passionate preaching, singing, praying, and crowds of fervent participants who stayed for days, worked up to a fever pitch by word and, especially, by song. At one of these meetings he met the Reverend H. Monroe Strickler and his wife, Sarah Soule Strickler, usually called Sallie. Since his acquaintance with the Stricklers influenced his life profoundly, I will spend a few pages introducing them and their families. Who were they?

Harrison Monroe Strickler, born 6 July 1843 and so less than a year older than William Hammill, was like William a middle son in a large, comfortable farming family. He grew up in Pace County, in the Valley of Virginia southwest of Prince William. His older brother was also a Methodist minister. Monroe Strickler went by his second name to avoid confusion with his father, for whom he was named. In the federal census of 1850, the senior Harrison Monroe Strickler was recorded as owning real estate worth $6,331. The slave schedules for that year show that he also owned three slaves. In 1860, the census valued his real estate at eight thousand dollars and his personal property at five thousand dollars, a good proportion of which must have been in his slaves, who now numbered five. They were a black woman, age thirty-five, a black man, age thirty-two, and three children ages ten, seven, and six, possibly a family.

Monroe Strickler was gifted from earliest childhood with a fabulous singing voice. As a twenty-year-old captain in the Confederate army, he brought an impressive number of soldiers to the faith "by his ministry of song and sermon," and after the war, though he was still not yet thirty, his reputation grew with every congregation he visited. His biographer waxed eloquent on the subject of Strickler's voice:

Amongst the singers of the Methodist Israel of his day, Brother H. Monroe Strickler stands for the peer of any.... The sweet echoes of his voice in many a familiar old hymn of the church

ring yet within our ears. To win men by the wonderful suasion
of blended soul-notes that ring in the voice in gospel song is
a masterful bit of art that may be used for God, and this very
thing did Brother Strickler in his long and splendid years of
ministry among us. . . . Years ago at a great meeting at Wesley
Grove, near Baltimore, he was called to the platform when there
had been no conversions, and after he had sung 'The Ninety and
Nine' there were thirty-five persons who came to the altar at that
service.[1]

So Monroe Strickler stood out in a faith where the power of song
could hardly be overstated:

When Methodism was born the pent lips of men were stilled,
long since, from spontaneous outbursts of song; the fountains
of religious enthusiasm had run dry; the experience of God in
the heart of man was an uncommon circumstance. . . . Charles
Wesley easily became the sweet singer of the revived Israel of his
day, and gave to Methodism, and through her to the universal
church, a new hymnody of spiritual warmth and power. Into
this hymnody was written the experience of personal conscience
conversion, justification by faith, [and] the witness of the
Spirit. . . . Methodism . . . has produced a people virile in faith,
enthusiastic in expression, evangelistic in spirit, going forth to
battle for the kingdom of God with banners flying and with the
challenge of ringing songs of Love's fine valor breasting the way
before her victorious hosts.

Inspired by high-flown sentiments like these and profoundly
moved by Monroe Strickler's expression of them in song, William
Hammill sought out Strickler's acquaintance at his first opportunity.
If they had not met before 1872, they certainly did so in the summer of that year, when the Methodist conference assigned Strickler

to the Prince William County circuit. Probably the entire Hammill family was present in the congregation that welcomed Monroe and Sallie Strickler to Prince William. Strickler made introductions easy, for in regard to personality he was "genial, hearty.... He lived on the sunny side of the street.... He was cheerful and happy and radiated sunshine all around him."

In short order, he and Sallie became frequent guests in the Hammill household. It could not have been long before the Stricklers introduced William to Sallie's younger sister Lucretia. Maybe she accompanied her sister and brother-in-law to Prince William at the time of their move, for her mother had died in the spring of 1872 and she might have welcomed a change of scene and some time away from her grieving father. It may also be that she had met William Hammill before 1872, and that her parents encouraged their relationship. They courted for two years or so before their marriage on 29 September 1874, about six months after her father's death that March. Monroe Strickler officiated at their wedding.

William's association with the Stricklers and his courtship of Lucretia Soule drew him into an intimacy with two of evangelical Methodism's prominent Virginia families. Sallie and Lucretia's father was Isaac Soule, a Methodist clergyman at the town of Ottobine in Rockingham County, which adjoins Pace County on the south. His wife, Elizabeth Smith, was born and raised in Rockingham County, where her family had settled in the mid-eighteenth century. Probably the Soules and Stricklers had known each other for years when Sallie and Monroe were married in 1866, while he was preaching on the Rockingham County circuit. Though Monroe was two years younger than she, in their parents' eyes they could not have been a more appropriate match.

Isaac Soule was a solid citizen in his community. In the 1850 federal census and slave schedules, his real estate was valued at seven thousand dollars and he owned one slave, a young woman of sixteen. In 1860, he owned real estate worth $6,615 and personal property worth $1,280, but apparently no slave. So the Soule and Strickler families lived at about the same level of income and prestige. The Stricklers had their son Monroe to boast of, and the Soules had their own illustrious connection, Isaac's older cousin Joshua Soule.

Joshua Soule, for many years a bishop of the Southern Methodist Church, was Isaac's third cousin once removed—a rather distant connection that nonetheless served Isaac very well in his own professional life. Bishop Soule was responsible for making the decision that divorced the Northern and Southern Methodist conferences as the Civil War approached. Southern Methodists were officially neutral on the question of slavery, which meant that they tacitly supported it. Northern Methodists were for the most part vehemently against the institution.

Joshua Soule's biographer justifies his position on slavery like this:

> The early ideals of the South were those conservative doctrines of the social order, that amenability to law and traditional authority and respect for the worth of the individual that completely described the creed of Joshua Soule on the intellectual side. He was opposed to slavery as such, was never the owner of a slave, nor can it be shown that he ever sought by word or deed to abet the institution.[2]

But of course, refusing to take an official position against slavery was in fact abetting it. And Soule did own slaves. The slave schedules of 1850 show him as the owner of three—a man of forty-five, a woman of twenty-eight, and one three-year-old child. Abolishing slavery was not in his personal interest, however he might protest that he simply did not want to break the civil law of the South.

Isaac and Joshua Soule were natives of Maine, whose forebear, George Soule, came to Plymouth Colony on the *Mayflower* as an indentured servant to Edward Winslow. Traditionally lumber dealers, ship builders, sailors, and sea captains, the Soules were Puritans to start with, then Presbyterians until Joshua converted to Methodism soon after 1800. He was a talented man who quickly rose in the Methodist hierarchy, moving frequently during his long career. A biographer describes him as "tall, dignified, and able," and continues: "Bishop Soule was a great man intellectually, of remarkable personal appearance, dignified and even ostentatious in bearing, of a strong and imperious will."[3] He died in Nashville, Tennessee, shortly after the Civil War ended, in 1867.

Isaac Soule, born in 1797, was sixteen years younger than Joshua. He served briefly in the War of 1812, then followed his cousin into the Methodist ministry and was sent to Rockingham County, Virginia, sometime before 1830. Methodist ministers were generally moved every few years from one circuit to another, but Isaac lived and worked his entire adult life in Rockingham County. He and his wife, Elizabeth, raised seven children, five boys and two girls. Lucretia Elizabeth was the youngest, born in 1846. Her older sister, Sarah Margaret, was born in 1841. The girls were probably named for two of Isaac's younger sisters, Lucretia and Sarah Soule, but Isaac was reticent about his early life and never said outright that it was so.

Isaac was well enough off to purchase a tract of land for each of his children as they came of age, and he invested in a large acreage in Iowa as well, where two of his sons eventually settled. Some descendants maintain that Isaac was a graduate of the University of Pennsylvania, but Penn has no record of him as a student. More likely, he attended a smaller seminary in the East before taking up his ministry. In any case he was reasonably well educated and he saw to it that his children were educated as well, probably at home, probably by him for the most part.

Though he lived forty years in the South, Isaac Soule never lost the down-East accent he grew up with. Remarkably, he passed that accent on to his youngest daughter—or she taught herself to model her speech after his, with or without his encouragement. Her children and grandchildren remembered that she spoke like a Yankee, with her father's crisp consonants and quick, assertive tone. She seems to have shared something of his personality as well.

A photograph of Isaac Soule as a young man shows him seated in an armchair, wearing a jacket with wide lapels and a large, dark-colored bow tie, looking severely at the camera. His hair and beard are very dark, nearly black, and so are his eyebrows and eyes. His forehead is white and broad, his cheeks high colored. He is good-looking, unquestionably, but it is the boldness of his gaze that is most striking. Apparently an uncompromising personality was a Soule family trait.

Isaac held himself and his family to a high, perhaps uncomfortable standard. He was a Yankee Methodist, a Puritan Methodist, not a sweet and sunny southern Methodist like his son-in-law Monroe Strickler. When his daughters packed for an overnight visit, Isaac inspected their valises for the telltale silk gown. Silk gowns meant dances, and dances were strictly forbidden. He sued his oldest son in a court of law over ownership of the Iowa land. When Elizabeth, his wife, died in 1870, he led the funeral procession mounted on an enormous white stallion, a gesture of respect that drew more attention to himself than to the deceased. And when he lay dying in March 1874, Isaac instructed his daughter Lucretia to marry Mr. Hammill, in full expectation that she would obey. She did obey, perhaps very happy to tie her future to a husband less imperious than her father.[4]

William was thirty years old and Lucretia was twenty-eight when they were married—not young by the standards of the time. Why were they still single? I think they shared a sense of duty to their parents, William because he was the only son at home, and Lou, as she was usually called, because she was the youngest child in the family, and a daughter. It may also be that Lou had not had many suitors in her girlhood, for judging by photographs taken in her late middle age, she had never been a beauty. She was short and plump, with her father's dark brown hair and eyes, and her right eye was crossed, wandering up toward the bridge of her nose. She must not have had vision in the right eye at all. Her bright intelligence, lively conversation, and strong will might have appealed to William, as well as membership in her solidly Methodist family. To Lou, William offered a secure future, an active faith, and her father's approval. Beyond that, he was tall and reasonably good-looking, with the Hammill gray-blue eyes. Kindly by nature, his quiet sense of humor complemented her assertiveness. They seem to have been very close throughout their fifty-two years of married life.

William and Lou lived with his family on the Hammill home place for four years after they were married. William continued running the mill and helping with the farm work, and Lou became well acquainted with his six sisters, especially his younger sister Catherine. Called Kate instead of Kitty like earlier Catherines in the family, she had been married in 1873. Though Kate was nine years younger than her brother and seven years younger than Lou, the sisters-in-law grew to be intimate friends. They shared the excitement of newly married life and the arrival of their first babies, Alice Cofrode in 1874 and Edith Hammill in 1875. Then they shared the tragedy of losing their little daughters. Both Alice and Edith died in 1876, perhaps of the same childhood infection. The deaths drew Lucretia and Kate even closer, so that their separation soon afterward must have been painful for both.

David Cofrode was an engineer, a road and bridge builder who had come to Prince William County from Philadelphia to repair infrastructure that had been destroyed in the war. Soon after their toddler's death, he and Kate moved back to Philadelphia. Their second child, Jesse Hammill Cofrode, was born there in July 1876. The Stricklers had moved out of the county to a new circuit late in 1874. The departures of these well-loved relatives might have encouraged William and Lou to consider moving on themselves. But they lingered another year or two; their second and third children, Isaac

Hugh and Ethel Elizabeth, were born in Occoquan, Isaac on 29 October 1876 and Ethel on 23 June 1878. Sometime after Ethel's birth, the family boarded the train for Topeka, Kansas.

Why did they leave Virginia? The answer is simple. William had a family to support. His father's farm could hardly continue to provide a livelihood for six grown children and their children as well. A modest economic boom at the close of the Civil War had given way to bust in the Panic of 1873. Driven by collapsing railway stocks and an unstable currency, the Panic was followed by four years of economic depression nationwide. People in Prince William County, Virginia, suffered along with everyone else.

The national economy began to revive around 1877, but recovery lagged in Virginia. As it had after the American Revolution one hundred years earlier, opportunity lay westward. William's parents encouraged him to move west; so did the pastor of their local church. The story goes that this Methodist preacher exhorted all the younger members of his congregation to leave Virginia if they could. His opinion carried a good deal of weight for deeply religious people like William and Lou.

Then, why move to Topeka? As their hometown preacher no doubt pointed out, Topeka had a new First Methodist Church where the family could find the Christian fellowship they so valued. And there were other advantages. Topeka was west, but not the frontier west. It was a railway hub, so Lou and William could travel fairly easily back to Virginia for visits or north to Buchanan County, Iowa, where Lucretia's brothers lived. Lucretia owned some land there herself, a gift from her father.

Topeka offered schools for the children and a growing economy that would welcome a new milling operation when William was ready to make the investment. On the face of it, Topeka was a logical choice. It might have occurred to William that he would not enjoy the dusty plains of the Midwest, but his personality inclined him not to rock the boat. He followed the lead of his parents, his pastor, and perhaps his wife, telling himself that he could adjust, like hundreds of other Virginians setting out for Kansas.

Once William and Lucretia decided they had to leave Virginia, the physical transition was not so difficult. The rail trip was short, and they probably did not take many household goods with them. Housing and work were easy to find in Topeka. William rented a house on Quincy Street, where the Topeka city directory lists him living in 1879.[5] He looked for and quickly found a job on the assembly line in a shoe factory. It might have been the Hyer Boot Company, which made cowboy boots for generations of cattlemen in the late nineteenth and early twentieth centuries, though no records give William's name.[6] While he worked, supporting the family and perhaps putting some money aside for the mill he hoped to build one day, Lou looked after the house and children. She probably sought companionship in the congregation of the Methodist church and tried to make a pleasant home for the family. For a time, she and William may have congratulated themselves on their easy shift from old to new.

But though Topeka had been a logical choice, emotionally it was a disaster. William hated Kansas. Where were the hills, rivers, and woodlands? Kansas horizons were desolate. There were no grand waterways, only narrow rivers and a few seasonal brooks. Summers were torturously hot with dust storms instead of rain. Winters were a succession of frigid blasts from north and west. He gave it two years, no doubt swallowing his misgivings while making every effort to cope. But in the end, he asserted himself. He wanted out.

Lou urged him to take a look at the land she owned near her brothers in Iowa. Iowa was green and well watered; maybe that would please him. But William would not hear of Iowa. It was prairie, and he wanted hills and woodlands. No pastor, no opinionated father or strong-willed wife was going to change his mind. As a middle son, he had been slow to step into the authority that a first-born son assumed as his right and duty. Now he took on the role that his father and grandfather were born to. He wanted out of the Midwest entirely. As head of the family, it was his decision to make. One might say that in making it, he became a man at last.

Where would he take his family? Washington Territory was in everybody's mouths in 1880. It was a land of mountains, forests, and waterways, wide open for settlement, with good, empty land begging to be claimed. But it was two thousand miles from Topeka, and no transcontinental railway could take them there. If they chose Washington Territory, they would have to travel two thousand miles by wagon train.

William didn't care. Washington Territory was where he wanted to be. Lucretia expected a third child in October 1880, but as a good Methodist wife she could not argue too strenuously. She sold a parcel of land in Rockingham County, Virginia, to help finance their trip. Like her Iowa property, it had been a gift from her father. The transaction was dated 16 June 1880.[7] It must have been very shortly afterward that William bought a wagon and a team of oxen and joined a train of sixty families traveling overland from Kansas City to Washington Territory. And so the Hammills became pioneers.

22

WASHINGTON TERRITORY,
A LAST FRONTIER

―――――――――― ❧ ――――――――――

ILLIAM AND Lucretia made their journey down the Oregon
Trail in the last decade of its active history. Steam power had
transformed commerce and transportation in the rest of the nation
by the Civil War or soon after, but political shenanigans and daunting terrain denied Washington Territory a transcontinental railway
until 1888. So it was that, in 1880 as in 1850, Washington "attracted
relatively small numbers of settlers, found little use for its rich natural resources, and maintained its commercial contact with the rest
of the world by sea."[1] Short local lines carried goods to and from
a handful of ports on Puget Sound, the Columbia River, and the
Pacific coast, but most settlers lived a frontier existence far from the
sound of a locomotive's whistle and a world away from the American consumer culture. As they toiled to secure a bare subsistence in
their scattered communities, these settlers dreamed of the boom that
the transcontinental railway would bring when it came through.

Expectations began to rise in 1870, when the Northern Pacific announced it would build a trunk line on the west side of the Cascades between the Columbia River and Puget Sound. At the same time, far to the east of the Cascades, that railroad began laying track from Duluth toward Bismarck, Dakota Territory, a first step toward closing the gigantic gap between Bismarck and the Cascade Range. Promoters issued a flood of pamphlets and broadsides touting the wonders of the Far West to attract the settlers who would make the railway a success. Ezra Meeker, an early and flamboyant resident of western Washington Territory, published a popular one in 1870, in "a compact form suitable for transmission through the mails." He

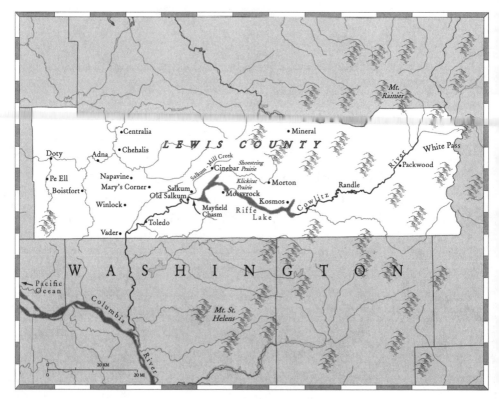

Lewis County, Washington

assured his readers that "the great aim has been to avoid overdrawn statements, and to give the resources as they are," and then proceeded to describe a paradise:

> Wheat, oats, barley and rye all mature well and produce abundant crops. . . . [Our wheat] is of most excellent quality, being pronounced by our millers as second to none on this continent, yet we do not raise a sufficiency for home consumption, because other and more profitable crops have engaged the attention of our farmers. Water is abundant, and of the purest quality. . . . [N]umerous water-privileges [are] not yet occupied, that can be improved as the wants of the settlers demand it.[2]

What an invitation for a miller! William Hammill may have ordered, read, and pondered Meeker's words as he sat on summer evenings in Virginia or Topeka, imagining those "water-privileges" that were going begging so far away. Thousands were tempted west by a skillful pen. Maybe he was one.

Meeker did his part to draw railway passengers, but the Northern Pacific bungled their side of the bargain. The financial panic of 1873 brought rail construction to a standstill. It was five years before the railroad recovered enough to continue work on its transcontinental line. Finally, in October 1878, it sent a surveying and engineering crew to the Cascades in search of a viable pass through the mountains.

Headed by Assistant Engineer Charles A. White, the crew first explored the Cowlitz Pass region southeast of Mt. Rainier. White and his crew spent some weeks surveying and staking a route in Lewis County not many miles east of William Hammill's future land claim, raising hopes to a fever pitch among those already living there. In the end, the railroad decided that the route would require too many tunnels and bridges to be practical. The pass was renamed White Pass for the man who surveyed it, and the search for a route moved to the north of Mt. Rainier.[3] In their disappointment, some

Lewis County settlers picked up and moved out. Others stayed, tantalized by the surveying stakes that stood for years afterward as if signaling that track might still be laid in their front yards.[4] William probably saw them as he traveled the area looking for land. Certainly he heard a good deal of heated talk about the railroad.

In 1881, the Northern Pacific decided that their route would cross the Cascades at Stampede Pass, in Kittitas County. By then a landowner on the Cowlitz, William like his neighbors would have greeted the news with a mixture of disappointment and optimism. It was a pity that the route would not go through Lewis County. On the other hand, so many settlers would come in on the train that there would be enough to populate all of western Washington.

People talked, argued, and made their plans for the post-railroad era while work on the track continued at a snail's pace. It was 17 December 1884 before the rails reached Yakima, and July 1888 before the Cascade Branch linked Yakima with Tacoma. By then, the Hammill family had been settled on their Cowlitz River land claim for six or seven years, listening for that locomotive's whistle all the while. Anticipation of the railroad spurred William's efforts to get settled from the moment he helped his pregnant wife and two small children out of their wagon at the end of their overland journey. He wanted to position himself to take advantage of the coming railroad boom, and he had a tremendous lot to do.

The Hammills arrived in Walla Walla, Washington Territory, a few days or weeks before 21 October 1880, the day their third child was born. Walla Walla lies in a grassy plain beside the Walla Walla River, about thirty miles east of its confluence with the Columbia. The settlement had long been a refuge and a jumping-off place for travelers headed down the treacherous thoroughfare of the Columbia River. The Hudson's Bay Company built a trading post at Walla Walla around 1800. A U.S. military fort followed in 1818. The Whitman Mission was built there in 1836, the westernmost outpost of Protestant faith in the far Northwest at that time.

Native Americans destroyed the mission in the Whitman Massacre of November 1847, convinced that white medicine had caused the measles epidemic that decimated their population earlier that year.[5] But the settlement was soon rebuilt. The site was simply too inviting for travelers who, decade after decade, stopped there for rest and refreshment before making their passage on land when they could, in wagon rafts or canoes when they could not, down the river toward Puget Sound, the Willamette Valley, and the Pacific.

Whether she delivered him in the shelter of their covered wagon or in the home of a local family, Lucretia must have been flooded with relief that she was not on the trail when baby John Henry was born. In Walla Walla, she had a midwife or even a doctor to attend her. Local women looked after her and the children while she recovered, and no more travel lay ahead, for a time at least. The plan was for Lou and the children to pass the fall and winter in Walla Walla while William traveled down the Columbia into western Washington to stake his land claim, find a job, and arrange a temporary home for the family until he could build them a cabin of their own.

As soon as his infant son was safely born and his family was situated for the winter, William took the wagon and oxen and headed downriver on the last leg of his journey. His destination was Tumwater, an industrial settlement at the south end of Puget Sound. To reach it, he traveled by water as much as possible to the Cowlitz Landing, where the Cowlitz River flows into the Columbia. The trip could take two months or longer for families traveling with animals and children. William probably made it to the Cowlitz Landing in three or four weeks, arriving at the town of Toledo in the short, dark days of early winter.

No family story has survived to give the details of his trip or explain when and how he found his land on Salkum Creek and the Cowlitz. I see him stopping for a few days at Toledo to talk to the locals about good land in the area. Of course he told them that he needed fast water for a millrace not too far from the big river. One of them might have mentioned the falls on Salkum Creek, maybe even offered to accompany him when he went to take a look. I imagine he left his oxen and wagon in Toledo and hiked the fifteen miles on foot. There were one or two families homesteading nearby that he could pass a night with—the Salem Plant family, for instance, who had purchased 420 acres near Salkum Creek in 1870. They probably looked forward to a visit from a traveler just as eagerly as the traveler looked forward to being received.

William's way was surely wet and muddy, his view of the river obscured by mist and late autumn foliage still clinging to the trees. But when he reached Salkum Creek, he liked what he saw—liked it very much. "Salkum" means "where the water boils up" in the language of the Cowlitz Indians. The waterfall was twenty-five feet high, powerful enough to drive an efficient, modern mill. The creek emptied into the Cowlitz just a mile or so below the falls, in flat meadowland that could accommodate a boat landing and other buildings. I think William staked his claim immediately and hastened to the nearest land office to register it. He paid the U.S. government about twenty-two dollars for 150 acres and a bit over, and only then hitched up his oxen to the wagon and headed up the Cowlitz Trail about sixty miles to Tumwater.

Tumwater, like Salkum, takes its name from a waterfall. The town grew up around the large falls created by the Deschutes River as it empties into South Puget Sound. "Tumwater" echoes the sound of the falling water in the trade language of Chinook. By 1880, several water-powered industries operated there, including two large gristmills. William might have known about those mills before he set out to Washington Territory. He easily found employment at one of them. He also found a cottage to rent for his family, in as settled an area as the territory could offer at that time.[6]

Tumwater in 1880 was a rough, raw, raggedy place, but it was not the wilderness. A railroad spur linked it to Gray's Harbor on the Pacific, and ship traffic could reach it via Puget Sound. It had access

The Cowlitz River at Toledo, Washington.

to goods from distant markets, so in Tumwater one could drink real coffee instead of the homesteaders' brew made from roasted grain or dried peas. And one could purchase milled flour in bags or barrels instead of grinding it painstakingly by hand. A Lewis County settler named Otto Mauermann described how both were done on homesteads in the early days: "My mother made coffee from dried peas, which she roasted.... We raised our own wheat, which was cut by hand and flailed out and cleaned in the wind, and flour for our bread was made by grinding it in coffee mills by hand."[7]

People who couldn't get by with flour they ground in their coffee mills traveled to Tumwater to buy it, carrying it home by pack animal or on their backs. Salem Plant, the settler at Salkum who became William's first neighbor, did this for a decade or more, until the trip became a family joke: "This journey took the greater part of a week as he walked carrying the flour on his back in a homemade packboard made of animal skin, rawhide and red cedar framing.... [He] used most of the flour for biscuits during his travel from Tumwater."[8]

If William Hammill felt somewhat uneasy about bringing his town-bred wife to live on a muddy, mostly vacant street in Tumwater, perhaps he comforted himself with the idea that at least she could make her biscuits from good white flour and wash them down with coffee just as they had done in Virginia. She certainly would not be able to do those things on their homestead, or not at first. With these and other notions in his mind, he turned back down the Cowlitz Trail and traveled again along the Columbia to retrieve his family. He hadn't been away more than three or four months, for the river was still frozen when he reached Walla Walla, and he drove the ox team and wagon into town across the ice.

He may have stayed a few days, resting and visiting with the families who had looked after his wife and children in his absence. But then he wanted to pack up and move on. In the hurry and flurry of loading the children and household goods into the wagon, Lou and William forgot to retrieve the baby from the neighbor woman who was watching him. They had to turn back for John Henry, just a few months old, and set out again for their temporary home in Tumwater.

Their winter journey down the Columbia would have been dramatic in the sleet and snow. I imagine them watching the high, dry, snow-dusted grassland east of the Cascades give way to Ponderosa and jack pine as the trail climbed the mountains' eastern slopes. As they descended through the gorge to the west of Mt. Hood, forests of western hemlock, red cedar, and Douglas fir crowded around them, heavy with deep, wet snow.

Then as now, snow turns to rain as one descends the mountains' western slopes. The air is moist and raw. Rushing brooks tumble down rocky beds. Undergrowth is thick; mountain shrubs, some still with leaves, tangle at one's feet. The earth is spongy. Great fallen logs decay on every side, heavy with moss. Moss hangs from the limbs of the trees above. The sky is distant, just a gray blur between the treetops. There are hills, lots of them, and waterfalls. Wherever the ground has been disturbed, there is mud.

Mud is ubiquitous in the Pacific Northwest at every season but high summer. It can be a very good thing for everyone but the housewife. Ezra Meeker's pamphlet praises western Washington's soil but omits to describe the rain that turns it into muck. He quickly moves on to the beauty of western forests, a safer topic:

> One-half of the surface of our Territory West of the Cascade Mountains, is a strong brown clay loam, fertile and productive, eminently calculated, when cleared up and judiciously farmed, to make, in our equable climate, a good wheat growing country, as well as all other cereals. . . . This region is principally timbered, . . . and in many places more beautiful or majestic forests were never viewed by man. This consists of fir, cedar, hemlock, spruce and pine, interspersed, in favorable localities, with alder, ash, crab-apple, wild cherry, and balm. Underneath all this is an intermixture of underbrush, consisting of hazle, tag-alder, willow, hard hack, vine maple, huckleberry, and an evergreen known as sal-lal.

I hope that Lucretia rose above her housewife's dismay and saw beauty and possibility beyond the splashing mud and drizzling mist that greeted her in February 1881. Surely she was relieved to set up housekeeping in their rented cottage, small and drab as it must have been, when at last they arrived in Tumwater.

The family passed a year and more in Tumwater. William worked at the gristmill and saved his money, then left Lou and the children in town while he went off to build a cabin for them on the homestead. In his absence, Lou was much distressed by a band of Indians who loitered around Tumwater cadging meals. One man in particular unnerved her. He was persistent and, as Lou put it, "so ugly."[9] She once gave him a piece of pie to get rid of him, and after that he would never leave her alone. At last a neighbor man shooed him away. But when, a few months later, William transported his family to the homestead, the same band of Indians with Lou's ugly nemesis were encamped on Salkum Creek not a mile from the cabin.

When Lou told this story to her grandchildren, they took it as funny a joke on her. But it certainly had not been funny to Lou. Her chagrin kept the incident alive in her mind for forty years. She never explained what she meant by "ugly," but a generation later, when a man called Indian John pestered her son's family, one of her grandchildren remembered him like this:

> He never knocked. Many a woman, including Mom, emitted a startled squeak upon looking up from her work to see him standing silently before her in the kitchen doorway. . . . He lived down on the river below Salkum—old, rotund and smelling of fish. I remember only once when he sat down at our table and ate with the family. It must have been a Sunday afternoon. He had no table manners. We nearly gagged at the sight, sound and smell of him.[10]

Perhaps the Indian who bothered Lou was also silent, fat, and reeked of fish. Startling and all too present, these men were among other things a reminder that not so long before, Salkum Creek and Tumwater and all the rest had belonged to their people, not hers.

While Lou stayed in Tumwater, dealing with Indians and other aggravations, William worked on their cabin on the Cowlitz. He built it on the bluff above the river, felling the giant cedars himself, trimming them up, and raising the squared-off logs into place with the help of neighbor men. Like the Virginia home he had left behind, the cabin and its surrounding farmyard could have been called River View. But it was a far cry from the comfortable household he had been raised in. The cabin consisted of two rooms with a loft above and a root cellar below ground in back where Lou could set out her milk pans as well as store her fruit and vegetables and home-canned goods. The big iron cookstove could heat all of it in that damp but rarely freezing climate. Whether relief or dismay prevailed when William settled his wife and children in the completed cabin, no story survives to say. Probably it was a mixture of both.

William soon built his boat landing on the Cowlitz and cleared land for planting. Still, the dense forest dominated his place and everyone else's. People eventually realized that the true riches of that country lay in its timber, but in William's day, the trees were an encumbrance and even a threat. A year or two after the Hammills were settled, they accompanied a neighbor man, a Mr. Mitchell, into the town of Chehalis to welcome Mitchell's bride, who was arriving by train from Canada. Many years later, Mrs. Mitchell told her children how frightening she had found the ride to her new home in Salkum. Huge trees crowded out the light along the mud track. They seemed sinister, "dripping with moss, and she was sure that every big clump of moss was a bear!"[11]

View of the Cowlitz River from the Hammill homestead site. William's boat landing is now the parking lot for a salmon hatchery.

This story, too, was told as a joke in later years, but was the incident funny to Mrs. Mitchell? Not likely. Lucretia Hammill held onto her Iowa land for twenty-six years after her move to Washington. She didn't sell out to her brother Henry until 1906. It might have comforted her to know through all those years that there was an alternative they could take, that life in a settled country was possible if Washington Territory proved too difficult a challenge.

When they moved into their cabin in the spring of 1882, William was thirty-eight and Lou was thirty-six. The children were six, four, and one. Twins, a boy and a girl, were born in 1884. Lou named them Harriet Cofrode and Harrison Strickler in remembrance of her beloved Virginia relatives, the Cofrodes and the Stricklers, showing that she was a woman of strong attachments who kept in touch with people back home. A fourth son, Edward William, was born in 1885, when Lou was nearly forty. A year or two later came a baby girl who lived just a few days. The couple's first baby had also been a girl who soon perished; Lou's childbearing years began and ended with baby girls who did not survive. The remaining six children, including John Henry, my grandfather, lived to marry and raise families of their own.

The Hammills were welcomed to the Salkum area by the Salem Plant family, among others. The Plants had been accustomed to traveling fifteen miles on foot to Toledo to pick up their mail, and nearly sixty miles to Tumwater when they needed flour. William Hammill's landing was a boon to them and other early settlers, for small Cowlitz River steamers could then ascend as far as Salkum, carrying mail and household goods for sale. People who lived north of the river canoed down Salkum Creek, tied up at the falls on William Hammill's claim, and walked the rest of the way to the landing to pick up their mail and buy bluing for the wash, hairpins and clothespins, sugar, coffee, flour, and other basics. Then they carried their purchases back to the falls, loaded them into their canoes, and made their way slowly upstream to their homes.[12]

The early 1880s brought a number of new families to the neighborhood: the Mitchells, the Bezemers, the Atwoods, and others. The Atwood homestead was just west of the Hammills, fronting on the river right next to William's landing. In the spring of 1885, Jacob Buesch purchased one acre of land from the Atwoods and one from the Hammills at the landing and built a grocery and drygoods store on the river. The Salkum Post Office opened in the fall on the same two acres.[13] The store and post office were accessible by road as well as by water, simplifying life for those who had traveled to the landing by canoe.

By the end of 1885, a modest commercial settlement had grown up around the Hammill landing. People called it Salkum after the nearby creek, and settlers continued to sift slowly in. Salem Plant gave land for a cemetery a short walk from the landing. The first burial there was that of the Hammills' baby girl around 1887. As his own children reached school age, William gave money to help build a one-room school. Sometime in the mid- to late 1880s, encouraged by Salkum's budding development and always listening to the promise of a railroad soon to come, William Hammill set about fulfilling his great western dream. He began to build his mill.

23

THE MILL ON SALKUM CREEK

―――――――――― ❧ ――――――――――

*T*HE HAMMILL mill had opened for business by 1891, as a photograph of that date attests. It might have opened a year or two earlier. The photograph shows a tall, spare structure of milled lumber with a sharply angled roof, standing on a dirt road where wagons and men pause before its wide doors. The hillside around it is littered with fallen saplings, debris that was left after the timber was cut for the mill. But what catches the eye is the immense steel flume stretching across the ravine between Salkum Creek and the mill's upper story, and the great wooden trestles that support it. The flume captured rushing water from the natural falls above, channeled that water across the ravine, and dropped it into the penstock, a vertical steel pipe that forced the water against the blades of a turbine below. The turbine then drove the sawing or grinding mechanism of the mill.

Turbine technology transformed the milling industry toward the middle of the nineteenth century, ending the era of picturesque old mills with gigantic vertical waterwheels rotating beside them. Water

turbines operating invisibly deep inside the mill were far more efficient and powerful. For example, in 1870 the Garland sawmill in
Lancaster, New Hampshire, ran nine enormous vertical waterwheels
that together produced a total of seventy horsepower to drive its five
saws. By 1880, the mill had replaced its nine waterwheels with four
state-of-the-art water turbines. They drove a ten-bladed gang saw
at seventy-five horsepower, utilizing a sixteen-foot drop of water
against the turbines.[1]

The Hammill mill operated at eighty-five horsepower with just
one turbine, for it had the advantage of a forty-eight-foot water
drop. Its very tall millhouse was built to accommodate that forty-
eight-foot penstock. The great flume was expensive, certainly, but
perhaps not as expensive as two or more turbines would have been.
So William Hammill made full use of that plunging waterfall on

The Hammill mill, c. 1891. ❧ Photo courtesy of Hal Hammill Jr.

Salkum Creek. Like the mill he had run for his father in Virginia, his mill was equipped for grinding grain and also sawing lumber. In winter and spring months, when ripe grain was not available, he could keep his equipment busy and his cash flow intact by producing and selling lumber for homes, barns, and other structures.

For processing the grain, the mill ran a smut machine and a bolting machine, a pair of French grinding burrs, and a silk sieve for sifting the flour.[2] The first two of these were and still are standard milling equipment. Smut machines clean the grain by fanning air through it, blowing off dirt and chaff. Bolters separate the bran from the grain and can be adjusted to produce various mixes of whole wheat and white flour. The silk sieve, on the other hand, was top of the line, giving a fine-textured white flour, and granite grindstones from France were considered the very best that money could buy.

Though the technical details are missing for William's wood saws, they would have been of equally high quality. As the photograph suggests, his mill was an engineering marvel in that frontier community. It had the potential to support a development boom in Lewis County and to make its owner a prosperous man.

Several years went into building the mill and its outbuildings, which included a plastered granary where wheat and flour could be stored. William had his priorities; the cabin his family lived in did not have plastered walls. The construction provided a good deal of entertainment as well as some employment for local men. Mrs. Buesch, wife of the grocery-store owner at the landing, described in a letter what a wonder it was when a great stern-wheeler built for heavy shipping came up the Cowlitz from Portland carrying equipment for the mill: "This boat so close to the Mayfield Chasm was a strange sight, and perhaps the first and last stern-wheeler that came."[3]

Mrs. Buesch observed that Mr. Hammill "put quite a lot of money" to his mill. No doubt he did; where did the money come from? For the most part, he probably built and paid as he went. But

I think some came from his father, probably in the form of equipment. Perhaps his father ordered and paid for the stone burrs from France that were shipped around the Horn to San Francisco or Portland, then to William's landing by steamer. Perhaps the water turbine made by Poole & Hunt of Baltimore—the one that bankrupted Hugh Hammill—had been purchased for William's mill. Did the father go broke helping his son to set up in business? Hugh was still hard at work in the 1880s; he lived nearly twenty years after William left Virginia, and he did not sell his farm until 1889. So the answer could easily be yes.

Tensions ran high as the mill went up. The equipment was complex, and it was coming from a host of different cities, by sailing ship, steamer, railroad car, and wagon. One family story captures William's anxiety and his wife's exasperation over a prolonged delay. The source of the story was John Henry, William's son, but it is told here by William's grandson, my father, to whom Lou and William were Grandma and Grandpa:

> About the only time [John Henry] saw his father angry was when they were working to get the mill ready. They had come to the house at noon for their dinner, and Grandpa said he could not understand why it was taking the man at Toledo so long to get the machine ready. Grandma replied, "If you don't stop taking him honey and a side of bacon every time you go to see about it, he will never get it done."
>
> Grandpa's anger flared at this remark but he made no reply. He turned to the boys and said, "We must get back to our work." At the unusual sight of their father's anger the boys followed meekly, and they worked through the long afternoon with no food since breakfast.[4]

There must have been other such moments, especially when in 1888 the transcontinental railroad began operating and the boom at last was on. Was the Hammill mill ready for the rush? I think it was almost ready, not quite ready ... then one day it was ready, and a new kind of excitement and tension reigned.

Between 1888 and 1893, the mood in western Washington was exuberant, even manic. As if to celebrate its entry into the modern era, in 1889 the territory became a state. In 1893 a second transcontinental railway, the Great Northern, began passenger service. Seattle boomed—it was "the boomingest city in the world!" One historian described how settlers from all over the United States packed the trains to Washington:

> For the poor farmer, there was a cheap rail ticket and cheap
> land, credit easy to come by, friendships easy to make, bankers,
> merchants, and neighbors eager to help him "get established." ...
> If a man came west with real money for investment ... he might
> organize a railroad company, build a lumber mill, a cannery, a
> brick factory, a land company, or even found a city.[5]

William Hammill was fortunate enough to belong in the second category. He and his family, old-timers now, welcomed newcomers and encouraged them to get settled so they could buy and sell along with everyone else.

In those giddy days, rumors flew. Lewis County was to be divided; at about eighty miles long and thirty miles wide, it was too big, too populous for a single county, so it would be divided and Mossyrock, that wondrously lucky village just east of Salkum, would be the new county seat. Every mile between the Canada and Oregon borders was studded with surveyors' stakes as hopeful speculators platted new towns and villages and people who were just off the train signed notes and bought a lot or two or three.[6]

Salem Plant, the settler who had waited longer than anyone else for civilization to come to Salkum, could not contain his excitement at the promise that lay ahead. The *Chehalis Bee* reported in March

1889 that Plant had walked into their newspaper office "to make a little kick":

> He says Chehalis feels so sure in her position, that all railroads to be built must pay her tribute that she forgets other towns. Salkum has hopes and promises of a railroad, and like Chehalis they can't miss her if they tap the Cowlitz valley or use the Cowlitz pass. . . . There is a wealth of timber and coal in the neighborhood of Salkum, while for many miles up and down the valley the land is of superior quality for hops, grass, grain, fruit and general farm products. . . . The Cowlitz valley is an empire of itself in position, resource, and extent, a garden in fertility, a mine of vast richness in coal and minerals, a field of unexcelled profit in lumbering, and can not long remain undeveloped. Her star is in the ascendant.[7]

The Northern Pacific had abandoned its plans for a Cowlitz Valley route more than a decade earlier, but citizens of the valley had not abandoned their hopes. Anything was possible! Everything was probable! I hear a note of mockery in the newspaper clip, but did its readers? I think they took every word as plain fact.

The Hammills felt the edge of excitement along with everyone else. William milled flour for the local people to start with—people like Salem Plant, who raised some wheat or needed more than the bushel or two of flour that they could buy at the Salkum store. Other customers came by wagon from settlements upriver, on the other side of the Mayfield Chasm. The mill was a tremendous convenience to those living in Silver Creek, Mossyrock, Mayfield, Cinebar, and other villages to the east because riverboats could not cross the rapids to reach them. They had been packing their flour from Tumwater for decades, and were heartily tired of doing so. If they couldn't make the round trip in the course of a day, the Hammills gave them supper and put them up in the barn for the night. That made a holiday interlude for settlers who rarely left their farms.

The Hammill family enjoyed the company most of the time. Some visitors they probably could have done without. One fellow, a Mr. Doss from Klickitat Prairie, north and east of Salkum, was known for his "humorous attitude." A story about him goes like this:

> [M]y Grandfather had a few sacks of wheat that he needed ground for bread and he asked Doss if he thought that the mill on Mill Creek in the Salkum area could grind that in time so he could get back home the same day. Doss said, "Hell yes! That is a fast outfit, they grind one grain of wheat and when they get through with that, they jump right on the next one!"[8]

It's true that the Hammill mill did not operate on Saturdays or Sundays. Sunday was the Lord's day, and on Saturdays William filed the grindstones to keep them in perfect repair. But on weekdays the mill most certainly did not grind wheat one grain at a time. Mr. Doss's witticism does not amuse me. It wouldn't have amused William, either. He needed good publicity and all the customers he could get.

I like to think that the mill's first few years were promising, showing modest growth and the expectation of more growth to come. But in the end it failed. William Hammill was out of the milling business by 1901. What happened? The family story runs thus: "(a) the rains that came at harvest time often got the grain wet and it was in poor condition when brought to the mill, (b) the wheat grown locally did not make the best flour, and (c) let's face it, Western Washington is not wheat climate!"[9]

So its failure was William's fault. He understood well enough how to build a mill, but not how to size up its chances for success in a new country. He was a technician, not a businessman. If he had had more savvy, he would have overcome his dislike of the high plains and found a homestead east of the mountains in that good wheat country near Walla Walla, where his mill might have succeeded.

But this explanation overlooks a major economic event of the 1890s, the Panic of 1893 and the four-year depression that followed. How short our memories are! William built his mill in the late 1880s, a period of rapid economic expansion. In the spring of 1893, a financial panic on Wall Street precipitated once again by railroad stock collapses forced the whole country out of its boom cycle and into bust. Washington State was hit especially hard. In the Puget Sound area, railway and mill closures resulted in huge numbers of unemployed men, maybe as much as 25 percent of the workforce.[10]

When Jacob Coxey, an Ohio quarryman, created his Industrial Army of the unemployed and planned a march on Washington, D.C., demanding government intervention on their behalf, Seattle mustered up fifteen hundred men to join him. More men joined from Tacoma, nearby. The idea was to meet at the town of Puyallup and head toward the capital on the Northern Pacific railroad. Predictably, the railroad refused to carry the men, and eventually most dispersed homeward. But these events and the panic that created them were the most dramatic and calamitous in Northwest history up to that time.

The "waves of catastrophe" brought about by the panic swept over Salkum as they did over larger towns.[11] Salem Plant, that early settler who anticipated the boom with such enthusiastic excitement, had taken out a note from a Chehalis bank in 1888. When the depression hit, he could not repay it. There was no demand for his crop of hops and no money to be had for additional financing, and he lost all but fifteen acres of his 420-acre spread.[12]

David Ainslie, who lived some miles southwest of Salkum near the community of Winlock, purchased eighty acres of timberland and built a sawmill there in the early 1880s. In 1884, he expanded his operation, financing a much larger sawmill, a hotel, several miles of railroad track, and a store, all on credit from a Portland, Oregon, bank. He incorporated as the town of Ainslie, and the Oregon bank was about to open a branch office there when the panic struck. The bank called the loan and the boomtown of Ainslie vanished practically overnight.[13]

Another townsite by the name of Ferry, located on the Cowlitz just above the Mayfield Chasm, met a similar fate. It was owned and promoted by a one-time Salkum resident, Klaus Bezemer, and his partner, a Mr. Bridges. An observer told the story: "There was the usual advertising as to the superior advantages of location, soil, climate, and resources. It was claimed that Mr. K. Bezemer was the author of the phrase or slogan 'tickle the soil with a hoe and it will smile with a harvest.'" Ferry had a sawmill, a blacksmith shop, a school, a store, a post office, and a Masonic temple—but when the panic hit, the town quickly faded away.

Many men who owned homesteads in the area were employed in the large lumber mills of Chehalis and Gray's Harbor. They boarded in those towns, visiting their families monthly or less often. Some who lost their jobs simply picked up and moved to other communities, abandoning their homesteads and even their wives and children. Immigration to the upper Cowlitz came to a shattering halt, then inched backward as settlers moved out instead of in. The commercial development that William Hammill had prepared for became a retreat. Population dwindled, erasing hopes that Salkum would develop just as Toledo had done a couple of decades earlier.

Traditionally, a miller was paid in "shares," or a percentage of the flour he produced for a customer. In a good market, he could sell that flour to families who did not grow their own wheat. But in the panic and the four-year depression that followed, people had no money for flour. They bartered for it when they could, and begged for credit when they could not. No doubt William kept a good many of his neighbors in flour at his own expense. More flour accumulated in his granary, unsold.

In a good market, a miller sells bran and other leavings to local farmers as animal feed. In a bad market, he feeds the leavings to his own hogs and cattle. William did this, driving his fattened hogs to Napavine and his cattle to Toledo, where railway spurs could carry them to city markets. But in that depressed economy, he could not get enough for his livestock to make raising them worthwhile. He slaughtered the animals for his own family's use. The Hammills ate very well during the depression—meat and flour aplenty. But they had no money to spend.

In a bad market, prices of commodities drop. The Northwest's exports of wheat and flour had begun to decline even in the late 1880s, but the market plummeted sharply in 1894.[14] That year, a price war raged over flour. Newspaper headlines shouted out, "Big news! Mills sell as low as $2.25 a barrel!" Just a few years earlier, a bushel of wheat brought seventy cents.[15] Figuring 4.5 bushels of wheat per barrel of flour, the price of flour had dropped more than 28 percent. The cheap flour may have helped scrimping consumers, at least in the short term, but millers' profits vanished, and wheat farmers' did, too.

On top of these problems came unusually bad weather. In the summer of 1894, heavy rains ruined crops just at harvest time. More newspaper headlines: "Walla Walla County suffers its only crop-failure; rain, having started in August, causes wheat to sprout in sack."[16] Rain like that in Walla Walla meant deluges west of the mountains. The Columbia flooded disastrously that year, pouring in peoples' windows and sweeping away buildings. One man remembered, "My brother and I took a sailboat and sailed all over what is now the site of Longview, Washington."[17] Smaller rivers in the Columbia watershed flooded, too. No wonder the family remembered that the wheat William received for milling was in poor condition. It had been soaked.

If the depression had subsided in a year or two, William Hammill's milling business might have recovered. But it continued through 1895 and 1896, two more years of "desperate hard times!"[18] It was too long. When the Klondike Gold Rush of 1897 precipitated another boom in the Northwest, many small businessmen found that the familiar economy of their world had been transformed. Suddenly railroads dominated commerce, and roads, not waterways, provided access to them. Towns prospered at railway hubs and along the highways that led to them. Consumers hitched their teams to their wagons and drove into town to visit the shops and buy their supplies.

Settlements like Salkum had been built in the expectation that the new era of railway commerce would coexist with water transport, even depend on it. But roads had become king instead. The Salkum post office moved north to the new White Pass highway. Jacob Buesch's grocery store and William Hammill's boat landing fell into disrepair. No more steamers came; their route once more stopped at Toledo, at the old Cowlitz Landing. At last even those steamers ceased to run. The upper Cowlitz remained nearly empty of traffic until the timber boom of the late teens and 1920s, when rafts of logs went careening downstream to the big sawmills at Longview and Kelso.

Still other factors were operating against William Hammill. During the years of depression, the ongoing experiment of wheat farming in western Washington collapsed for good. "Bitter experience" had taught that the forested lands west of the Cascades could not compete with the eastern prairies in raising grains.[19] The *Evergreen State Souvenir*, published for the Washington State exhibit at Chicago's Columbian Exposition of 1893, puts it this way: "Wheat and oats yield splendidly [west of the Cascades], and the quality ranks A1 ... yet grain-raising, except oats, is not generally followed, because other crops are far more profitable."[20]

For William to succeed, he would have needed to operate like the big flouring mills at Tumwater, which "import large quantities of wheat from Oregon and California, in addition to that obtained from the farmers, and supply not only the local demand ... but ship to British Columbia and the Northern markets."[21] But this major commercial operation is not at all what William had in mind, nor was he financially capable of it. He wanted to operate a local mill for his neighbors in the community, like the ones that were scattered throughout the East when he was a boy—like the one his father ran for so many years in Virginia. But his neighbors stopped growing wheat. When the economy improved enough to give them a little money to spend, they purchased their flour in Chehalis and enjoyed the visit to town. The opportunity for a mill like William's passed right out from under him. He took a gamble on how the economy of a frontier region would develop, and he lost his bet.

Of course, it could have been worse. William did not lose his land or his mill equipment. He sold off some of the machinery, perhaps including that costly water turbine, and he used the plastered granary for storage and extra sleeping space. The rest of the mill slowly settled back into the damp soil beneath it. In 1925 it washed away when a mill dam upstream burst apart during heavy rains.

By then, William had sold out and was living in the city of Olympia, just a few miles from Tumwater, where he had begun his Northwest adventure more than forty years earlier. In 1923, a lumbering firm called the Chehalis Mill Company had bought him out, paying him fifteen thousand dollars, or about $166 an acre, for his excellent timberland and his location on the Cowlitz. Considering that the land had cost him virtually nothing, it was an excellent return. The money enabled him and his wife to enjoy the comforts and conveniences of a modern home in town during their last years.

Did William's father know that the mill was in trouble? Hugh died in 1896, during the depression that followed the panic. William's sisters notified him by letter, addressing him as "Billy," and they say of their father, "He knew his time had come." So Hugh died alert and aware. He probably did know that William was struggling, but he died before the mill closed its doors for good.

In the end, both father and son saw their milling ventures collapse. The great difference was that Hugh sold out at the age of seventy-nine, at the end of his working life. William was fifty in 1894, fifty-six in 1900. He had thirty years to live after the failure of his mill, and a wife and children to support. He could not fold up and get out as his father had done. Instead, he and his family eked out a living by farming that rich though stony soil along the Cowlitz.

For the first time in three generations, the Hammill family had no trade—no blacksmithing, no wagon building, no lumber or flour milling—to help support them. They had no wildly profitable cash crop to take to market, as the first John Hammill had with tobacco. Nor could they lease out a part of their land for rental income, as the first Hugh had done; there would simply have been no takers.

They had a great big garden and cherry trees; they had chickens and eggs. William ran a dairy herd and sold the milk to the creamery in Chehalis. He raised hogs, too, some for home use, and some to sell. He may have sold his honey when he could. They had trout, salmon, and bass from the river and kept a fine table, but they had little money to spend. Like their Scots forebears who transplanted themselves to Ireland nearly three hundred years earlier, they lived as frontier farmers, wiping the mud from their boots at night and the wet mist from their faces by day. In this, they were like their neighbors, but they were living a very different life from the one they had known in Virginia, a very different life from the one they had hoped to create.

How did William think about the mill in after years? How did he tell the story to himself, in the privacy of his thoughts? Chagrin and disappointment must have ebbed with time, until he could chuckle silently over life's ironic tricks. But sometimes, as he hauled another load of gravel or milked another cow, the beauty of the mill must have come before his eyes. The perfection of those French grinding burrs, the sleek drop of the penstock, the power of the steel turbine as the water rushed against it, the wondrous sight and sound of ripe wheat pouring into the hopper, the flour, light and white, dancing through the sieve—ah, it had been a beautiful thing, that mill. All

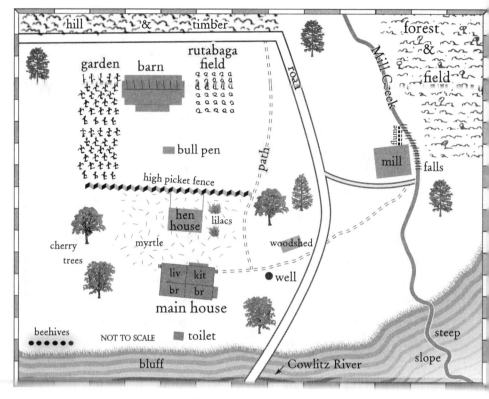

The Hammill homestead.

the years it stood empty on the creek, it must have reminded him of his southern boyhood, his young man's dreams, and his love for the trade he had been raised in. It linked him to his past. The one legacy of his efforts is that Salkum Creek is now called Mill Creek, a reminder that his mill once operated there.

24

WILLIAM AND LUCRETIA
HAMMILL, PIONEER FOLK

───────── ❧ ─────────

*L*IKE EARLIER generations of the Hammill family, William and
Lucretia did not think about how they might present their
choices to those who came after them. The very idea would have
seemed like an absurdity to them. We were just trying to get along,
they would say to anyone who asked. Nor does any document reveal
them accidentally, as William's father, Hugh, was revealed in his
court testimony after the Civil War. But there are some clues to
their appearance and personalities in a collection of reminiscences
from friends and family who knew them in their later years, and
in a handful of photographs taken in the last few decades of their
lives.

These are wonderful things, yet they present two aspects of one
conundrum. First, what can representations of people in their old
age tell us about them in their youth? And second, what can the
recollections of children reveal about adult motives and concerns?

People change in looks and in character as they grow old, and children remember what they see and hear in the moment, as it pertains to them. They give no context, no interpretation.

The Centralia, Washington, *Daily Chronicle* carried a picture of William and Lucretia in its bicentennial edition of 4 July 1976. In it, the couple stands in their dooryard like Grant Wood's farmer and his wife, relics of a bygone era even when the photograph was taken around 1923. William is tall, gaunt, dressed in his work overalls with a great white beard spread over his chest, his narrow face deeply lined, his eyes deep-set, his wavy white hair cut rather long. He may or may not be smiling; something about his face suggests it, but too much beard and mustache is in the way to be sure.

Short and plump, with a round, unsmiling face and her hands clasped perhaps nervously before her aproned waist, Lucretia stands slightly apart from her husband. Her hair is pulled tightly back, her skirt nearly brushes the ground. They are pioneer folk, like thousands of others still living in the Northwest in the 1920s. Their clapboard house stands behind them. The original hewn-log cabin had burned around 1920, and their adult children helped them build this new home of milled lumber. It even boasts a small covered porch.

In another photo of Lou alone, taken perhaps in 1900 when she was in her early fifties, she wears a Sunday dress of silk with a ladylike tucked bod-

Lucretia Soule Hammill, c. 1900.
Photo courtesy of Roxie Hammill Wilcox

ice and an elegant white lace bow tie at her throat. Her jaw is firm, her mouth stern with just a hint of smile. Only her left eye meets the camera.

William and Lucretia Hammill on their homestead, 1923.
Photo courtesy of Hal Hammill Jr.

Another, somewhat later photo shows her in a blouse with a rich satiny collar, wearing glasses. The glasses cannot hide the fact that she was cross-eyed. Not a word of family lore concerns this defect. Like many other conditions that today would be considered intolerable, in her lifetime that crossed eye was simply a given. One wonders what other physical shortcomings went without mention in this family's long history, and what they might explain if they could be seen.

Beside this little gallery of photos I place a group of reminiscences typed up years after William's death by one of his grandsons, my father. The first ones describe the old man's formidable strength:

> Grandpa was a large, powerful man, probably six feet, two inches tall and weighing 225 pounds. Seemingly, he was inexhaustible. His physical prowess was legendary. One of those legends concerns a day, one of those innumerable days, when Grandpa and two of his grown sons were hauling rocks. . . .
> The sons were tired and cross with this tedious, never-ending job. They began to quarrel about something real or imagined. Grandpa was patient and extremely taciturn. Finally, he lost his patience but not his taciturnity. Without a word, he grasped each son by the nape of the neck and knocked their heads together. For the rest of that load nobody said a word. . . .
>
> Grandpa was the best man in the community with the scythe or cradle. Every farmer in the area wanted him to mow their hay and to cradle, bundle and shock their grain. He could do as much of this work as two or three ordinary men. When the new, mechanical reaper, so the story goes, was first being demonstrated in the community, one farmer, watching it perform, said to another, "If I can't get Mr. Hammill this summer, I think I'll try to get this machine." [A second] version is that one farmer said, "I believe that machine goes as fast as Mr. Hammill." "Yes," responded the other, "but it doesn't cut as wide a swath."

His last great physical feat occurred when he was in his late 70s, shortly before he sold the farm and moved to Olympia. He was leading his bull, "Duke" to water when the animal, without warning, attacked him from the rear. Although knocked down and injured by the first impact, Grandpa seized the bull's horns and struggled with him, holding his own with him pretty well until help arrived.

[Another time,] one of Grandpa's cows disappeared. A few days later we learned that she was with the herd of a neighbor who lived about a mile up the river. After milking the next morning, Grandpa saddled up his two work horses, Fanny and Polly. He climbed up on Fanny and held Polly while I climbed up into the saddle. Then he started off through the woods toward the neighbor's place, calling his cows to follow. And they did. When we got to the neighbor's fence, the wandering cow dashed quickly up to the fence, wanting to join her own herd. The neighbor let her out. Grandpa turned around and started back home, calling his cows behind him, with me bringing up the rear on Polly. When we got home I tried to get off Polly, but my coat got caught on the saddle horn and held me suspended, kicking and squirming but unable to get free. Grandpa came, chuckling silently, reached up with one hand, and lifted me down as easily as if I were a baby.[1]

These passages do indeed portray William's amazing strength and stamina, the legacy in part of handling heavy mill equipment all his life. His habit of silence is evident, too—good-humored most of the time, but with limits. Besides these personal details, my father's recollections capture vivid moments in the daily round of a farming community at the turn of the twentieth century. But they indicate little about William's interactions with adults. From the child's point of view, he is a kindly giant of formidable powers. Like the white-bearded figure in the pioneer photograph, he would not be out of place in a fairy tale.

This next passage describes the original hewn-cedar cabin that William built about 1882. It burned down around 1920, when my father was a child of eleven:

It seemed low, dark, and at least partially covered by vines. It smelled . . . of leather, home-made bread, cookies, and apple butter, and honey. . . . I remember the root house well, especially the pans of milk which sat in rows on shelves until the cream had risen and had been skimmed off. The cream went into butter, coffee, cooking, etc. The skimmed milk went mostly into the hogs, calves, and chickens, although some of it was used for cottage cheese, and for letting sour to become clabber. Being mostly underground, the root house was always cool and dark.

Nearby was the well, with its windlass, rope, and moss-covered wooden bucket. Once, I was stunned when hit on the head by the handle of the windlass. I was probably 8–10 — so small that the handle of the windlass, at the top of its orbit, was higher than my head. And, in reaching up above my head, I lacked the strength to push the windlass over the top. On this occasion, the handle slipped from my grasp, flew around, and struck the top of my head which boasted a lump the size of an egg for some time.

A bluff about 150 feet high flanked the creek and river. At one point the house stood within 100 feet of the bluff. Beehives, perhaps a dozen of them, stood by the bluff which also served as a stage, from which Grandpa called his cows, when milking time approached. When he called, the cows would answer, their faint mooing wafting up . . . from the distant river bottom. In half an hour they would be at the barn, ready for their rutabagas and/or hay.

Grandpa robbed the bee hives himself. What tasty honey it was! No wonder Grandma's biscuits were so good. . . . As if it

were yesterday, I can see that large kitchen—the three of us
eating, or Grandpa, after the meal, sitting gaunt and stooped,
pondering, or chuckling into his white beard, or napping a few
minutes before he and I returned to the field.

And Grandma—tiny, white haired, shuffling about her
kitchen on her bent, feeble legs, mumbling to herself, being too
nearly deaf to realize that she might be heard by others.[2]

Again, my father provides invaluable information of the kind
a child collects, washed with adult nostalgia for a vanished past. I
notice William's rapport with his cows and horses, a talent that has
fallen by the wayside in most modern lives. My father once taught
me how to call cattle, hoping to keep me quiet on a car trip. The call
was "soo boss." It wouldn't surprise me to learn that William's great-
great-grandfather John in Maryland and earlier forebears in Ireland
and Scotland called their cows in exactly the same way.

Here is one more passage describing the homestead, this one by a
granddaughter, my Aunt Roxie:

It was a beautiful walk down the puncheon road which led past
the church and to the Hammill farm. One walked along under
the majestic trees where it was nearly dark at midday. Ferns
and dainty wild flowers grew in the dense shade, and there was
the "Sheep's Sorrel," a plant resembling clover, but with much
larger leaves from which we sucked the acid-sweet juice. Along
the bank of the road grew nettles, and the tall beautiful "Devil's
Club" with its bright red berries and sharp thorns. Here, too,
were the salmon berries, so called because of their bright yellow
color and berries shaped like large raspberries. There were many
of the huckleberry bushes native to our region. These had small
light green leaves and small bright red berries. . . .

I remember [the well's] wooden bucket and the cool water
which tasted so pure and sweet. The cedar lining of the well

naturally attracted insects, so three or four trout were kept in the water to devour them. Sometimes, when lowering the heavy, water soaked bucket into the well it would strike and kill one of the trout. We watched, and if one was seen floating on the surface, we dipped it out and put in another.

Behind the house were the big cherry trees. The ground there was level but full of gravel, and Grandma had planted the ground cover known as myrtle over that area. It made a beautiful carpet with its evergreen foliage and purple flowers. A path led through the trees to the high bluff where the honey bees were kept. We children were always warned not to go near the bees. . . . The only form of ornamental planting I remember, aside from the myrtle I have mentioned, were the two old fashioned lilacs that grew in front of the chicken house. One was white and the other purple.[3]

Roxie is alive to the irretrievable loveliness of this home place and to the delights of a childhood passed within it. Like my father, she remembers a fairyland in which a tiny, white-haired grandmother and towering but beneficent grandfather are exactly what one would expect.

In Roxie's eyes, even William's rigorous Methodism is charming. She recounts an incident from the first years of her marriage: "Grandpa stood on the front porch looking at the hay in the shock in our field. He asked what kind it was, said it was a heavy crop for volunteer hay, then after a short pause he said, 'You didn't shock it on Sunday, did you?'"[4] Fifty years earlier, when William gave the orders and his sons obeyed, the question would have made them squirm. Now it has no force—to his granddaughter, it is quaint and nothing more.

These children adored their grandparents, that is clear, and they were raised in a region of exquisite natural beauty whose memory grew more luminous as the decades passed. Inevitably, their recollections reveal little about William and Lucretia as they were in themselves, as adults, coping with a frontier existence in the last decades of the nineteenth century. For that, a contemporary voice is needed—the voice of an individual who shared their lives in that community as an adult himself.

Happily, such an individual exists. He is the Reverend William J. Rule, a Methodist minister who was appointed to three years on the Upper Cowlitz circuit beginning in late December 1893. Fifty years later he took the trouble to sit down and write about his experiences. His little book, *Riding the Upper Cowlitz Circuit*, touches on the area's early history, its people, and his efforts to bring spiritual comfort in adverse times. His sweet temper and determination coupled with a profound ignorance of frontier life quickly won over the hardscrabble settlers he lived and worked with. In capturing the texture of daily experience with humor and insight, he wins over today's reader as well.

William J. Rule arrived in Lewis County, Washington, as a young man in his very early twenties. Judging by his photographs, he was about five feet, two inches tall and as thin and light as a child, with a mustache on his upper lip to show that despite appearances he had reached adulthood. He had finished his seminary training in the state of Michigan in the spring of 1893 and had reported for duty in Seattle as the Methodist Conference directed. He spent several months as the circuit preacher in a mill town on Puget Sound, and when the mill closed for winter, the Seattle Conference sent him off to the Upper Cowlitz. They gave him a train ticket to Chehalis and directions to a livery stable near the station that would furnish him with a horse for the rest of his journey. They explained that the circuit needed a young man unencumbered by a family, but they didn't tell him why.

Rule arrived at Chehalis on December 21 to find that the livery had only one horse available, furnished with a sidesaddle. The horse had been readied for a schoolmarm who never appeared. No matter;

Rule climbed up and rode off. Years later he commented, "It was not very comfortable but it made little difference to me. It was the first time I was on a saddle of any kind."

He describes his winter journey south from Chehalis to Jackson Prairie, about sixteen miles, then east along the Cowlitz forty miles more to the Big Bottom area and the hamlet called Vance (now Randle):

> It was not raining but the atmosphere was heavy with a clinging dampness and soon it became a drizzle, possibly "The Oregon Mist" I had heard about. . . . I cannot describe the landscape for I never saw it; no traffic danger—I had met or passed no one so far. . . . Before long I was on rising ground, the atmosphere was a little clearer, the road less muddy, but more water holes. There were floating puncheon in places and sometimes a root of a tree that the road man overlooked stretched its length clear across the highway. At last I heard and saw things.
>
> I heard men making various kinds of calls. I saw two wagons then. What a sight! Turkeys and more turkeys! The drivers, friendly but inquiring fellows, asked me why I was riding on a side-saddle. . . . They said that they hailed from a very fine place that had a wonderful future. Its name was Mossy Rock and that the town (perhaps they did not say "town" but as I had all my life lived in towns, I could not conceive of any place of importance being other than a town) was to become the County Seat when Lewis County was divided which was a sure thing and with a most wonderful future. . . . Neither did they give me any information as to where I might find a restaurant along the way. I was anxious to see one even then and there.

Of course, there was no restaurant any closer than Chehalis. The turkey drivers could have told him so, but they were hastening to get their fowl to market for peoples' Christmas dinners. Soaking wet, famished, and exhausted, Rule at last rode into a farmyard that stood beside the road. The kindly family who lived there took him in, fed him and his horse, and gave them both shelter for the night. The next morning he continued his journey, slowly realizing that the places of importance in his new life would be farmsteads and cottages, not towns, and that he would be preaching in barns or from a big cedar stump in a clearing, not in churches as he had imagined.

Rule did not reach Vance until Christmas Day. By then, "all ideas of towns and even villages had been erased from my mind." One member of the Vance congregation welcomed him with the comment that "the circuit was a hard one and he doubted if I was strong enough to perform the exacting labors." But Rule was undaunted. He found a cheerful young family to stay with, said good-bye to his horse and the uncomfortable sidesaddle, and began working up his Sunday sermon. People were impressed.

By the middle of January 1894, Brother Rule had been loaned a pony with an appropriate saddle, had learned to ride him "real fast," and had traveled once around his entire circuit. That was a distance of a hundred miles at least, as he had to reach farms on both sides of the river. The pony swam across the Cowlitz, and Rule traveled by canoe. Paddling in wind and rain against the strong current was another skill he had to master in a hurry, and he had some narrow escapes. Nevertheless, he says of that first winter:

> I was in a new, strange, delightful world. I was charmed by these hospitable people. My walks through the trails brought surprises at every turn—even skunk cabbage and devil's clubs had their interest, the enormous stems and great height of the vine maple from which hung the massive curtains of moss as they joined the beds of moss on the ground below. What a retreat for quiet and study as you lounged on these natural couches!
>
> I soon found that these new rude homes just from the axe, froe, and planes were supplied with the choicest of books, and

the newspapers from the settlers' former homes kept us all in touch with the doings of the world.[5]

Rule's stipend from the conference was five dollars a month, just enough to get by on. He comments, "I had the same as the people had to eat and drink. I soon learned to relish the 'coffee' they made out of parched wheat and other grains.... Suitable clothing and footwear was nearer to a problem than anything else—so much horseback riding in all kinds of weather, mostly drizzle, roads, and trails."[6]

In November 1894, badly needing to replenish his wardrobe, Rule rode his pony to Tacoma "to see if I could not get a bargain in clothes and shoes, and on Pacific Avenue I saw goods on sale at amazingly low prices and the display covered the sidewalks" symptoms of the depression as it strengthened its hold. On the street, soapbox speakers "were proving that overproduction was the cause of our want and that our poverty was the result of our plenty." Rule bumped into an acquaintance who asked how he could give a Thanksgiving sermon when there was so little to be thankful for.

Brother Rule managed to do it. He argued that there were shortages and want, but not "in the products of nature. There had been no war, no pestilence, no famine." He continued:

[T]he real fact was that there had been overproduction for which let us thank God for His goodness. The lack was money and other mediums of exchange which was purely a human fictional device that would not and could not be relied upon. We are a very wise people, we Americans, but we are not smart enough yet to equally distribute what a generous Creator had so lavishly given and according to His economy "Here is enough for each/ Enough for all/Enough for evermore." So we will sing in closing "Praise God from whom all blessings flow."[7]

Did this argument comfort his congregation? Given that there was nothing any of them could do to fix the situation, perhaps it helped.

Rule spent what he calls "a reasonable share of my time" in the Hammill household over the three years of his Lewis County ministry. His choice of adjective makes me wonder if he spent quite a bit of time there—all that he could. He comments on "the Christian fellowship, the refinement" of their home, and on William Hammill, "the father of this household, so tall, so quiet, so dignified and interesting with his fine sense of humor," mentioning the same personal qualities that my father pointed out.

Then he speaks of Lucretia:

> Mrs. Hammill was quite a character too, well informed, so apt in her replies. Sister Hammill thought that there was a dearth of teaching in the church on the training of children, too little was said on this important subject and that it was my duty to give attention to the matter. I told her that I was not the one to do it. If I went to preaching on this subject, the congregation would say, "There it is again, it takes bachelors and old maids to tell you how to raise your young ones." She was still insistent and duties must be done, then I said, "I will read John Wesley's sermon on 'The Raising of Children.' She replied, instantly, "What did John Wesley know about it more than yourself? He had no children."[8]

These passages are revealing of both William and Lucretia, possibly more deeply than Reverend Rule understood. William was a Virginia gentleman, bred to courtesy. His dignity and quiet sense of humor went right along with the southern accent he retained even in the rude Northwest. Lucretia, on the other hand, was a Yankee like her father. She could be feisty to the point of bad manners, as her indignant comment about John Wesley showed. She was disappointed that Reverend Rule did not ask her what to say to the erring parents in their community. She had an opinion to give in every situation she encountered, offered in her rapid-fire northern speech.

Such deep differences might have driven the couple apart. Instead, his Virginia courtesy and her Yankee stubbornness served them both by turns. Maybe Lou's toughness encouraged William to be more assertive. Other times, William's gentle manner must have smoothed down feathers that Lou had ruffled up. And the Methodist faith that drew them together in Virginia kept them united throughout their long marriage, possibly with a little boost from Reverend Rule. His frequent presence in their household invited a kind of discussion and fellowship they hadn't enjoyed in years.

I am sure they sat over Lou's good dinners and talked over details of Methodist doctrine and the progress of the church. By the family fireside, they chatted about the needs of the local congregation, laughed at the antics of the children, and ended their evenings with impromptu Bible readings, hymns, and prayers. These simple pleasures must have helped to take away the sting of hard times and William's disappointment in the performance of his mill. Like money and credit, it too was a "human fictional device" that could not be relied on. God's gifts were more valuable: good health, plenty to eat, a crackling fire on the hearth, and happy children underfoot.

The Upper Cowlitz community that Reverend Rule describes had not changed very much three decades later, at the time the family memories that open this chapter were enacted. Of course, local men had fought in the Spanish-American War and in World War I. Old and young had perished in the influenza epidemic of 1918. As the lumber boom got underway in the teens and 1920s, men spent more time in the woods and less on their farms. The gasoline engine began to work its influence. Yet the community remained small, closely knit, made up of hardworking rural folk with high standards of behavior and a respect for education, but hardly any money to spend.

This was the community my father was raised in, the one he shared with his grandparents in the first decades of his life and the last of theirs. He spent two summers living with William and Lucretia when he was eleven and twelve, helping his grandfather with the farm work. Late in his own life, he described those weeks. Speaking of William's largest field, the one in the river bottom, my father says:

[It] was originally strewn with water-worn rocks of all sizes. For 25 years Grandpa and the boys utilized their spare time hauling those rocks and dumping them on the creek bank. At the time my memory begins, the rocks were gone, with nothing left but a seemingly endless expanse of fine soil. . . . [There] he raised beets, turnips, carrots, and rutabagas for his cows. First, when the plants were small, we got down on our hands and knees to thin them and transplant them. Then, as the plants grew larger, we weeded them—still on our hands and knees. Finally, we rose up to our feet to hoe them. I thought that lunch time and quitting time would never come. In that huge field we were as nothing, while time, space, and the sun were eternal.

My father says of these weeks, "They were not unhappy. Indeed, they were among the most memorable of my life, creating within me the greatest respect and admiration I have ever held for anyone, with the possible exception of my father."[9] The kind of work they did, wordless, patient, endlessly cycling across seasons, years, generations, is what made our species flourish on earth. Humans still depend on it, though most people in the first world have little experience or understanding of what it entails.

What did William think about as decade after decade passed, each made up of days like those my father described? At times he must have mused over his boyhood in the South: his father, his wife as a bride, the exuberant chatter of his six sisters. He might have called up his brother Rueben's face or heard in his mind Monroe Strickler's astonishing voice soaring from the pulpit. When sunlight or rain sparkled on the Cowlitz, he might have remembered sunlight and rain on the Potomac, on the Occoquan.

Perhaps, when his mind drifted over the mill, he concluded that the Lord did not mean for him to transplant that part of his life to the West. Perhaps he said so to his wife. She might have scolded in return, "Pshaw, William, you didn't think it out. You didn't see what stood around you, the reality of this rainy country. No wheat was ever going to grow here. And the Lord helps those who help themselves."

But then I see her go into her big, dim kitchen to fix their supper. Late afternoon sun angles across the wood-planked floor. She puts out biscuits and honey, cold sliced ham, a dish of beans or greens. She sets a pitcher of buttermilk on the table, and a big wedge of cherry or huckleberry pie. They have coffee made from grain or coffee made from coffee beans, boiled in an enamel pot and served with sugar and cream. William pats her shoulder as they sit down, and they take hands as he blesses the food before them. They had enough, I think they were content.

OF LUCRETIA and William's six children, only one stayed in Salkum. This was Harrison Strickler Hammill, named for the Virginia relatives who had been so important to his parents. Though he had been a tiny, fragile baby, Harrison—or Hallie, as he was called in the family—outlived his siblings, including his twin sister, by many years. He and his wife, Patty, raised their children on a farm to the north of his father's homestead, between Highway 12 and the hills behind town. The old farmhouse still stands there along the highway, abandoned but not yet derelict, awaiting an uncertain future like the town itself.

Some years after William and Lucretia were gone, Hallie and his son Hal Jr. went down to the old homestead site to take a look

William Hammill in an Olympia, Washington, city park, c. 1926.
❦ Photo courtesy of Roxie Hammill Wilcox

around. The big mill door lay in the mud as it had since the flood of 1925. Near it they found a chunk of granite millstone, which they retrieved and set in the garden as a memento of the past. Beside it they placed another treasure, an Indian grinding stone or metate that had been turned up by the plow in Hallie's field a good distance from the river.

When I visited Hal Jr. at his home in Kent, Washington, near Seattle, he showed me these relics standing side by side in his woodsy front garden. Hal is an old man now, and he was glad to find a family member of a later generation who looked on the stones with a reverence like his own. They are real, those stones—utterly real and unarguable in a family history so long, yet so devoid of objects to hold it firm in the flood of experience rushing down the centuries.

EPILOGUE

─────────────── ❧ ───────────────

THE FAMILY story does not end with Lucretia and William Hammill. Five generations more have followed them into the present and are thriving there. But by 1923, when William sold his farm, the world—even in the frontier West—was very different from the one the Hammills had lived in for many centuries. The frontier had settled up. Trades had become industries, and artisans who once operated their own small businesses now labored in other mens' factories. The strategy of combining a trade with farming, once a mainstay of American livelihoods, became less and less viable. It was hard to make a living as a farmer. People sold their land and moved into towns and cities, trading one kind of independence for another.

Hammills today who live in Portland and Seattle, in Alexandria and the District of Columbia, still enjoy the landscape that the family sought out for so much of its history. But now those wooded hillsides and rivers offer a comfortable familiarity—they make a place feel like home. No Hammills depend on water for transport anymore, or on water power, or on their own timber for construction or running a lumber business. In those ways too, William and Lucretia were the last to live as their parents, grandparents, great-grandparents, and countless generations before them had lived. That is one reason I close this account with them.

Before I began this research, Lucretia and William Hammill and their son John Henry, my grandfather, had only the dimmest presence in my mind, for I did not know them personally. But I knew John Henry's wife very well. Crissie Hammill was my grandmother. She was a steady presence in my childhood and beyond, for she lived until I was twenty-two. I also knew Lou and William's grandchildren. My father, his sisters and brothers, their spouses and children made the thicket of kin I grew up in. So it could be said that with the deaths of Lou and William, the mysteries that engaged me in this story were dissolved. Or, more accurately, they have been replaced by different mysteries, different stories. That is another reason to end here.

When I told my friends about this project, they warned me that I would turn up illicit liaisons, illegitimate births, horse thieves, scoundrels, and liars of every stripe. But that didn't worry me. I worried that the family I was about to discover would prove to be staid and unimaginative, or perpetually down on their luck, or unable to read or write from one generation to the next.

I was convinced that the immigrant John Hammill came to America as an indentured servant and a Presbyterian, maybe a vehement one. That evangelical strain might have been translated very early to the Methodist faith, maybe in the family's second generation as Americans, when the movement first came to Maryland's Eastern Shore.

I imagined that every Hammill who left one home for another had been driven by desperation, not drawn by visions of an even better life that could be had at not too much cost. In all these things I could not have been further from the mark. The family I discovered was not a group of strangers with habits and beliefs that were alien to mine. In fact, they were very much like me.

All the Hammills in this account could read and write. In Ireland, some were clerks and lawyers. Others were businessmen with gentlemanly educations. John the immigrant was a surveyor who grew up in a parish that prided itself on its schools and who later taught school in Maryland. No Scots Hammill who could serve as a steward or bailiff to a great house could have failed to read and write. Obviously the grammar-school master at Aberdeen in 1418 was fluent in English and Latin too. And William de Hameville—what about him? I like to think that he, not a scribe, signed his name and set his seal to his charters.

The Hammills were adaptable, always on the lookout for some new scheme that might advance their prosperity. John Hammill had the enterprise to leave Ireland, then worked as a schoolmaster, surveyor, and planter in Maryland, whichever suited the moment and his pocketbook. His son Hugh left Maryland for Virginia, experimented with running a public house, and then leased tobacco land instead of buying it, a less expensive option that did not tie up what capital he had.

The second Hugh was positively flamboyant as a businessman. In his lifetime, he operated a farm, a blacksmith shop, a grist and lumber mill, and, for a time, the Hammill Hotel. He sold lumber on contract to the government and transported it on his own boats. During the Civil War, he sold liquor to soldiers and civilians and hay to the Union army. After the war, he purchased army surplus steamers and with his son Edward ran them as pleasure craft for tourists between Alexandria and Occoquan. William Hammill worked in a shoe factory and as a miller until he could build his own grist and lumber mill. When that did not work out, he made a living as a dairy farmer. William and his grandfather, the second John Hammill, are the two who fared least well, economically speaking. But that does not mean they did badly. The family prospered when outside circumstances permitted them to do so. They did not produce widows or orphans who became wards of the state. They took care of their own.

The Hammills were not horse thieves, either. Their communities respected them. Besides teaching school, John the immigrant surveyed, witnessed documents, and gave numerous depositions in court, showing that his talents were appreciated in Charles County. Among his peers, the Civil War–era Hugh Hammill was regarded as a generous neighbor, a worthy citizen, and a keen, shrewd businessman. His son William was admired as a skillful farmer and a courteous, entertaining host. Several Irish Hammills stood out in their communities. As for the Scots Hammills, the little that can be known about them suggests that they, too, were recognized and secure in their world.

To put all this succinctly, the Hammills appear to have been middle class, always. The documentary evidence portrays their home lives as stable; they did not take social risks. As far as can be known, they got married and stayed married. Their children were born in wedlock. No wives or husbands had notorious love affairs, or ran away, or fell so deeply into debt that they could not support their families. Was black Lizy Hammill a Hammill by blood? She might have been a freed slave, no more.

As middle-class people, they put their livelihoods first. When Hugh stood before the commissioners of southern claims after the Civil War, he responded very simply to their doubts about his behavior during the conflict. He told them, "I had my all there—everything that I had worked for all my life-time was there." In his view, there was nothing more to be said. Political loyalties, theories of government, the merits or demerits of slavery, all the considerations so important to the commissioners didn't mean a thing to Hugh. Not compared to his family's economic well-being.

In religion, the family was moderate. They were Protestants, but not dissenters or nonconformists. As Espiscopalians, they belonged to Britain's mainstream faith. They didn't have to defend their religion or practice it in secret. They didn't sign their names to covenants in blood. They left Scotland and Ireland as members of the established church, and they stayed in that church until late in the nineteenth century, when Methodism became respectable. Only then did the Hammills leave the Episcopal Church behind.

Even in regard to personal traits, the Hammill proclivities seem middle class.

A talent for mathematics and engineering surfaces across the generations, in trades like surveying, blacksmithing, and milling as an industrial art. So does an aptitude for social occupations—schoolteaching, running an ordinary or boarding house, running a hotel. The Scots Hammills who held positions in gentlemanly households and the Irish ones who acted as agents for ladies in distress, even the earliest knights who waited on their lords' commands might be seen to share this trait. I personally think that Hammills, including myself, excel as middle managers, expediting and implementing what others decide. They do not have the self-assertion or indeed the arrogance that leadership requires. Hammills are too amiable and too deliberative for that.

And some have a verbal gift. William Hammill the pamphleteer did. Hugh of Ballyatwood, the tireless letter writer on behalf of Lady Alice, did too. Hugh of the American Civil War loved a story, loved to write a letter, and was loquacious to a fault. Though few who read this account can know it, I have a son who is just as voluble and opinionated. My father and his sister wrote very well and I think surprised themselves in how much they enjoyed the work. Maybe it could be said that they kept on going after it was time to quit. Perhaps the same could be said of me.

However, one last question begs to be answered. How Scots-Irish were the Hammills? Certainly they meet the basic definition: Scots who migrated to Northern Ireland at the time of the Plantation of Ulster, then moved on to America before the Revolution. They share some habits that are Scots to the bone. One is frugality. With the possible exception of the Civil War Hugh Hammill, those who appear in this account lived simply and accumulated few personal possessions. I don't know of a single object that has passed down the generations to my cousins or to me. Another is dogged perseverance. Hammills work hard and don't give up, and they expect others to do the same. Both qualities were fostered by centuries in a country known for bad weather, poor soils, and reckless feuding that destroyed livelihoods and discouraged accumulation of more than bare essentials. There was no alternative but to pick oneself up and start again.

But they emphatically do not share other defining traits of the Scots-Irish. They were not religious dissidents. They were not inclined to belligerent self-defense. None fought in the American Revolution or against Native Americans on colonial borders; only one served briefly in the War of 1812. None that I know of made military careers. "Noble Hugh Hamill of Lifford" who defended Londonderry so bravely in 1689 was forced into that role by default and lived to regret it in the end. Hugh Hammill of the Civil War era voted a moderate ticket, hoping to avoid armed conflict between the states. Hugh's brother Stephen showed a radical spirit, for he was an abolitionist. Yet he did not fight. He blacksmithed for the Union until his early death in 1862.

I do not know what William Hammill's politics might have been, but he was too polite to stand up to the machinist who was delaying his progress on the mill. He took him sides of ham and jars of honey instead. Nor, at sixteen or seventeen years old, did he defy his father and run away to fight on either the Union or the Confederate side in the Civil War. I asked Hal Hammill if he thought William had voted as a Populist in elections around the turn of the twentieth century. Hal reflected, then said no, he didn't think William was inclined that way. I imagine he was right.

These Hammills show a mildness, an acquiescence to the status quo, and a respect for authority that the Scots-Irish abhorred.

Those Scots were "born fighting," as Jim Webb demonstrates in his wonderful book by that name. They were rough, tough, and ruthless, passionate and terrifying. The Hammills have never been like that, as far as I can see.

Taking the longest view, out at the twiggy end of a very long limb, I would say that the family described in this account shows little of the Celtic belligerence that characterizes the Scots-Irish personality and culture. Rather, it demonstrates a possibly Norman respect for hierarchy, a comfort with traditional social structure that may have been born in feudal times. The established social norms worked for them, and they supported those norms over a cascade of centuries, from the Anglo-Norman William de Hameville to his American namesake William Hammill.

And this brings me to my conclusion. Family culture is deeply conservative. It perpetuates itself across political upheavals and vast demographic shifts, despite the social mobility that Americans so prize. In politics, religion, naming, and habits—extravagance or frugality, persistence or volatility, belligerence or mildness—parents pass their preferences to their children, often without a word. Children absorb them, and they become the values that shape generations. These preferences or assumptions resist analysis. Like air and water, they are nearly invisible, yet our lives are built around them. That's why I say, haul out your stories; look them over and see what you find. What is so elusive in each of us can sometimes be captured in the family group. What the present hides, the past can show.

Acknowledgments

꧁

$\mathcal{F}$IRST, I would like to thank the archivists and librarians who so generously gave me their time and advice as I came to grips with the complexity of historical research. The volunteers at the Lewis County historical library in Chehalis, Washington, and Dolores Elder of Historic Occoquan Inc. were unfailingly helpful and supportive. Don Wilson and Beverly Veness at Bull Run Regional Library in Manassas, Virginia, patiently enlightened and directed me, as did Scott Parham, archivist at the Prince William County Courthouse in Manassas. Suzanne Levy of the Virginia Room at the Fairfax County Library, Robert Barnes at the Maryland State Archives, and Dr. William Roulston of the Ulster Historical Foundation provided valuable information and gently steered me away from sandtraps and mistakes. And Mary O. Klein of the Maryland Diocesan Archives let me in out of a Baltimore snowstorm and shared both documents and lunch with me one January day.

Thanks, too, to Katherine Bateman, who made her way through more than one draft of this book and advised me both as a reader and as a historian, and to members of my two book groups, who read or listened to big chunks of narrative and offered suggestions that I nearly always took. Special thanks to JoAnn Burger and her mother, Milla Boczar, of Los Angeles, cousins I had not seen in decades who put me up, entertained me, and helped to sort and copy important documents from their family archives. Likewise to Hal Hammill Jr. of Kent, Washington, whose information about the Lewis County Hammills proved so invaluable, and to my Baltimore cousin, Pam Boyle, a jolly coadventurer and generous hostess on several occasions.

My thanks as well to Jeanne Lockridge Mueller, Jeanne Graham, Chris Herbert, and Bernadette Fort for the encouragement that only true friends can provide, and to Curt Matthews, my husband, who was a mostly cheerful chauffeur and companion on many an expedition around Chesapeake Bay and Northern Ireland. He was a valiant reader and stalwart advocate of this project from the start.

And last, my thanks to the staff at Chicago Review Press. I deeply appreciate their editorial care, authorial support, and all the good ideas they offered along the way.

Notes

---

1 Origins

1. For these and more geographical details, see Samuel Lewis, *A Topographical Dictionary of Scotland* (1846). British History Online, http://www.british-history. ac.uk/source.aspx?pubid=308. Search on Beith.

2. Dane Love, *Ayrshire: Discovering a County*. Ayr: Fort Publishing Ltd., pp. 87–89.

3. James Paterson, *History of the County of Ayr: With a Genealogical Account of the Families of Ayrshire*. Ayr: George Dick (1847), vol. I, p. 275. Digitized by Google Book.

4. Many Web sites describe the Cunningham clan history. A good one is http:// cunninghamfamily.homestead.com/coatofarms.html.

5. George Robertson, *A Genealogical Account of the Principal Families in Ayrshire, More Particular[l]y in Cunninghame*. Irvine: Cunninghame Press (1823), pp. 372–73. Digitized by Google Book. Robertson describes the Hammill coat of arms as it appeared above the doors of Roughwood: "—Quarterly; first, *Gules*, a mullet, *Or*; second, *Azure*, a crescent, *Argent*; third, *Argent*, a shake-fork, *Sable*; fourth, *Gules*, a fleur de lis, *Or*. –Crest, a fleur de lis. Supporters, two serpents, pendant et vigilans." *Gules* is red; *Or* is gold. *Azure* is blue, *Argent* is silver, and *Sable* is black.

6. Robertson says he is quoting verbatim from Chalmers's *Caledonia* (1807), for which Google Book holds an index but at the moment no text. I have not been able to find *Caledonia* in a library.

7. The Register: Tordiff, *Register & Records of Holm Cultram* (1929), pp. 34–37. http://www.british-history.ac.uk/report.asp?compid=49493.

8. Robertson, p. 372.

9. Patrick Hanks and Flavia Hodges, eds., *A Dictionary of Surnames*. New York: Oxford University Press (1988), under Hamill.

10. Robertson, p. 373.

11. Robertson, p. 377; also "The Hamill Family in Ireland," a printout from the Internet of research carried out by Robert Williams of the organization Ulster Ancestry. For a time this information was posted on a Web site called *Writings of Robert Hamill*.

12. David Carpenter, *The Struggle for Mastery: Britain 1066–1284*. Oxford: Oxford University Press (2003). See p. 395ff. for an excellent summary of the evolution of knighthood in the British Middle Ages.

13. Hanks and Hodges, eds., *A Dictionary of Surnames*, under Montgomery.

14. Paterson, vol. I, p. 292.

15. See the Genuki Web site at http://www.peerage.org/genealogy/Baronies.htm# under the heading "Loss of right to sit in Parliament."

16. Wikipedia is a handy place to look for an explanation of "forty shilling freehold" and what it implied for leaseholders. Many other online sources touch on it as well.

17. Paterson, vol. I, pp. 292, 279.

18. Robertson, p. 377.

19. http://www.colonialhall.com/witherspoon/witherspoonElizabeth.php.

20. Paterson, vol. I, p. 275.

2 A POSSIBILITY OPENS

1. James G. Leyburn, *The Scotch-Irish, a Social History*. Durham: University of North Carolina Press (1989). See pp. 7, 9, 26.

2. Leyburn, p. 89.

3. Leyburn, p. 88.

4. Rev. George Hill, ed., *An Historical Account of the Plantation of Ulster at the Commencement of the Seventeenth Century*. Belfast: McCaw, Stevenson & Orr (1877), pp. 58, 69–70. Digitized by Google Book.

5. Leyburn, p. 111.

6. Patrick Macrory, *The Siege of Derry*. Oxford: Oxford University Press (1980), p. 94.

7. David Stewart, "The Scots in Ulster: Their Denization and Naturalisation, 1605–34." Reprinted in *Familia: Ulster Genealogical Review*, 1995 (no. 11).

8. Ulster Historical Foundation, http://www.ancestryireland.com. See 17th Century Records: Scottish Settlements in Ulster: Early Scots Settlers in the County of

Antrim. Matthew Hammill is listed as a tenant of the Earl of Antrim in the Barony of Dunluce, 1615.

Raymond Gillespie, *Colonial Ulster: The Settlement of East Ulster, 1600–1641.* Cork: Cork University Press for the Irish Committee of Historical Sciences (1985), p. 77. Gillespie mentions John Shaw and the fact that he paid his rents in kind rather than cash to the Earl of Antrim.

9. George Hill, ed., *The Montgomery Manuscripts (1603–1706), Compiled from Family Papers by William Montgomery.* Belfast: James Cleeland and Thomas Dargan (1869), pp. 130–42. Digitized by Google Book.

3 Scots-Irish Pioneers, 1606–1641

1. *The Montgomery Manuscripts*, pp. 58, 59, 62, 66.

2. *The Montgomery Manuscripts*, pp. 63–65.

3. *The Montgomery Manuscripts*, pp. 130–42.

4. See Family and Local History (Bill Macafee's Web site), http://billmacafee.com/index.htm. This Web site provides searchable indexes to the 1630 muster rolls and the 1669 hearth money rolls for North Antrim. Several Hammills are listed in these, but no Matthew Hammill.

5. *The Montgomery Manuscripts*, p. 141.

6. Gillespie, p. 143, quoting M. Perceval Maxwell, "Strafford, the Ulster Scots and the Covenanters," *HIS* xviii (1973), pp. 547–48, fn. 118.

7. Leyburn, p. 125.

8. Leyburn, pp. 125.

9. *The Montgomery Manuscripts*, pp. 165, 171, 189ff.

10. *The Montgomery Manuscripts*, p. 408.

11. *The Montgomery Manuscripts*, p. 347.

12. Charles A. Hanna, *The Scotch-Irish or the Scot in North Britain, North Ireland, and North America.* 2 vols. New York: G. P. Putnam's Sons (1902). Vol. I, p. 605.

13. *The Montgomery Manuscripts*, p. 438.

14. *The Hamilton Manuscripts: Containing Some Account of the Territories of the Upper Clandeboye, Great Ards and Dufferin in the County of Down.* T. K. Lowry, ed. (1867). Ulster-Scots Agency (2006): E-book PDF edition, pp. 102–5.

15. *The Hamilton Manuscripts*, E-book PDF edition, pp. 108, 109, 111.

16. Public Record Office of Northern Ireland (PRONI), County Down Wills, microfilm reel 637, T/753/1, Hans Hamill, 1772; T/810/302, Hans Mark Hamill, 1796.

17. http://freepages.genealogy.rootsweb.com/~donegal/dkr5.htm. PRONI, Deputy Keeper's Reports, Co. Donegal references G–H. D 1759, Hamill, Hugh, Ballindrait, 1679–80.

18. These and other details are given in William J. Roulston, *Restoration Strabane, 1660–1714: Economy and Society in Provincial Ireland*. Maynooth Studies in Local History, Number 72. Dublin: Four Courts Press (2007), pp. 37–38. Hugh Hammill's approximate death date was provided by Dr. Roulston in an e-mail of November 2007.

19. For a Creighton genealogy, see http://www.stirnet.com/HTML/genie/british/cc4rz/crichton05.htm.

20. T. H. Mullin, *Families of Ballyrashane: A District in Northern Ireland*. Belfast: News Letter Printing Co., Ltd. (1969). Rev. Mullin summarizes Hammill family occupations on pp. 207–9.

4 HUGH AND WILLIAM HAMMILL AND THE SIEGE OF DERRY

1. Rev. John Graham, M.A., *History of the Siege of Derry, and Defence of Enniskillen, in 1688 and 1689*. Philadelphia: James M. Campbell (1844), p. 13.

2. Graham, pp. 14, 49, 55.

3. Graham, pp. 20, 41.

4. Brian Lacy, *Siege City: The Story of Derry and Londonderry*. Belfast: The Blackstaff Press (1990), pp. 127–28.

5. Patrick Macrory, *The Siege of Derry*. New York: Oxford University Press (1980), p. 174.

6. Graham, p. 150.

7. William Hamill, *A View of the Danger and Folly of Being Publick-Spirited, and Sincerely Loving One's Country*. London (1721), pp. 11, 12. Courtesy of the British Library.

8. Graham, p. 189.

9. Hamill, pp. 12–13.

10. Graham, pp. 195, 223.

11. Graham, pp. 235–36.

12. Macrory, pp. 344–45.

13. Hamill, p. 67.

14. http://www.proni.gov.uk/records/private/erne.htm, Colonel Abraham Creighton (d. 1706) and General David Creighton (1671–1728), Lifford Estate and Lifford Borough.

15. Hamill, p. 72.

16. Hamill, pp. 5, 6.

5 JOHN HAMMILL THE IMMIGRANT

1. See http://billmacafee.com/hearthmoneyrolls/1669hmr.htm for hearth money roll returns and North Antrim muster rolls and poll tax returns. For Neale Hamill and

the other Presbyterian Hammills, see http://www.rootsweb.com/–nirant/Belfast/hometowns.htm, "Home Towns of Ulster Families, 1691–1718," under Neil Hamill.

2. Samuel Lewis, *Lewis's Topographical Dictionary of Ireland* (1837), under Ballywillin. The entire text can be found online at http://www.from-ireland.net/lewis/allcounties.htm.

3. *Ordinance Survey Memoirs*, volume 33: Londonderry, XII (1831), pp. 32, 36.

4. *Lewis's Topographical Dictionary*, Ballywillin.

5. A Web site shows photographs and gives a pleasant commentary about the church's past. Go to http://www.bbc.co.uk/northernireland/yourplaceandmine/antrim/ballywillan_graves.shtm.

6. T. H. Mullin, *Families of Ballyrashane: A District in Northern Ireland*. Belfast: News Letter Printing Co., Ltd. (1969), pp. 207–9.

7. See note 1 above.

8. See Thomas M. Truxes, *Irish-American Trade 1660–1783*. Cambridge: Cambridge University Press (1988), pp. 127–32.

6 John Hammill, Tidewater Planter

1. *A New Map of Virginia, Maryland, and the Improved Parts of Pennsylvania and New Jersey*, by J. Senex (London, 1719). Taken from Jean B. Lee, *The Price of Nationhood: The American Revolution in Charles County*. New York: W. W. Norton & Company (1994), p. iv.

2. Lois Green Carr et al., *Robert Cole's World: Agriculture & Society in Early Maryland*. Chapel Hill: Omohundro Institute of Early American History and Culture, University of North Carolina Press (1991), pp. 17–19.

3. For this historical summary and the statistics, I have relied on Lee, *Price of Nationhood*, chapter 1 and Appendix.

4. Jack D. Brown et al., *Charles County, Maryland: A History, Bicentennial Edition*. Hackensack, NJ: Custombook Inc. (1976), p. 4.

5. Elias Jones, *The Revised History of Dorchester County, Maryland*. Baltimore: Read-Taylor Press (1925), p. 261.

6. Lee, *Price of Nationhood*, p. 24.

7. Charles County Land Records, Lib. L, vol. 2, fols. 329, 361, indenture, John Hamil to John Magrah, 13 June 1727.

8. Regina Combs Hammett, *A History of St. Mary's County, Maryland, 1634–1990*. St. Inigoes, MD: privately published (1991), p. 294.

9. Brown, *Charles County, Maryland: A History*, p. 237.

10. Robert E. and B. Katherine Brown, *Virginia 1705–1786: Democracy or Aristocracy?* East Lansing: Michigan State University Press (1964), p. 10.

11. William B. Sprague, *Annals of the American Pulpit*. New York: Arno Press and the *New York Times* (1969), vol. 5, p. 11.

12. Sarah S. Hughes, *Surveyors and Statesmen: Land Measurement in Colonial Virginia*. Virginia Surveyors Foundation, Ltd. (1979), p. 18.

13. Elise Greenup Jourdan, *Early Families of Southern Maryland*. Westminster, MD: Willow Bend Books (1999), vol. 8, pp. 191–95.

14. Harry Wright Newman, *Some Smoots of Maryland and Virginia*. Washington, D.C.: privately published (1936). Online in its entirety at http://www.usgennet.org/family/smoot/book/0001.html. See Edward Smoot, Gent. (1724–95).

15. Charles County Land Records, Lib. Z, vol. 2, fol. 324, deed of gift, 12 October 1751.

16. Angelique Day and Patrick McWilliams, eds., *O.S. Memoirs Co. Antrim V*, Belfast: Institute of Irish Studies in association with the Royal Irish Academy, Dublin (1990–98). Memoirist Thomas Fegan, June 1838, vol. 16, p. 32.

17. An interesting Web site on Ballyrashane Parish in Northern Ireland refers to a Curry and several Hamills as informants in its bibliography. See http://www.nireland.com/Dolina/ballybibliography.html.

18. Charles County Land Records, Lib. Z, vol. 2, fol. 327, division of Partner's Purchase between Dr. John Curry and John Hamill, 20 February 1748–49; Society of Jesus Box 35, folder 107 Z1–Z8, grant of Lord Calvert to John Howard and John Hamill, Partner's Purchase, resurveyed 4 September 1738.

19. Elise Greenup Jourdan, *Early Families of Southern Maryland*. Westminster, MD: Willow Bend Books (1999), vol. 7, p. 157.

20. Karen Mauer Green, compiler, *The Maryland Gazette 1727–1761*. Galveston, TX: Frontier Press (1990), p. 253.

7 SARAH HAMMILL AND HER HOUSEHOLD

1. Jean B. Lee gives a very nice summary of women's legal status in *Price of Nationhood*, p. 59.

2. Charles County Land Records, Lib. O, vol. 2, fols. 429–30, James Abernathey to John Hamill, 4 January 1739 [actually, 1740].

3. Charles County Land Records, Lib. Z, vol. 2, fol. 324, deed of gift, 12 October 1751.

4. Daniel J. Boorstin, *The Americans: The Colonial Experience*. New York: Vintage Books (1958), p. 133.

5. Charles County Prerogative Court (Accounts), Maryland State Archives S531, fols. 411–13, estate of John Hamill, 19 June 1767.

6. "Everywhere the great bulk of movable property was in slaves and livestock." Lois Green Carr and Lorena S. Walsh, "The Standard of Living in the Colonial Chesapeake," *William & Mary Quarterly*, vol. 45, ser. 3 (1988), p. 142.

7. Carr and Walsh, "The Standard of Living in the Colonial Chesapeake," p. 142.

8. Allan Kulikoff, *Tobacco and Slaves: The Development of Southern Cultures in the Chesapeake, 1680–1800*. Chapel Hill: Omohundro Institute of Early American History and Culture, University of North Carolina Press (1986), pp. 407–8.

9. Carr and Walsh, pp. 135–59.

10. Carr and Walsh, p. 138.

11. See note 5 above. Sarah Hammill's death is mentioned on fol. 413.

12. Maryland State Archives, Vestry Book, William & Mary Parish, Charles County, 8 June 1752.

13. Lee, *Price of Nationhood*, Table 1, p. 266.

8 Things Fall Apart

1. John Jr. and John Sr.'s wills can be found in Charles County Wills, Lib. AD, vol. 5, fol. 158, fols. 300–302. Sarah Hammill's death is mentioned in Charles County Prerogative Court (Accounts), Maryland State Archives, S531, fol. 403, estate of John Hamill, 17 June 1767. Stephen and William Chandler's estates are summarized in V. L. Skinner Jr., *Abstracts of the inventories of the Prerogative Court of Maryland*: [18th century] Westminster, MD: Family Line Publications (1988–91), vol. 13, p. 90; vol. 15, p. 32.

2. Daniel J. Boorstin, *The Americans: The Colonial Experience*. New York: Vintage Books, 1958, pp. 219–20.

3. Eugene Fauntleroy Cordell, *The Medical Annals of Maryland 1799–1899, Prepared for the Centennial of the Medical and Chirurgical Faculty*. Baltimore: Press of Williams & Wilkins Co. (1903), pp. 652–54.

4. Cordell, *The Medical Annals of Maryland 1799–1899*, p. 654.

5. Arthur Pierce Middleton, *Tobacco Coast: A Maritime History of Chesapeake Bay in the Colonial Era*. Baltimore: Johns Hopkins University Press (1984), p. 13.

6. Stephen Hammill's accounts appear in Charles County Prerogative Court (Accounts), Maryland State Archives, S531, fols. 316–18, 390–91, 444. The reference to Richard Ratcliff appears on fol. 318, 23 June 1768.

7. Middleton, *Tobacco Coast*, p. 13.

8. Alan L. Karras, *Sojourners in the Sun: Scottish Migrants in Jamaica and the Chesapeake, 1740–1800*. Ithaca: Cornell University Press (1992), pp. 93–99.

9. Mentioned in Colin James, *John Hamill Poston, His Ancestors and Descendants* (1959), privately published pamphlet, and in a personal letter from Colin James dated 18 February 1971.

10. Maryland State Archives, S1587, Patent record BC and GS 40, pp. 302–3. Hammills [sic], Stephen, 1768. The details of this patent are a bit complicated. The whole tract is "to be held of Panguiah Manor" for a yearly rent of nineteen shillings and two

pence payable at Michaelmas. When Stephen died, only Ashbrooke's Rest stayed in his estate. I suppose the additional acreage reverted to the Manor.

11. Jonathan Boucher, p. 126, and George Washington, pp. 125–28, quoted in *The Encyclopedia of Dumfries, Virginia*, by Robert Hedges VIIII at http://www.ecsd. com/-rhhedgzi/1770.html.

9 HUGH THE HEIR

1. Prince William County Land Records, Deed Book U, fol. 149. Indenture dated 4 April 1780: William Tebbs to Hugh Hammill.

2. BfBonham Web site: The Family Snitch. Shaw of Charles County, Maryland, and Orange County, South Carolina, Generation Two. http://homepages.rootsweb. com/-bfbonham/shaw/shaw0001.htm.

3. These and several other transactions are documented in the land records of Charles County. Most are summarized by Elise Greenup Jourdan in *Early Families of Southern Maryland*, vol. VIII, pp. 293–94. See also Charles County Land Records, Lib. O, vol. 3, fols. 418, 475, 543; Lib. S, vol. 3, fol. 130. One transaction not mentioned in the text is the sale of a slave named Deptford, who belonged to Hugh's father, John. Deptford may have come to the Hammills from Sarah's father, John Chandler, who patented a parcel of land called Deptford in 1731 (Charles County Land Records, Lib. P, vol. 8, fol. 202).

4. Charles County Land Records, Lib. Z, vol. 2, fol. 324.

5. Newman, *Some Smoots of Maryland and Virginia*, http://www.usgennet.org/family/ smoot/book/0001.html. See Edward Smoot, Gent. (1724–95).

6. Charles County Land Records, Lib. S, vol. 3, fols. 502, 528.

7. Charles County Land Records, Lib. S, vol. 3, fol. 664.

8. Alan L. Karras, *Sojourners in the Sun: Scottish Migrants in Jamaica and the Chesapeake, 1740–1800*. Ithaca: Cornell University Press (1992), p. 194.

9. Charles County Land Records, Lib. S, vol. 3, fol. 497.

10. Lee, *Price of Nationhood*, p. 137.

11. S. Eugene Clements and F. Edward Wright, *The Maryland Militia in the Revolutionary War*. Silver Springs, MD: Family Line Publications (1987), pp. 158–65.

12. Bettie S. Carothers, compiler, *1776 Census of Maryland; 1778 Census of Maryland*. Chesterfield, MD (1972?). Also Gaius Brumbaugh, *Maryland Records, Colonial, Revolutionary, County and Church: From Original Sources*. Baltimore: Williams & Wilkins Co. (1915). Vol. 1, section 2, pp. 298ff.

13. Bettie S. Carothers, compiler, *Nine Thousand Men Who Signed the Oath of Allegiance in Maryland During the Revolution*. No date. Chesterfield, MO.

14. Newman, *Some Smoots of Maryland and Virginia*. See William Groves Smoot (1755–1800).

15. British sources give the royal governor's name as John Murray, Earl of Dunmore. American sources refer to him as John Murray Dunsmore, dropping his title and adding an *s* to his surname.

16. Dee E. Andrews, *The Methodists and Revolutionary America, 1760–1800: The Shaping of an Evangelical Culture*. Princeton: Princeton University Press, 2000. For women's involvement in the movement, see especially chapter 4, "Evangelical Sisters." For the doings of the itinerant preachers, see especially chapter 2, "The Wesleyan Connection."

17. Newman, *Some Smoots of Maryland and Virginia*. See Captain John Smoot (1748–93).

10 GOOD-BYE TO CHARLES COUNTY

1. Quoted in Lee, *Price of Nationhood*, p. 6.

2. Charles County Land Records, Lib. O, vol. 2, fol. 165.

3. Kulikoff, *Tobacco and Slaves*, pp. 127–30.

4. Kulikoff, Allan, *From British Peasants to Colonial American Farmers*. Chapel Hill: University of North Carolina Press (2000), p. 133.

5. Kulikoff, *From British Peasants to Colonial American Farmers*, p. 135.

6. Neale Hamill Shaw is mentioned in Regina Combs Hammett, *History of St. Mary's County, Maryland, 1634–1990*. St. Inigoes, MD: privately published (1991), p. 344; also in Brown, *Charles County, Maryland: A History*, p. 95. The Episcopal Archives of Maryland in Baltimore hold several letters and other documents written by and about Neale Hamill Shaw in the course of his employment as rector and master in All Faith Parish. The letters quoted are dated 8 June 1810, 4 June 1819, and 1 June 1822.

11 CROSSING THE POTOMAC

1. Edward Smoot's lease for this land is reproduced on the Smoot Family Association Web site at http://www.usgennet.org/family/Smoot/va/PrinceWilliam17640525.

2. This extremely useful bit of information comes from the *Prince William Reliquary*, an online publication dedicated to the history and genealogy of Prince William County, published by RELIC, the local history room at the Bull Run Regional Library in Manassas, Virginia. "Dumfries District Court Land Causes 1793–1811," Tebbs vs. Barron. *Prince William Reliquary*, vol. 3, no. 2 (April 2004), p. 50. Philip Shaw is given an approximate birth date of 1731 in the BfBonham Web site: The Family Snitch. Shaw of Charles County, Maryland, and Orange County, South

Carolina, Generation Two. http://homepages.rootsweb.com/~bfbonham/shaw/shawooo1.htm#t3.

3. Thomas was a grandson of that Barton Smoot who purchased land from John Hammill in 1742. His will is reproduced in the Smoot Family Association Web site at http://www.uogonnot.org/family/Smoot/va/PrinceWilliam1783020. It mentions his children, his slaves, and his tract at "Bristoe's Land." For more about the Bristoe Tract, see Darlene L. Hunter, "The Bristoe Tract—Rent Rolls, Map and History," *Prince William Reliquary*, vol. 3, no. 4 (2004), pp. 81–88. See also Harry Wright Newman, *Some Smoots of Maryland and Virginia*. Washington, D.C.: privately published (1936). Online in its entirety at http://www.usgennet.org/family/smoot/book/0001.html, Captain Barton Smoot (1688–1744).

4. Hugh Hammill was living on Partner's Purchase in Charles County late in 1764, when this information is given in his father, John's, will. He first appears in Prince William County records in 1778, when he requests a license from the county to open an ordinary. Because it was so easy to travel between the two counties in question, he might have lived in Prince William for a decade or more while conducting business in Charles County.

5. Paul Weir, a Washington, D.C., newspaper reporter, made a brief typewritten genealogy now in my possession. Weir was the husband of Lillian Hammill, youngest daughter of Edward Hammill. Edward was the oldest son of Hugh Hammill, grandson and namesake of the Hugh Hammill who crossed the Potomac in the mid-1770s.

6. The Ancestry.com Web site (http://www.Ancestry.com) gives a full account of the fate of the 1790 and 1800 censuses of Virginia.

7. Virginius Dabney, *Virginia: The New Dominion: A History from 1607 to the Present*. New York: Doubleday & Company Inc. (1971), p. 415.

8. Joan W. Peters, compiler, *Prince William County, Virginia Tax Lists/1782 Tax Lists* (1996). Noncirculating material available at RELIC, Bull Run Regional Library, Manassas, VA.

9. For example, "Carte de la Virginie ou Precis de la Campagne de 1781," which indicates the route of the "marche forcée de Baltimore a Richemond par le Gal. de la Fayette avec son detachement," including several ordinaries. MapPhoto France. Available at Newberry Library, Chicago, IL.

10. Ordinaries were often run in rented or leased houses, as this quote shows: "The tax on an ordinary may be determined by the actual rent of the house and furniture." Ronald Ray Turner, *Prince William County Virginia Business Licenses 1806–1899*. Manassas (1998), p. 6. Noncirculating material, available at RELIC, Bull Run Regional Library, Manassas, VA.

11. Prince William County Virginia Circuit Court Archives: Court Order Book 1778–84. "At a Court Continued and Held for Prince William County the Seventh Day of September 1779."

12. "The Encyclopedia of Dumfries, Virginia, 1740–1750," by Robert Hedges VIIII. Entry for April 26, 1745. This unique and very useful work can be found at http://www.ecsd.com/~rhhedgz1/1740-59.HTML.

13. May 16, 1780, Petition to the Virginia House of Delegates. *Magazine of Virginia Genealogy*, vol. 30, no. 3 (1992), pp. 182–83.

14. Prince William County Land Records, Deed Book U, fol. 149. Indenture dated 4 April 1780: William Tebbs to Hugh Hammill. The family surname is actually spelled Hammill every time it is mentioned.

15. Prince William County Land Records, Deed Book T. Indenture dated 6 January 1777: William Tebbs to James Graham, for a tract "lying and being … on the north side of the piney branch of broad run."

16. Willard F. Bliss, "The Rise of Tenancy in Virginia," *VMHB* LCIII (1950), p. 431.

17. For example, see Willard F. Bliss, noted above, and Gregory A. Stiverson, *Poverty in a Land of Plenty: Tenancy in Eighteenth Century Maryland*. Baltimore: Johns Hopkins University Press (1977), pp. 23–24; 45–46.

18. Bliss, "The Rise of Tenancy in Virginia," p. 440; Allan Kulikoff, *Tobacco and Slaves*, p. 134, footnote 30.

19. Robert E. Brown and B. Katherine Brown, *Virginia 1705–1786: Democracy or Aristocracy?* East Lansing: Michigan State University Press, 1964, pp. 131–33.

20. Brown and Brown, p. 23.

21. *Virginia Journal & Alexandria Advertiser*, 9 November 1786: "Valuable Lands for Sale." Advertisement placed by Thomas Blackburn for "1260 acres on the Broad Run of Occoquan." Ronald Ray Turner, *Newspaper Abstracts 1784–1860*. Manassas (2000), p. 11.

22. Bliss, p. 439. He is referring to tenants on Carter's Piney Ridge tract, also in the Northern Neck.

12 Life and Death on Revolution's Doorstep

1. *The Encyclopedia of Dumfries, Virginia*. From the papers of General George Washington, vol. 2, including a letter from Col. Henry Lee to Gov. Jefferson dated April 9, 1781; a letter from George Mason to Gov. Jefferson dated May 14, 1781; and a letter from Gen. George Washington to Col. Henry Lee dated September 10, 1781. http://www.ecsd.com/~rhhedgz1/1781.html.

2. Quoted in Edith Sprouse, *Colchester: Colonial Port on the Potomac*. Fairfax, VA: Fairfax County Office of Comprehensive Planning in cooperation with Fairfax

County Historical Commission (1975, 1992), p. 73. The original sources are: Marquis de Chastellux, *Travels in North America in the Years 1780, 1781 and 1782*, vol. 2, p. 615; *Alexandria Gazette*, 5 September 1857.

3. No document states the fact of her death, much less the particulars of it. Hugh Hammill's second marriage, to the widow Elizabeth Maddox Smoot, is given in the Paul Weir genealogy mentioned earlier, as are the birth years of Hugh's sons by his second wife, John and Stephen.

4. An influenza pandemic for 1782–83 is referenced in Cyndi's List at http://www.cyndislist.com/disasters: Natural & Man-Made.

5. Charles County Land Records 1782–86, fols. 263–65.

6. Prince William County, Virginia, Personal Property Tax Lists, 1782–99. Library of Virginia microfilm publication, reel 288 (1782–1810).

7. Charles County Land Records, Lib. S, vol. 3, fol. 497.

8. John J. McCusker and Russell R. Menard, *The Economy of British North America 1602–1789*. Chapel Hill: North Carolina Press (1985), p. 359.

9. McCusker and Menard, pp. 374, 366.

10. Lee, *Price of Nationhood*, pp. 242–44.

11. McCusker and Menard, p. 359.

12. Kulikoff, Allan, *Tobacco and Slaves*, pp. 430–31.

13. Prince William County Deed Book X, fol. 275. Quoted in Leslie Davis Dawson, *History of the Dawson-Davis Family and Related Families of Fairfax and Prince William Counties, Virginia*, revised ed. Plainfield, NJ: privately published (1984), p. 105.

14. "Dumfries District Court Land Causes 1793–1811," Lithgow vs. Carr. *Prince William Reliquary*, vol. 4, no. 3 (July 2005), p. 74.

15. *Prince William County Will Book H, 1792–1803*. Abstracted by June Johnson Whitehurst. Fairfax, VA, privately published (1985), p. 32.

16. Prince William County Land Records, Deed Book T, 1774–79, fols. 152–53. Indenture dated 6 November 1800: Willoughby Tebbs to Charles Shaw.

17. Sprouse, *Colchester: Colonial Port on the Potomac*, pp. 101–2.

14 The Second John Hammill, Citizen of the New Republic

1. It seems likely that they were already living in Occoquan in 1831, when John purchased that black and white cow from the estate of William Selecman.

2. Charles G. Muller, *The Darkest Day: The Washington-Baltimore Campaign During the War of 1812*. Philadelphia: University of Pennsylvania Press (2003), pp. 133ff.

3. *Virginia Militia in the War of 1812, from Rolls in the Auditor's Office at Richmond*. Richmond (1852), vol. 2, p. 596.

4. Dawson, *History of the Dawson-Davis Family and Related Families of Fairfax and Prince William Counties, Virginia,* p. 209.

5. "The net revenue collected in Virginia increased nearly seventy percent, comparing the year 1815 with the average of the five years 1800–1804." Henry Adams, quoted in *Garry Wills, Henry Adams and the Making of America.* New York: Houghton Mifflin (2005), p. 378.

6. Inventory and sale of the estate of William Selecman, dated 7 November 1831. Prince William County Virginia Circuit Court Archives, Will Book O, fols. 11–15.

7. Prince William County, Virginia, Personal Property Tax Lists. Library of Virginia microfilm publication, reels 289 (1811–32) and 290 (1833–50).

8. Nan Netherton et al., *Fairfax County, Virginia: A History.* Fairfax, VA: Fairfax County Board of Supervisors (1978), p. 242.

9. This information is given in Elizabeth McIntosh Hammill's application for a Bounty Land Warrant, dated 7 October 1854. In it, she also mentions that she was married on 5 April 1809. I take the material from Dawson, *History of the Dawson-Davis Family and Related Families of Fairfax and Prince William Counties, Virginia,* p. 209.

10. Microfilm publication M2094, Southern Claims Commission Approved Claims, 1871–80: Virginia. Reel 35, Prince William County. Washington, D.C.: National Park Service, Virginia Genealogical Society, and National Archives and Records Administration (2005). Hugh Hammill's claim, number 18565, is the first on the reel, pp. 1–158. He gives his birth date on p. 58.

11. Margaret B. Binning, compiler, *Index to Death Records of Prince William County Prior to 1912,* Vol. 1 (A–K). RELIC: Manassas, VA (2001).

12. She did not belong to John's son Hugh, for the woman slave Hugh owned in 1850 was only forty-five that year. Federal Slave Schedule, Prince William County, Virginia, 1850. *Prince William Reliquary,* vol. 4, no. 1 (January 2005), p. 20.

13. Thomas L. Selecman letter dated 6 January 1868, from Prince William County Courthouse at Manassas: Miscellaneous Assorted Papers, Box 39, 2 pages.

14. T. H. Mullin, *Families of Ballyrashane,* p. 209. The coachbuilders are shown in an unpaginated photo insert, in an undated photo captioned "Hamills, the coachbuilders." They are standing beside a bread coach or van in front of their shop. The shop sign reads "C. Hamill, prop."

16 THE SECOND HUGH HAMMILL, A KEEN, SHREWD MAN

1. These details are given by Hugh's great-niece, Margaret Maddox Finch, in her unpublished typescript of reminiscences written about 1970. Mrs. Finch mailed the

typescript to my aunt, Roxie Hammill Wilcox, in response to Roxie's letter asking for information about the Virginia Hammills. Roxie included the reminiscences in her unpublished typescript *Hammill and Soule Families* (1970), in my possession.

2. A useful summary of the act can be found online at http://valley.vcdh.virginia. edu/claims/about3CC.html.

3. Hugh Hammill's claim can be found in a microfilm edition of the original manuscript. It is not available in print. Claim 18565, Hugh Hammill. Microfilm publication M2094, Southern Claims Commission Approved Claims, 1871–80: Virginia. Reel 35, Prince William County. Washington, D.C.: National Park Service, Virginia Genealogical Society, and National Archives and Records Administration of the United States (2005).

4. Virginius Dabney, *Virginia: The New Dominion: A History from 1607 to the Present*. New York: Doubleday & Company Inc. (1971), p. 277.

5. *Alexandria Gazette*, 21 October 1822; 4 February 1823; 10 June 1828; 22 January 1840. From *Newspaper Transcripts, Prince William County, Virginia, 1784–1860*. Ronald Ray Turner, ed. Manassas (2000), pp. 114, 116, 136, 179.

6. Ronald Ray Turner, *Prince William County Virginia. Clerk's Loose Papers, Volume II. Selected Transcripts 1808–1860, Deeds and Slave Records*. Manassas (2004), pp. 183–84 (October 1845).

7. Edith Moore Sprouse tells Agnes's story in *Colchester: Colonial Port on the Potomac*. Fairfax: Fairfax County Office of Comprehensive Planning in cooperation with the Fairfax County History Commission (1975, 1992), p. 111.

8. Library of Virginia, Records of the Executive Branch. Record Group 3—Office of the Governor. Executive Papers of Governor John Buchanan Floyd, January 1, 1849–January 1, 1852, Box 397.

9. Prince William County Deed Book 20, p. 279 (Spinks/Hammill); Deed Book 21, p. 100 (Fisher/Hammill); Deed Book 23, p. 114 (Selecman/Hammill).

10. The 1850 Virginia Census Nonpopulation Schedules show Hugh Hammill as the proprietor of a blacksmith shop built with a capital investment of five hundred dollars and employing three men, at that time probably still apprentices. So he was not milling lumber in 1850. Library of Virginia: Virginia 1850 Nonpopulation Schedules, microfilm publication T-1132 #4.

11. The 1860 Virginia Census Manufacturing Schedule indicates that on 1 June 1860, Hugh Hammill operated a sawmill and gristmill as well as a blacksmith shop. As in 1850, the capital investment in blacksmithing was five hundred dollars. He had invested a thousand dollars in the mills. At that time he was producing sixty thousand feet of plank and 675 bushels of meal annually, employing two men in the mills and one in the blacksmith shop. By 1860, the employees were no longer apprentices but

his own sons. Library of Virginia: Virginia 1860 Manufacturing Schedule, "Products of Industry," microfilm publication T-1132 #4.

12. Hugh's son William told his daughter-in-law, Lucretia Fuller Hammill, that the house he grew up in had fourteen fireplaces. Lucretia passed it along to younger relatives, among them my aunt, Roxie Hammill Wilcox. The name River View is given in the return address of a letter that Hugh Hammill wrote to H. A. Tayloe on 9 December 1873. It is letter 13 in the collection referenced below.

13. *Records of Ante-Bellum Southern Plantations from the Revolution Through the Civil War, Series M, Part 1: The Tayloe Family.* General Editor: Kenneth M. Stampp. A microfilm project of University Publications of America, an imprint of CIS. Bethesda, MD: compilation © 1995 by Virginia Historical Society. Reel 14, section 81, letters 1 & 2, March 1858.

14. The flagpole incident and its aftermath are described in Dolores Elder, "Uncivil Occoquan," pamphlet, 16 pp., unpaginated, dated November 2004. Available from Historic Occoquan Inc., Box 65, 413 Mill Street, Occoquan, VA 22125.

17 THE CIVIL WAR COMES TO PRINCE WILLIAM COUNTY

1. For the Potomac Flotilla and the Confederate Blockade, see Mary Alice Wills, *The Confederate Blockade of Washington, D.C. 1861–1862.* Prince William County, VA: The Prince William Board of County Supervisors and the Prince William County Historical Commission (1975), pp. 15–45. For the Albemarle Light Horse Cavalry action, see Dolores Elder, "Uncivil Occoquan," p. 7.

2. This is the first of a great many passages from Hugh Hammill's claim that will appear in the next few chapters. The claim is unpublished and cannot be referred to except in the microfilm edition I referenced earlier. I give the dates of depositions and of every session before the commissioners, though these dates can be confusing. New material was presented at every juncture, and it was often out of chronological order. Also, I make the identity of every speaker or deposer very clear. With few exceptions, I do not give page references, as they seem to me to obstruct more than they clarify. One day perhaps this and other transcripts of claims can be published in book form and made available to a wide audience. Then page references might be practical.

3. *The Local News* (Fairfax County, VA), 26 November 1861, citing "a letter in the *Washington Star*" that reported the arrests.

4. A useful biography of Colonel Randall can be found online at http://www.rootsweb.com/~vermont/WashingtonCoHistory12.html.

5. Lieutenant Clark's history of the regiment can be found online at http://www.vermontcivilwar.org/units/13/. The quoted material in these passages comes from Clark's account.

6. This would have been December 1862. The 13th Vermont left northern Virginia in May 1863 and never returned. This is just one of several places in his testimony where Hugh Hammill lost track of dates.

18 A VIRGINIAN IN A YANKEE COURT

1. This deposition is not dated. Tucker recorded it and submitted it with his report of 3 January 1876. Probably he took it the same day as Rolls's or Payne's deposition.
2. Wills, *The Confederate Blockade of Washington, D.C. 1861–1862*, p. 61.
3. Dolores Elder provides this detail in "Hugh Hammill, Reluctant Escort." *The Mill Racer*, vol. V, no. 9 (April/May 2008), p. 2.

19 NOTHING TO DO AND NOTHING TO DO IT WITH— THE WAR'S LAST YEARS

1. When Edward Hammill visited his brother William in Washington State in 1922, he told the family that he blacksmithed in the family shop before the war, and his brothers worked in the mills. Roxie Hammill Wilcox includes this detail in *Hammill and Soule Families*, p. 8.
2. These death dates and some details are easily found at http://ancestry.com, searching under Birth, Marriage & Death Records by the name of the deceased. Death dates can be found through the Library of Virginia Digital Library Program, though fewer details are given. Search County and City Records, Vital Statistics, Death Records Indexing Project, under the name of the deceased at http://ujux.lva lib.va.us. The Library of Virginia also holds microfilm editions of Virginia birth, marriage, and death registers with all the details that were provided at the time of registration.
3. Margaret Maddox Finch tells several stories about her great-uncle John Hammill in her personal reminiscences. He fought on the Confederate side in the war. When he came down with typhoid in 1864, he sought refuge with the Lynn family. While he was ill, Union soldiers came through the neighborhood, looking for Rebels. Mrs. Lynn ran upstairs, told John to play dead, and covered him up with a sheet. The soldiers came in and stuck their bayonets into the mattress and pillows, but not into John.
4. *New York Times*, 3 March 1866. ProQuest Historical Newspapers, *New York Times* (1851–2003), p. 4. "Maryland: Government Sale of Steamers. Baltimore, Thursday, March 1." Digitized. Maybe H. F. was a typographical error for H. E. Then the initials stood for both Hammill captains, Hugh and Edward.
5. The earliest mention of a Hammill-owned steamer I know of is this: "Messrs. Hugh Hammill & Son are building a very fine steamer designed for freighting on the Potomac. It is 90 feet, length of keel, 24 foot beam." *Alexandria Gazette*, 4 October

1869. Ronald Ray Turner, ed., *Prince William County Newspaper Transcripts 1865–1875.* Manassas (2001), p. 66.

6. Prince William County Will Book R, p. 36. The will makes specific bequests and concludes: "I give & bequeath to Hugh Hammill all the remainder of my property of every description & kind and do hereby appoint him my executor."

7. These details are given in Susan Annie Plaskett, *Memories of a Plain Family, 1836–1936.* Washington, D.C.: Franklin Press (1936). See chapter 4: The Athey Line (unpaginated in my photocopy). Plaskett says that the third Harley sister was named Catherine, not Caroline.

8. Deed of Trust dated 7 March 1831 between Silas and Theodosia Beach, Michael Cleary, and Joseph and John H. Janney. Prince William County Deed Book 12, pp. 301–2.

9. Library of Virginia, *Land Tax Records: Prince William County.* Microfilm reel 260, 1824A–1838B. Copy at RELIC, Bull Run Regional Library, Manassas, VA. Under Occoquan Town Lots for the year 1830, fourteen lots are listed under Joseph and John H. Janney "of Est. of Ellicott." Two of these lots are valued at $1,175 to $1,200 with a note: "buildings added." The next year, 1831, four more of the original fourteen lots have "new buildings," and one, number 13 in the list, indicates "buildings increased," with a new value of $1,000 to $1,200. In 1832, lot number 13 counting down the list is one of a group of three lots with a note: "Number reduced by sale to Beach." Lot 13 is again valued at $1,000 to $1,200. My guess is that this is the improved lot that the Janney brothers sold to Silas Beach.

10. Library of Virginia, *Land Tax Records: Prince William County.* Microfilm reel 262, 1851–61. Copy at RELIC, Bull Run Regional Library, Manassas, VA. Robert L. White or his estate paid the taxes on the hotel building between 1852 and 1867. John Athey paid the taxes prior to 1852.

11. "Hugh Hammill is lately got a fine house on this old street which I am informed he wishes to fix up for a Public House, as soon as the changes is made." Thomas L. Selecman letter dated 6 January 1868. Prince William County Courthouse at Manassas: Miscellaneous Assorted Papers, Box 39, 2 pages. Transcribed by Earnie Portia.

12. *Washington Post* (1877–1954). 8 July 1878. ProQuest Historical Newspapers, *Washington Post* 1877–1991, p. 4: "Occoquan's Attractions." This article also mentions a steamer, *Harbinger*, operated by "mine host Hammill," and a new outdoor dance floor and pavilion adjoining the hotel. Digitized.

13. Prince William County Deed Book 29, p. 272.

14. *Records of Ante-Bellum Southern Plantations from the Revolution Through the Civil War, Series M, Part 1: The Tayloe Family.* General editor: Kenneth M. Stampp. A microfilm project of University Publications of America, an imprint of CIS. Bethesda,

MD: compilation © 1995 by Virginia Historical Society. Reel 46, section 265, letters dated 6 June 1872, 11 June 1862; section 269, letter dated 9 December 1873. Reel 56, section 7, letter dated 22 January 1875; section 10, letter dated 25 February 1875, letter dated 9 March 1875; section 4, affidavit dated 31 March 1875, letter dated 23 March 1874; section 8, tax receipts dated 17 December 1871, 18 August 1874, 2 January 1875. A Guide to the Microfilm Edition with a genealogical chart as an Appendix can be accessed as a PDF at 2481_/AnteBellSouthPla#E4272.pdf. Or search on Series M: Selections from the Virginia Historical Society, and follow the prompts to access the Appendix.

15. M1407, Southern Claims Commission Barred Claims. National Archives and Records Administration (1985) (CD). Claim no. 10415, file 2777, scans 003–048; file 1031, scans 054–063.

16. Anthony Trollope, *An Editor's Tales*. London: Penguin Books (1993), "Mary Gresley," p. 53.

20 HUGH TAKES CARE OF HIS CHILDREN

1. Prince William County Deed Book 30, p. 265.

2. For the lot assessments, see Land Tax Records: Prince William County. Lower District Town Lots. Microfilm reels 260 (1824–38), 261 (1839–50), 262 (1851–61), 532 (1860–70). Copies at RELIC, Bull Run Regional Library, Manassas, VA. For the indenture between Hugh and Edward Hammill, see Prince William County Deed Book 33, p. 102.

3. They were the parents of ten children, but four of them, all sons born between 1860 and 1870, died very young, at least one by drowning in Occoquan Run.

4. Prince William County Deed Book 33, p. 333.

5. Prince William County Deed Book 31, p. 563.

6. These death dates and some details are easily found at http://ancestry.com, searching under Birth, Marriage & Death Records by the name of the deceased. Death dates can also be found through the Library of Virginia Digital Library Program, though fewer details are given. Search County and City Records, Vital Statistics, Death Records Indexing Project, under the name of the deceased at http://ajax.lva.lib.va.us. The Library of Virginia also holds microfilm editions of Virginia birth, marriage, and death registers with all the details that were provided at the time of registration.

7. The four women can be found living together in Precinct 5, Washington City, in the U.S. censuses of 1900 and 1910. In 1920, Jennie and Nellie are listed, together with their sister Catharine Cofrode and her son Jesse H. Cofrode. Apparently Kate and her unmarried son moved back to Washington, D.C., after Kate was widowed

and her daughter Eleanor was married. In 1930, only Jesse H. Cofrode is listed. The five sisters were presumably all deceased by then.

8. *Washington Post* (1877–1954): 13 July 1889; ProQuest Historical Newspapers, p. 3. Digitized.

9. Roxie Hammill Wilcox gives the text of this advertisement in *Hammill and Soule Families*, p. 9. She says it ran in the county newspaper, but gives no specific information. I have not yet been able to find it.

10. The Baltimore County Public Library Legacy Web site at http://external.bcpl/lib.md.us/hcdo/dfdocs/photopage.cfm?id=12385 shows drawings of the Poole-Leffel turbine waterwheel and gives some background on the company.

11. Margaret Maddox Finch quotes Wade Hampton Hammill in her unpublished reminiscences, giving no information as to her source. Roxie Hammill Wilcox repeats the comments in *Hammill and Soule Families*, p. 6. A *Washington Post* article dated 15 February 1911 alludes to the controversy but not to Hammill: "Save Heroes' Graves," *Washington Post* (1877–1990), ProQuest Historical Newspapers, p. 16. Digitized.

21 A VIRGINIAN WEIGHS HIS OPTIONS

1. Quoted passages concerning Monroe Strickler are taken from W. D. Keene Jr., ed., *Memoirs—200 Years! 1785–1987* (Decorah, IA: Amundsen Publishing, 1988), "Reports," H. Monroe Strickler, pp. 125–28.

2. Horace M. DuBose, D.D., *Life of Joshua Soule*. Methodist Founders Series, Bishop Warren A. Candler, ed. Nashville: Publishing House of the M.E. Church South, Smith & Lemar, Agents (1911), p. 237. Digitized by Google Book.

3. Edited Appletons Encyclopedia, © 2001, Virtualology, at http://famousamericans.net/joshuasoule/

4. These details are given in *Hammill and Soule Families*, pp. 82, 84.

5. *Radges' Directory of the City of Topeka for 1878–79*, p. 95. Courtesy of Kansas State Historical Society.

6. For a quick rundown on the Hyer Boot Company, see http://www.kshs.org/cool/coolboot.htm.

7. *Hammill and Soule Families*, p. 82.

22 WASHINGTON TERRITORY, A LAST FRONTIER

1. Dorothy O. Johansen, *Empire of the Columbia: A History of the Pacific Northwest*, second edition. New York: Harper & Row, Publishers (1967), p. 301.

2. Ezra Meeker, *Washington Territory West of the Cascade Mountains, Containing a Description of Puget Sound and Rivers Emptying Into It* (Olympia, W.T.: 1870), pp. 9–10, 17, 19, 38. This fifty-two-page pamphlet is bound into Meeker's 1921

publication, *Seventy Years of Progress in Washington* (Tacoma, WA: Allstrum Printing Co., © 1921), after p. 381.

3. "RR Surveys Were Rugged Work," "West Side Survey Disappoints," "Clearwater Survey Not Feasible." Settling the Big Bottom series, *Centralia Daily Chronicle*, 3 September, 5 September, and 6 September 1969.

4. Reverend William J. Rule, *Riding the Upper Cowlitz Circuit Fifty Years Ago, 1893–1896, with a Brief Account of Methodism in Lewis County, Washington* (Seattle: University Printing Company, 1945), p. 9: "[T]he great incentive was the expectation of a branch of the Northern Pacific Railway from Yakima down the Cowlitz Valley to Gray's Harbor to which the numerous surveyors stakes on the proposed route abundantly testified. When the scheme failed many moved from the valley and many stayed—some too long, they said."

5. For a brief history of the Mission and Massacre, see http://www.historylink.org/index.cfm?DisplayPage=output.cfm&File_Id=5192.

6. The city of Tumwater, Washington, supports a useful Web site detailing the history of the area at http://www.ci.tumwater.wa.us.

7. U.S. Government, Works Progress Administration, *Told by the Pioneers: Tales of Frontier Life as Told by Those Who Remember the Days of the Territory and Early Statehood of Washington* (Olympia? 1937–38, 3 vols.), vol. 3, p. 117.

8. "The Plant History, by Tom Plant." *Memories from Family Albums of School District #206, Bi-Centennial Edition*, compiled by Mossyrock Grange #355. Centralia (1976), p. 85.

9. Roxie Hammill Wilcox, *Hammill and Soule Families*, p. 19.

10. Kenneth Hammill, *This Is My Life*, 1983. Unpublished typescript in my possession, p. 54F.

11. Lois Hammill, *The Hammill Family History*, 1975. Unpublished typescript in my possession, p. 35.

12. "Pioneer Family Marks 110th Year in Salkum." *Centralia Daily Chronicle*, undated newspaper clipping from family papers. Probably published 1998.

13. See *Hammill and Soule Families*, p. 29, and *Riding the Upper Cowlitz Circuit*, p. 34.

23 THE MILL ON SALKUM CREEK

1. This and more information about the Garland sawmill can be found at http://www.garlandmill.com.

2. Roxie Hammill Wilcox, *Hammill and Soule Families*, pp. 29–32. The source for this information, Lloyd Bergman, uses the word *penstroke* instead of *penstock*. No such milling term exists, as far as I can find.

3. *Hammill and Soule Families*, p. 29, and Reverend William J. Rule, *Riding the Upper Cowlitz Circuit Fifty Years Ago, 1893–1896, with a Brief Account of Methodism in Lewis County, Washington* (Seattle: University Printing Company, 1945), p. 34.

4. *Hammill and Soule Families*, p. 29.

5. Norman H. Clark, *Washington: A Bicentennial History* (New York: W. W. Norton and the American Association for State and Local History, 1976), pp. 61–62.

6. *Riding the Upper Cowlitz Circuit*, p. 24.

7. "Salkum's Claims." *Chehalis Bee*, 22 March 1899.

8. "The Landes Family." *Memories from Family Albums of School District #206, Bi-Centennial Edition*, compiled by Mossyrock Grange #355. Centralia (1976), p. 235.

9. Lois Hammill, *The Hammill Family History*, 1975. Unpublished typescript in my possession, p. 36.

10. HistoryLink.org, in its *Online Encyclopedia of Washington State History*, gives a useful summary of the Panic at http://www.historylink.org/essays/output. cfm?file_id=2030.

11. *Washington: A Bicentennial History*, p. 67.

12. "The Plant History, by Tom Plant." *Memories from Family Albums of School District #206, Bi-Centennial Edition*, compiled by Mossyrock Grange #355. Centralia (1976), p. 85.

13. "Panic of 1893 Broke Ainslie." *Centralia Daily Chronicle*, undated clipping in my possession.

14. Dorothy O. Johansen, *Empire of the Columbia: A History of the Pacific Northwest*, second edition. New York: Harper & Row, Publishers (1967), pp. 20, 360.

15. O. B. Sperlin, ed., *Building a State: Washington, 1889–1939*. Tacoma: Washington State Historical Society (1940), pp. 23, 89–90.

16. *Building a State*, p. 88.

17. U.S. Government, Works Progress Administration, *Told by the Pioneers: Tales of Frontier Life as Told by Those Who Remember the Days of the Territory and Early Statehood of Washington* (Olympia? 1937–38, 3 vols.), vol. 3, p. 99.

18. *Building a State*, p. 90.

19. *Empire of the Columbia*, p. 317.

20. J. O. Hestwood, *Evergreen State Souvenir: Containing a Review of the Resources, Wealth, Varied Industries and Commercial Advantages of the State of Washington*. Chicago: W. B. Conkey Co. (1893), p. 16.

21. Ezra Meeker, *Washington Territory West of the Cascade Mountains, Containing a Description of Puget Sound and Rivers Emptying Into It*, p. 38. Bound into Meeker's *Seventy Years of Progress in Washington*, Tacoma, WA: Allstrum Printing Co. (1921).

24 WILLIAM AND LUCRETIA HAMMILL, PIONEER FOLK

1. Kenneth Hammill, *This Is My Life*, pp. 30, 33.
2. *This Is My Life*, p. 31.
3. *Hammill and Soule Families*, pp. 20–21, 41.
4. *Hammill and Soule Families*, p. 15
5. *Riding the Upper Cowlitz Circuit*, p. 8.
6. *Riding the Upper Cowlitz Circuit*, p. 49.
7. *Riding the Upper Cowlitz Circuit*, pp. 27–28.
8. *Riding the Upper Cowlitz Circuit*, pp. 34–36.
9. *This Is My Life*, pp. 29, 32, 33.

INDEX

NRTH